TEACHER WRAPAROUND EDITION
BEGINNING

Experiencing Choral Music

UNISON, 2-PART/3-PART

Developed by

HAL•LEONARD® CORPORATION

W9-CZI-058

 Glencoe

New York, New York   Columbus, Ohio   Chicago, Illinois   Peoria, Illinois   Woodland Hills, California

The portions of the National Standards for Music Education included here are reprinted from *National Standards for Arts Education* with permission from MENC–The National Association for Music Education. All rights reserved. Copyright © 1994 by MENC. The complete National Standards and additional materials relating to the Standards are available from MENC, 1806 Robert Fulton Drive, Reston, VA 20191 (telephone 800-336-3768).

A portion of the sales of this material goes to support music education programs through programs of MENC–The National Association for Music Education.

The McGraw·Hill Companies

Copyright © 2005 by Glencoe/McGraw-Hill, a division of The McGraw-Hill Companies. All rights reserved. Except as permitted under the United States Copyright Act, no part of this publication may be reproduced or distributed in any form or by any means, or stored in a database or retrieval system, without prior written permission from the publisher.

Printed in the United States of America.

Send all inquiries to:
Glencoe/McGraw-Hill
21600 Oxnard Street, Suite 500
Woodland Hills, CA 91367

ISBN 0-07-861104-0 (Student Edition)
ISBN 0-07-861105-9 (Teacher Wraparound Edition)

1 2 3 4 5 6 7 8 9 045 09 08 07 06 05 04

Table of Contents

SECTION		National Standards								
Selection	**Concepts and Skills**	**1**	**2**	**3**	**4**	**5**	**6**	**7**	**8**	**9**
LESSONS										
We Want To Sing	Sing expressively; perform two-part music.	a, b				e		a, b	a	
Spotlight On Posture	Performance techniques—posture.	b								
My America	Perform in 3/4 meter; relate music to other subjects; American heritage.	a, c				a, c			b	a, b
Spotlight On Arranging	Arrange melodic and rhythmic phrases.				b					
Spotlight On Breath Management	Sing accurately with good breath control.	b								
Music Alone Shall Live	Identify and perform a canon; read and write music notation.	a, b, c				a, d	a			
Singabahambayo	Relate music to society; read and perform syncopation; South African music.	c		c		a				b, c
Spotlight On Diction	Performance techniques—diction.	b							b	
Good Cheer	Describe music from Medieval period; read and write music in 6/8 meter; interpret musical content through drama.	c	a		a	a			b	a
Winter's Night	Relate music to culture; singing diction; music from the Arctic region of Sampi.	b, c		c	a					a
Radiator Lions	Describe music from the Contemporary period; use non-traditional notation to read, write and perform music; rondo form.	a, b, c			a	a, b, c	c	b		
Spotlight On Vocal Production	Performance techniques—vocal production.	b								
Jesu, Joy Of Man's Desiring	Describe music from the Baroque Period; read and write triplets; sing phrases expressively.	b, c, d				a, c, f	a	b	a	b
Da pacem Domine	Identify canon; demonstrate step-wise and skip-wise motion.	c, d				a, d	c			
Spotlight On Vowels	Performance techniques—vowels.	b								
Sanctus	Describe music from the Romantic Period; demonstrate melodic contour; sing independently in duets.	a, b, c, d	a			c	b	b		a, b
Spotlight On Pitch Matching	Accurate intonation.	b								
Alleluia	Describe music from the Classical period; sing melismas correctly; read and perform sixteenth notes.	a, b, c, d			a	a, c	a, b	b		a, b
Spotlight On Melismas	Performance techniques—singing melismas.									
Waters Ripple And Flow	Read rhythmic patterns with triplets and sixteenth notes; compose rhythmic phrases; music from diverse cultures.	a, b, c, d			a	a, c, d		b	a	

SECTION		National Standards								
Selection	Concepts and Skills	1	2	3	4	5	6	7	8	9
MUSIC & HISTORY										
Renaissance, Baroque, Classical, Romantic and Contemporary periods	Describe, listen to and analyze music from the five main historical periods.						a, b, c, e, f		a, b, c, d, e	a, c, d, e
Spotlight On Concert Etiquette	Apply concert etiquette in a variety of settings.							a, b		
CHORAL LIBRARY										
An American Folk Song Spectacular!	Read and perform eighth notes; identify by ear and notate melodic patterns; use dramatic storytelling to interpret music.	a, b, c, d	b	c		a, c, d	a, c		b	a, b, d
Blues, Blues, Blues	Compose and perform rhythmic patterns in swing style; explore and perform blues style.	b, c			a	a, c, d	a	b		
Spotlight On Improvisation	Create rhythmic and melodic phrases. Improvise melodic embellishments.	a, c		a, b, c						
Brand New Day	Extend the vocal range; sing with expression; music in major tonality.	a, b, d				a, b		b	a	
Consider Yourself	Sing chromatic pitches accurately; read and write music notation in compound meter.	a, b, d			a	a, b, d	b	b		a
Hine ma tov	Perform music in minor tonality; compose rhythmic phrases; music of Hebrew culture.	a, b, c, d			a	a, b, c, d		a		a
Spotlight On Careers In Music	Describe music-related vocations and avocations.							a, b		
Little David, Play On Your Harp	Define *imitation*; syncopated and non-syncopated rhythms; African American spiritual.	a, b, c			a		a, b, c	b		a, c
Pokare Kare Ana	Correct diction and syllabic stress; music in relation to history and culture.	a, b, c, d	a	a	a, b	a, b, c		b		a
Río, Río	Recognize the difference between unison and part-singing; relate other subjects to music; develop criteria for the evaluation.	a, b, c, d		b		a, b, c	b	b	b	
Sourwood Mountain	Identify musical form; sing with expression and technical accuracy; read sixteenth notes.	a, b, c, d	a			a, b, c	c	a, b	b	a
Tinga Layo	Sing in three-part harmony; standard notation for dynamics; calypso style of the West Indies.	a, b, c, d		b		a, b, c		b	b	a, b
Spotlight On Changing Voice	Describe characteristics of vocal timbre individually and in groups.							a, b		
Unity	Extend the vocal range; read and perform sixteenth notes; gospel style.	a, b, c, d		b, c		a, b, c		b		a, b
Yonder Come Day	Sing with good breath support; evaluate performances; music from the Georgia Sea Islands.	a, b, c, d		b, c		a, b, c	c	b	a	a, c

National Standards Middle School Grades 5–8

The National Standards for Music Education were developed by the Music Educators National Conference. Reprinted by permission.

MUSIC

The period represented by grades 5–8 is especially critical in students' musical development. The music they perform or study often becomes an integral part of their personal musical repertoire. Composing and improvising provide students with unique insight into the form and structure of music and at the same time help them develop their creativity. Broad experience with a variety of music is necessary if students are to make informed musical judgments. Similarly, this breadth of background enables them to begin to understand the connections and relationships between music and other disciplines. By understanding the cultural and historical forces that shape social attitudes and behaviors, students are better prepared to live and work in communities that are increasingly multi-cultural. The role that music will play in students' lives depends in large measure on the level of skills they achieve in creating, performing and listening to music.

Every course in music, including performance courses, should provide instruction in creating, performing, listening to and analyzing music, in addition to focusing on its specific subject matter.

1. **Content Standard:** Singing, alone and with others, a varied repertoire of music
   Achievement Standard:
   Students
   a. sing accurately and with good breath control throughout their singing ranges, alone and in small and large ensembles.
   b. sing with *expression and *technical accuracy a repertoire of vocal literature with a *level of difficulty of 2, on a scale of 1 to 6, including some songs performed from memory.
   c. sing music representing diverse *genres and cultures, with expression appropriate for the work being performed.
   d. sing music written in two and three parts.
   Students who participate in a choral ensemble
   e. sing with expression and technical accuracy a varied repertoire of vocal literature with a level of difficulty of 3, on a scale of 1 to 6, including some songs performed from memory.

2. **Content Standard:** Performing on instruments, alone and with others, a varied repertoire of music
   Achievement Standard:
   Students
   a. perform on at least one instrument[1] accurately and independently, alone and in small and large ensembles, with good posture, good playing position and good breath, bow or stick control.
   b. perform with expression and technical accuracy on at least one string, wind, percussion or *classroom instrument a repertoire of instrumental literature with a level of difficulty of 2, on a scale of 1 to 6.
   c. perform music representing diverse genres and cultures, with expression appropriate for the work being performed.
   d. play by ear simple melodies on a melodic instrument and simple accompaniments on a harmonic instrument.
   Students who participate in an instrumental ensemble or class
   e. perform with expression and technical accuracy a varied repertoire of instrumental literature with a level of difficulty of 3, on a scale of 1 to 6, including some solos performed from memory.

3. **Content Standard:** Improvising melodies, variations and accompaniments
   Achievement Standard:
   Students
   a. improvise simple harmonic accompaniments.
   b. improvise melodic embellishments and simple rhythmic and melodic variations on given pentatonic melodies and melodies in major keys.
   c. improvise short melodies, unaccompanied and over given rhythmic accompaniments, each in a consistent *style, *meter and *tonality.

4. **Content Standard:** Composing and arranging music within specified guidelines
   Achievement Standard:
   Students
   a. compose short pieces within specified guidelines,[2] demonstrating how the elements of music are used to achieve unity and variety, tension and release, and balance.
   b. arrange simple pieces for voices or instruments other than those for which the pieces were written.

c. use a variety of traditional and nontraditional sound sources and electronic media when composing and arranging.

5. **Content Standard:** Reading and notating music
Achievement Standard:
Students
   a. read whole, half, quarter, eighth, sixteenth and dotted notes and rests in 2/4, 3/4, 4/4, 6/8, 3/8 and *alla breve meter signatures.
   b. read at sight simple melodies in both the treble and bass clefs.
   c. identify and define standard notation symbols for pitch, rhythm, *dynamics, tempo, *articulation and expression.
   d. use standard notation to record their musical ideas and the musical ideas of others.

6. **Content Standard:** Listening to, analyzing and describing music
Achievement Standard:
Students
   a. describe specific music events[3] in a given aural example, using appropriate terminology.
   b. analyze the uses of *elements of music in aural examples representing diverse genres and cultures.
   c. demonstrate knowledge of the basic principles of meter, rhythm, tonality, intervals, chords and harmonic progressions in the analyses of music.

7. **Content Standard:** Evaluating music and music performances
Achievement Standard:
Students
   a. develop criteria for evaluating the quality and effectiveness of music performances and compositions and apply criteria in their personal listening and performing.
   b. evaluate the quality and effectiveness of their own and others' performances, compositions, arrangements and improvisations by applying specific criteria appropriate for the style of the music and offer constructive suggestions for improvement.

8. **Content Standard:** Understanding relationships between music, the other arts and disciplines outside the arts
Achievement Standard:
Students
   a. compare in two or more arts how the characteristic materials of each art (that is, sound in music, visual stimuli in visual arts, movement in dance, human interrelationships in theatre) can be used to transform similar events, scenes, emotions or ideas into works of art.
   b. describe ways in which the principles and subject matter of other disciplines taught in the school are interrelated with those of music.[4]

9. **Content Standard:** Understanding music in relation to history and culture
Achievement Standard:
Students
   a. describe distinguishing characteristics of representative music genres and styles from a variety of cultures.
   b. classify by genre and style (and, if applicable, by historical period, composer and title) a varied body of exemplary (that is, high-quality and characteristic) musical works and explain the characteristics that cause each work to be considered exemplary.
   c. compare, in several cultures of the world, functions music serves, roles of musicians[5] and conditions under which music is typically performed.

Terms identified by an asterisk (*) are explained further in the glossary of *National Standards for Arts Education,* published by Music Educators National Conference, © 1994.

1. E.g., band or orchestra instrument, *fretted instrument, electronic instrument
2. E.g., a particular style, form, instrumentation, compositional technique
3. E.g., entry of oboe, change of meter, return of refrain
4. E.g., language arts: issues to be considered in setting texts to music; mathematics: frequency ratios of intervals; sciences: the human hearing process and hazards to hearing; social studies: historical and social events and movements chronicled in or influenced by musical works
5. E.g., lead guitarist in a rock band, composer of jingles for commercials, singer in Peking opera

INTRODUCTION

Experiencing Choral Music is a four-level series designed to build music literacy and promote vocal development for all students and voice categories in grades 6–12. The series is a multitextbook program supported with print materials and audio listening components that enable students to develop music skills and conceptual understanding, and provides teachers with a flexible, integrated program.

Experiencing Choral Music presents beginning, intermediate, proficient and advanced literature for various voice groupings: unison, 2-part/3-part, mixed, treble, and tenor/bass. All selections in *Experiencing Choral Music* are recorded three ways: full performance with voices, accompaniment only, and individual part-dominant recordings. The program also includes companion *Sight-Singing* textbooks that present a sequential approach to musical literacy and is directly correlated to the literature books. This comprehensive choral music program includes student texts, teacher wraparound editions, teacher resource binders, and rehearsal and performance audio recordings designed to enhance student learning while reducing teacher preparation time.

Experiencing Choral Music is a curriculum that provides your students with a meaningful, motivating choral music experience, and will help you and your students build choral music knowledge and skills. For example:

Experiencing Choral Music connects to . . . the National Standards

The National Standards are correlated to each lesson for quick-and-easy identification and reference. The performance standards related to singing and reading notations are explicit in each lesson, and by using the extension activities, teachers can connect the musical elements through improvisation and composition. Analysis and evaluation are an active and consistent component of lessons throughout the series. Additional student activities connect the lessons to the other arts, as well as provide a consistent historical and cultural context.

Experiencing Choral Music connects to . . . Skill Development

Through the Links to Learning exercises, students build vocal, theory and artistic expression skills necessary to perform each piece. Rhythmic, melodic and articulation skills are developed as needed for expressive interpretation. Students are encouraged to develop listening skills and use their perceptions to improve individual and group performance.

Experiencing Choral Music connects to . . . Creative Expression/Performance

Student performance provides opportunities for young musicians to demonstrate musical growth, to gain personal satisfaction from achievement, and to experience the joy of music making. To help develop skills, *Experiencing Choral Music* provides vocal, theory and artistic expression exercises which help prepare students to successfully sing each piece. Conceptual understanding is built throughout the teaching/learning sequence, as the performance is prepared.

Experiencing Choral Music connects to . . . Historical and Cultural Heritage

Experiencing Choral Music provides a vehicle to help students gain knowledge and understanding of historical and cultural contexts across the curriculum. These concepts are presented in the Getting Started section of each lesson. Also, historical connections through art, history, timelines, performance practices and listening examples are made in Music & History.

Experiencing Choral Music connects to . . . the Arts and Other Curriculum Areas

Choral music provides a rich opportunity to connect the musical experience to other art disciplines (dance, visual arts, theater), and to enhance the learning in other subject areas.

PROGRAM PHILOSOPHY

Responding to New Trends in Choral Music Education

Experiencing Choral Music is consistent with current educational philosophy that suggests:

- Performance is a product that should be the end result of a sound educational process, building conceptual understanding and skills as the performance is prepared.
- Students are motivated through materials and concepts that are connected to their own lives and interests, and should be exposed to high-quality, challenging musical literature.
- Students learn best when they are active participants in their learning, and when they clearly understand and help set the goals and objectives of the learning outcome.
- Students understand concepts better when they have background information and skills that allow them to place their learning into a larger context.
- Students need to actively manipulate musical concepts and skills through improvisation and/or composition in order to fully assimilate and understand them.

- Students improve when they receive fair, honest and meaningful feedback on their success and failures.
- Students should be encouraged to assess themselves individually and as a group, learning to receive and process constructive criticism, leading to independent self-correction and decision making.

Scope and Depth of Music Literature

Most students are capable of performing more difficult material than they can sight-read. Therefore, the literature in *Experiencing Choral Music* is drawn from many periods and styles of music. The wide range of composers and publishers ensures variety, and allows for various skills and concepts to be developed as each new piece is encountered. The high standards set in *Experiencing Choral Music* provide selections that are inherently powerful and exciting for students. The *Sight-Singing* textbooks provide additional literature for sight-singing purposes. Written in a sequential manner, this component will present students with a developmental process for learning to read music.

Addressing the National Standards

The National Standards for Arts Education, published in 1994, launched a national effort to bring a new vision to arts education for all students. The National Standards provide a framework for achievement in music, with outcomes suggested for grades 4, 8, and 12. *Experiencing Choral Music* addresses the National Standards in several ways.

The most obvious and predominant National Standards addressed in choral ensemble are: (1) singing and (5) reading and notation. However, good performance requires musical understanding that only occurs when all aspects of musical experience are incorporated. The preparation of vocal performance is enriched and deepened by involvement in all nine of the National Standards.

As you teach with *Experiencing Choral Music,* there will be frequent opportunities to deepen or extend student learning through: (2) playing through creating accompaniments, (3) improvisation, (4) composition and arranging, (6) analyzing, (7) assessing, (8) linking with other arts and other academic disciplines, and (9) understanding historical and cultural contexts. The National Standards identified for each lesson and the Extension activities provided in the Teacher Wraparound Edition help you become aware of the National Standards, and the depth of learning that will occur as you implement this choral music program.

Promoting Music Literacy

Experiencing Choral Music promotes music literacy throughout the lessons. Literacy includes oral and aural aspects of music communication—reading, writing, singing and listening. Each lesson begins with Getting Started that (1) connects the song to the student, and (2) frames the historical and cultural aspect of the music to be performed. From there the students are directed to the Links to Learning which are divided into three categories: Vocal, Theory and Artistic Expression. These exercises emphasize reading development and artistic expression. These may be rhythmic, melodic, harmonic or a combination thereof; and are directly related to the objectives of the lesson. The exercises lead directly into the musical selection. Students are encouraged to sight-sing in every lesson. Sight-singing is approached as a challenge and a means to musical independence for the student.

Literacy goes beyond simply reading pitch and rhythm, extending to the expressive elements of music and appropriate interpretation. Through Artistic Expression, students will be asked to explore interpretive aspects of music making, and are encouraged to suggest their own ideas for phrasing, dynamics, and so on. Through careful listening and constructive critique of their own work, they will gradually become more discriminating about the quality of performance and the impact of that performance on the audience.

Including Authentic Student Assessment

The assessment in *Experiencing Choral Music* is systematic, objective and authentic. There is ongoing informal assessment by teacher observation throughout the lessons. The text is written as a series of action steps for the student, so there are many opportunities for the director to hear and see the level of accomplishment.

Students will find objectives at the beginning of each lesson, and evaluation activities at the end. The Evaluation questions and activities are always related directly to the lesson objectives, and allow students to demonstrate their understanding. By answering the questions, and demonstrating as suggested, students are involved in *self-assessment*. Many times, students are involved in their own assessment, constructing rubrics or critiquing their performance to determine what level of success has been achieved, and identifying the next challenge.

The *Teacher Wraparound Edition* includes lesson objectives, and each lesson is taught so the concepts and skills are experienced, labeled, practiced and reinforced, then measured through *formal assessment*. These assessment tasks match the lesson objectives, allowing students to demonstrate understanding of concepts and skills through performance, composition or writing. Students are frequently required to produce audio- or videotapes. This authentic assessment keeps testing of rote learning to a minimum, and allows measurement of higher-level application of knowledge and skills. A portfolio can be constructed for individual students, groups or the whole ensemble, to demonstrate growth over time.

Connecting the Arts and Other Curriculum Areas

Lessons in *Experiencing Choral Music* integrate many appropriate aspects of musical endeavor into the preparation of a piece. Students compose, improvise, conduct, read, write, sing, play, listen/analyze and assess on an ongoing basis that builds understanding, as well as high standards. In this way, the many aspects of music are integrated for deeper learning.

As one of the arts, music can be linked to other arts through similarities and differences. Throughout the text, and particularly in the historical section, music is compared and contrasted with other arts to determine aspects of confluence and the unique features of each art.

As one way of knowing about the world, music can be compared with concepts and skills from other disciplines as seemingly different as science or mathematics. The integrations between music and other disciplines are kept at the conceptual level, to maintain the integrity of both music and the other subjects. For example, mathematical sets of 2, 3, 4, 5 and 6 might be explored as a link to pieces with changing meter; or the text of a piece might become a starting point for exploration of tone painting. In Music & History, a time line connects music to social studies, and a list of authors for each period provides a link to language and literature.

Providing a Variety of Student Activities

Experiencing Choral Music begins with the choral experience, and builds understanding through active participation in a range of activities including singing, playing, improvising, composing, arranging, moving, writing, listening, analyzing, assessing and connecting to cultures, periods or disciplines. Lessons are written with the heading "Direct students to . . ." so there is always an emphasis on learning by doing. In this way the teacher becomes a guide and places the responsibility for learning on the student. When students are engaged in meaningful and challenging activity, they are more likely to learn.

Fitting Your Classroom Needs

With *Experiencing Choral Music*, your students will be clear about purpose and direction, have multiple routes to success, and be involved in their own learning. The lessons will guide you and your students to share in the excitement of music making, and help you to grow together. The lessons are written the way you teach, and allow you to maintain and strengthen your routines, while adding flexibility, variety and depth.

ORGANIZATION AND FLEXIBILITY

Each *Experiencing Choral Music* text is divided into the following sections:
- Lessons
- Music & History
- Choral Library

Lessons

The Lessons are designed to be taught over a period of time. They are divided into three categories: Beginning of the Year, Mid-Winter, and Concert/Festival. Each lesson is developed around a piece of authentic and quality music literature. The lesson includes background information, vocal examples, sight-reading and rhythmic or melodic drills, all of which are directly related to preparation of the piece. Objectives are clearly stated, and a motivational opening activity or discussion is provided. The Teacher Wraparound Edition outlines a carefully sequenced approach to the piece and clear assessment opportunities to document achievement and growth.

Music & History

Music & History provides narrative and listening experiences for each of the five main historical periods. A *narrative lesson* provides a brief and interesting exposition of the main characteristics of the period outlining the achievements and new styles that emerged. A time line guides the student to place the musical characteristics into a larger historical and cultural context. The listening lesson includes both vocal and instrumental *listening selections* from the period, with a guide to student listening. A listing of the historical pieces to be sung from the period are cross-referenced from the Music & History divider page. Combined, these components give historical context of the period across the arts, then apply the context to musical literature.

Choral Library

The Choral Library provides the same comprehensive student lesson featured in the Lessons. The additional literature features multicultural selections, patriotic and seasonal selections, American folk music, African American spirituals, Broadway show tunes, and light concert pieces that can be used to enhance the repertoire of your choral music performance.

Overview of Lesson Objectives

Each lesson has objectives that emphasize and build conceptual understanding and skills across the lessons. The objectives in this book are:

LESSON OBJECTIVES	
Title	**Objective**
We Want To Sing	• Sing expressively. • Perform two-part music.
My America	• Perform music in 3/4 meter. • Relate music to other subjects. • Perform music of American heritage.
Music Alone Shall Live	• Identify and perform a canon. • Read and write music notation.
Singabahambayo	• Relate music to society. • Read and perform syncopation. • Perform music representing South African culture.
Good Cheer	• Describe and perform music from the Medieval period. • Read, write and perform music in 6/8 meter. • Interpret musical content through drama.
Winter's Night	• Relate music to culture. • Sing with good diction. • Perform music representing the Arctic region of Sampi.
Radiator Lions	• Describe and perform music from the Contemporary period. • Use nontraditional notation to read, write and perform music. • Identify rondo form.
Jesu, Joy Of Man's Desiring	• Describe and perform music from the Baroque period. • Read and write triplets. • Sing phrases expressively.
Da pacem Domine	• Identify and perform a canon. • Explain and demonstrate step-wise and skip-wise motion.
Sanctus	• Describe and perform music from the Romantic period. • Identify and demonstrate melodic contour. • Sing independently in duets.
Alleluia	• Describe and perform music from the Classical period. • Sing melismas correctly. • Identify, read and perform sixteenth notes.
Waters Ripple And Flow	• Read rhythmic patterns with triplets and sixteenth notes. • Compose rhythmic phrases. • Perform music from different cultures.
An American Folk Song Spectacular!	• Read and perform rhythmic patterns with eighth notes. • Identify by ear and notate melodic patterns. • Use dramatic storytelling to interpret musical content.

LESSON OBJECTIVES	
Title	**Objective**
Blues, Blues, Blues	• Compose and perform rhythmic patterns in swing style. • Perform music that represents the blues style.
Brand New Day	• Extend the vocal range. • Sing with expression. • Perform music in major tonality.
Consider Yourself	• Sing chromatic pitches accurately. • Read and write music notation in compound meter.
Hine ma tov	• Perform music in minor tonality. • Compose rhythmic phrases. • Perform music that represents the Hebrew culture.
Little David, Play On Your Harp	• Define *imitation*. • Identify and perform syncopated and nonsyncopated rhythms. • Perform music that represents the African American spiritual.
Pokare Kare Ana	• Perform music with correct diction and syllabic stress. • Understand music in relation to history and culture.
Río, Río	• Recognize the difference between unison and part-singing. • Relate other subjects to music. • Develop a criteria for the evaluation of music.
Sourwood Mountain	• Identify musical form. • Sing with expression and technical accuracy. • Read rhythmic patterns with sixteenth notes.
Tinga Layo	• Sing in three-part harmony. • Identify and perform standard notation for dynamics. • Perform music that represents the calypso of the West Indies.
Unity	• Extend the vocal range. • Read and perform rhythmic patterns with sixteenth notes. • Perform music in the gospel style.
Yonder Come Day	• Sing with good breath support. • Evaluate the quality and effectiveness of performances. • Perform music from the Georgia Sea Islands.

STUDENT TEXT

The comprehensive student lessons are structured as follows:

- **FOCUS** . . . tells the student the main concepts and skills addressed in the lesson. By having only a few main goals, students and teacher will keep focused on these objectives as work progresses.

- **VOCABULARY** . . . gives the student an opportunity to build a musical vocabulary essential for clarity of thought in communicating about music to others.

- **LINKS TO LEARNING**

Vocal . . . allows the student to explore the melodic and vocal skills that are directly related to some aspect of the upcoming musical selection. Also includes melodic sight-singing examples.

Theory . . . builds rhythmic, theory and basic reading skills through exercises that are directly related to the musical selection about to be learned. Through sight-reading practice every day, students gain confidence and skills to become independent readers.

Artistic Expression . . . provides interpretive aspects of music making, such as phrasing, dynamics, stylistic performance practices, movement, and artistic expression through drama, writing and the visual arts. Through interest and active participation, the student is then led logically into the piece.

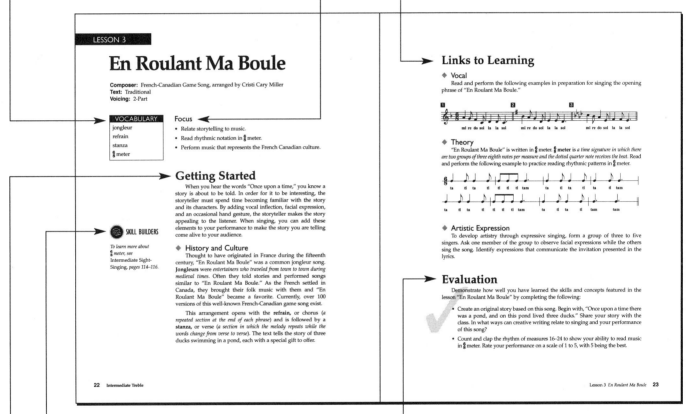

- **SIDEBAR REFERENCES** . . . provide additional information about the lesson through:
  Skill Builders . . . reference to *Sight-Singing* textbook
  Music & History . . . reference to the history section
  Spotlights . . . reference to a featured Spotlight page

- **GETTING STARTED** . . . provides a motivating introduction to the piece of music, related to the student's perspective. The History and Culture provides background information on the selection, the composer and/or the cultural context.

- **EVALUATION** . . . gives the student ways to assess accomplishment, growth and needs, for both self and group. Through careful listening and constructive critique of their own work, they will gradually become more discriminating about the quality of performance and the impact of that performance on the audience.

Lessons

The student lessons, through which students systematically build musical skills and conceptual understanding, comprise the first twelve selections of the text. They are presented in three general categories: Beginning of the Year, Mid-Winter, and Concert/Festival.

Music & History

The Historical section of the text provides a survey of Western music history through exploration of the culture and music of the five overarching periods: Renaissance, Baroque, Classical, Romantic and Contemporary. Each period is addressed in the following ways:

- **Historical Narrative Lesson** . . . provides a brief, student-oriented historical context of the period through visual art, architecture, historical events, musical developments, artistic characteristics, musical personalities and listening selections.
- **Historical Listening Lesson** . . . provides one choral and one instrumental listening selection to give students an aural experience with the styles, sounds and forms of the period. Recordings are provided to aid student learning.

Choral Library

The Choral Library maintains the same comprehensive lesson format of the Lessons and comprises the final twelve selections of the text. The additional literature features multicultural selections, patriotic and seasonal selections, American folk music, African American spirituals, Broadway show tunes and light concert pieces.

Glossary

The glossary provides brief, accurate definitions of musical terms used in the text.

TEACHER WRAPAROUND EDITION

National Standards Connections

Experiencing Choral Music affords multiple opportunities to address the National Standards. Correlations among lesson content, extension activities and bottom-page activities are listed to make obvious the relationship between lesson activities and the standards.

Suggested Teaching Sequence

Each lesson is organized to follow a logical progression from Getting Started through Evaluation, while providing maximum flexibility of use for your individual situation. Each lesson is linked to one musical selection, and provides learning opportunities based on the inherent concepts and skills required to understand and perform the piece. The lessons of the Teacher Wraparound Edition are structured as follows.

- **Overview** . . . Gives the teacher a brief analysis of the music being taught, including composer, text, voicing, key, meter, form, style, accompaniment, programming ideas and vocal ranges for each voice part.
- **Objectives** . . . Two or three concrete, measurable objectives form the skeletal structure for the lesson, allowing an interconnected approach to lesson segments.
- **Vocabulary** . . . Vocabulary terms are those used during the lesson and music terms used in the music to build understanding and skills.
- **Links to Learning** . . . The Links to Learning of the lesson includes exercises that focus on vocal, theory and artistic expression elements of the upcoming song. It provides rhythm and vocal, as well as sight-singing exercises. They are designed to sequentially develop vocal and sight-singing skills, and lead directly into the upcoming piece. These exercises may all be done before the piece is introduced, or they may be presented cumulatively, one each day, and concurrent with developing understanding of the piece.
- **The Lesson Plan: Suggested Teaching Sequence** . . . The Suggested Teaching Sequence is divided into three section: Introduce, Rehearse, and Refine. At the end of each section, Progress Checkpoints are provided for quick informal assessment of the materials covered to that point. Introduce often refers to the Links to Learning exercises on the student page and provides meaningful ways to introduce a new song to students. Rehearse includes a list of recommended steps to teach the piece through a variety of teaching techniques. Refine puts it all together and prepares the students for performance of the piece. The Performance Tips provide teachers with the polishing nuances that transform the notes on the page into an expressive performance experience.

Informal Assessment, Student Self-Assessment, and Individual and Group Performance Evaluation

Informal Assessment is done by teacher observation during the lesson. Each objective is observable, and the text indicates the checkpoint for teacher assessment.

Student Self-Assessment is accomplished through student evaluation of their individual performance based on an established set of criteria.

Individual and Group Performance Evaluation requires the student to demonstrate a skill or understanding through individual or group evaluation. This is directly related to the Evaluation found in the student lesson. Individual and Group Performance Evaluation can be done by the teacher, student, peers or a combination thereof. Frequent audio- or videotaping is suggested as an effective means of evaluation. The tapes may be compiled into a portfolio that shows growth and developing understanding over time.

Bottom-Page Activities

Bottom-page activities in each lesson afford a plethora of background information, teaching strategies and enrichment opportunities.

- *Teacher 2 Teacher* provides a brief description of the main features of the lesson.
- *Enrichment activities* provide musical activities that go beyond the basic lesson including composition, improvisation, and so forth.
- *Extension activities* expand the lesson to the other arts or other disciplines.
- *Teaching strategies* reinforce concepts or skills presented in the lesson, or elaborate on classroom management techniques.
- *More about* boxes provide background historical, cultural, and/or biographical information.
- *Curriculum connections* provide strategies to help students build bridges between music and other disciplines.
- *Vocal development strategies* give detailed information about specific techniques that facilitate vocal production and style.
- *Music literacy strategies* help students expand their ability to read and analyze music.
- *Cultural connections* provide cultural information related to the lesson.
- *Connecting to the arts* boxes provide strategies to help students connect music to the other arts.
- *Community connections* provide activities that extend into the community.
- *Careers in music* boxes provide information about career opportunities in music.
- *Online* directs students and teachers to **music.glencoe.com**, the Web site for *Experiencing Choral Music*.

TEACHER RESOURCE BINDER

The *Teacher Resource Binder* contains teaching materials designed to reduce teacher preparation time and maximize students' learning. The following categories are provided to assist with meeting the individual needs and interests of your students.

- **Teaching Masters.** The *Teaching Masters* support, extend and enhance the musical concepts and skills presented in the text lessons. Included are strategied focusing on composing, arranging, evaluating, analyzing, writing, multi-arts, culture and language pronunciation guides.
- **Evaluation Masters.** The *Evaluation Masters* provide performance assessment criteria, rubrics and other pages to help teachers and students with individual group, and ensemble assessment.
- **Music & History.** The *Music & History Masters* include full-color overhead transparencies of the visual art pieces introduced in each of the historical sections. They also include characteristics of the period, biographies of composers and other teaching strategies.
- **Vocal Development Masters.** The *Vocal Development Masters* provide important information about the voice. Included are numerous warm-up exercises that may be used throughout the year. Each exercise is recorded and included on the *Sight-Singing CD*.
- **Skill Builders Masters.** The *Skill Builders Masters* reinforce the development of fundamental skills, knowledge and understanding in areas such as rhythm, notation, music symbols, conducting patterns, improvisation, Kodály hand signs, time signatures and meter.
- **Sight-Singing Masters.** The *Sight-Singing Masters* are directly correlated to the *Sight-Singing* textbooks. They provide reproducible evaluation activity sheets for assessment and review.
- **Kodály, Dalcroze, Interdisciplinary.** Teaching strategies with a focus on Kodály, Dalcroze and Interdisciplinary are presented in this section.
- **Reference Resources.** The *Reference Resource Masters* serve as a resource bank for the teacher and provides a library of resource materials useful in supporting instruction.
- **Listening Selections CD.** *Listening Selections CD* provides full recordings of the vocal and instrumental historical listening lessons from the student text.
- **Sight-Singing CD.** The *Sight-Singing CD* provides a piano accompaniment track for practice songs and sight-singing exercises found in the student text of *Experiencing Choral Music: Sight-Singing*. The CD also includes the accompaniment track to the vocal warm-up exercises in the Vocal Development section.

EFFECTIVE TEACHING CHECKLIST

Teaching can be a rewarding as well as a challenging experience. The following is a compilation of suggestions and tips from experienced teachers. Review this list often.

Preparation

- Good planning leads to a successful rehearsal.
- Establish high expectations from the start – students want to succeed.
- Establish a routine and basic standards of behavior – and stick to it!
- Follow your planned routine every rehearsal (e.g., opening cue that rehearsal has begun, warm-up, sight-reading, repertoire, evaluation). Younger choirs in particular respond well to structure in a rehearsal.
- Plan, plan, plan.
- Develop long-range planning (the entire year's goals and activities, the semester, the month) and short-range planning (weekly plans and the daily lesson as they fit within the entire year's goals).
- Vary teaching strategies: modeling, peer coaching, large group, small group, cooperative learning, individual instruction, student conductors, independent practice.
- Study the score well. Anticipate problem areas.
- Be able to sing any one part while playing another.
- Know the vocal ranges of each member of the chorus.
- Select appropriate music to fit those vocal ranges.
- Remember: out-of-range results in out-of-tune singing.
- Select music of appropriate difficulty for the group.
- Plan evaluation techniques in advance.
- Have all necessary supplies and equipment ready (music in folders or ready to pass out, tapes cued, director's folder handy, recording equipment set, etc.) before the lesson begins.
- Plan to make beautiful music at least once during every rehearsal.

Presentation

- Begin each lesson with singing rather than talking.
- Make all parts of the lesson musical—including warm-ups and sight-reading.
- Rehearse a cappella. Use the piano as little as possible.
- Remember: Delivering information is not necessarily teaching.
- Display a positive attitude.
- Communicate effectively and concisely.
- Enthusiasm is essential.
- Make learning an enjoyable experience.
- Respect legitimate effort on the part of every student.
- Be the best musician you can be.
- Laugh often.

Pacing

- Be 30 seconds mentally ahead of the class at all times.
- Know where the lesson is going before it happens.
- Vary activities and standing/sitting positions.
- Plan a smooth transition from one activity to the next.
- Avoid "lag" time.
- If a "teachable" moment occurs, make the most of it.
- Avoid belaboring any one exercise, phrase, or activity—come back to it at another time.
- Always give students a reason for repeating a section.
- Provide at least one successful musical experience in every rehearsal.

Evaluation

- Assess student learning in every lesson (formally or informally).
- Vary the assessment activities.
- Consider evaluating individual as well as group effort.
- Tape the rehearsals often (audio and/or video).
- Study the rehearsal tapes: (1) to discover where overlooked errors occur, (2) to assist in planning the next rehearsal, or (3) to share findings with the students.
- Provide students with opportunities to evaluate themselves.
- Teach critical listening to the students by asking specific students or a group of students to listen for a specific thing (balance of parts in the polyphonic section, a correct uniform vowel sound on a particular word or words, rise and fall of phrase, and so forth).
- Constantly evaluate what's really happening. (We often hear what we want to hear!)
- Listen, listen, listen.

TEACHER WRAPAROUND EDITION

Experiencing Choral Music

BEGINNING

UNISON, 2-PART/3-PART

Developed by

HAL•LEONARD® CORPORATION

McGraw Hill Glencoe

New York, New York   Columbus, Ohio   Chicago, Illinois   Peoria, Illinois   Woodland Hills, California

The portions of the National Standards for Music Education included here are reprinted from *National Standards for Arts Education* with permission from MENC–The National Association for Music Education. All rights reserved. Copyright © 1994 by MENC. The complete National Standards and additional materials relating to the Standards are available from MENC, 1806 Robert Fulton Drive, Reston, VA 20191 (telephone 800-336-3768).

A portion of the sales of this material goes to support music education programs through programs of MENC–The National Association for Music Education.

Glencoe

The **McGraw·Hill** Companies

Copyright © 2005 by Glencoe/McGraw-Hill; a division of The McGraw-Hill Companies. All rights reserved. Except as permitted under the United States Copyright Act, no part of this publication may be reproduced or distributed in any form or by any means, or stored in a database or retrieval system, without prior written permission from the publisher.

Printed in the United States of America.

Send all inquiries to:
Glencoe/McGraw-Hill
21600 Oxnard Street, Suite 500
Woodland Hills, CA 91367

ISBN 0-07-861104-0 (Student Edition)
ISBN 0-07-861105-9 (Teacher Wraparound Edition)

1 2 3 4 5 6 7 8 9   045   09 08 07 06 05 04

Credits

LEAD AUTHORS

Emily Crocker
Vice President of Choral Publications
Hal Leonard Corporation, Milwaukee, Wisconsin
Founder and Artistic Director, Milwaukee Children's Choir

Michael Jothen
Professor of Music, Program Director of Graduate Music Education
Chairperson of Music Education
Towson University, Towson, Maryland

Jan Juneau
Choral Director
Klein Collins High School
Spring, Texas

Henry H. Leck
Associate Professor and Director of Choral Activities
Butler University, Indianapolis, Indiana
Founder and Artistic Director, Indianapolis Children's Choir

Michael O'Hern
Choral Director
Lake Highlands High School
Richardson, Texas

Audrey Snyder
Composer
Eugene, Oregon

Mollie Tower
Coordinator of Choral and General Music, K-12, Retired
Austin, Texas

AUTHORS

Anne Denbow
Voice Instructor, Professional Singer/Actress
Director of Music, Holy Cross Episcopal Church
Simpsonville, South Carolina

Rollo A. Dilworth
Director of Choral Activities and Music
    Education
North Park University, Chicago, Illinois

Deidre Douglas
Choral Director
Labay Junior High, Katy, Texas

Ruth E. Dwyer
Associate Director and Director of Education
Indianapolis Children's Choir
Indianapolis, Indiana

Norma Freeman
Choral Director
Saline High School, Saline, Michigan

Cynthia I. Gonzales
Music Theorist
Greenville, South Carolina

Michael Mendoza
Professor of Choral Activities
New Jersey State University
Trenton, New Jersey

Thomas Parente
Associate Professor
Westminster Choir College of Rider University
Princeton, New Jersey

Barry Talley
Director of Fine Arts and Choral Director
Deer Park ISD, Deer Park, Texas

CONTRIBUTING AUTHORS

Debbie Daniel
Choral Director, Webb Middle School
Garland, Texas

Roger Emerson
Composer/Arranger
Mount Shasta, California

Kari Gilbertson
Choral Director, Forest Meadow Junior High
Richardson, Texas

Tim McDonald
Creative Director, Music Theatre International
New York, New York

Christopher W. Peterson
Assistant Professor of Music Education (Choral)
University of Wisconsin-Milwaukee
Milwaukee, Wisconsin

Kirby Shaw
Composer/Arranger
Ashland, Oregon

Stephen Zegree
Professor of Music
Western Michigan State University
Kalamazoo, Michigan

EDITORIAL

Linda Rann
Senior Editor
Hal Leonard Corporation
Milwaukee, Wisconsin

Stacey Nordmeyer
Choral Editor
Hal Leonard Corporation
Milwaukee, Wisconsin

Table of Contents

Music & History

Choral Library

TO THE STUDENT

Welcome to choir!

By singing in the choir, you have chosen to be a part of an exciting and rewarding adventure. The benefits of being in choir are many. Basically, singing is fun. It provides an expressive way of sharing your feelings and emotions. Through choir, you will have friends that share a common interest with you. You will experience the joy of making beautiful music together. Choir provides the opportunity to develop your interpersonal skills. It takes teamwork and cooperation to sing together, and you must learn how to work with others. As you critique your individual and group performances, you can improve your ability to analyze and communicate your thoughts clearly.

Even if you do not pursue a music career, music can be an important part of your life. There are many avocational opportunities in music. **Avocational** means *not related to a job or career*. Singing as a hobby can provide you with personal enjoyment, enrich your life, and teach you life skills. Singing is something you can do for the rest of your life.

In this course, you will be presented with the basic skills of vocal production and music literacy. You will be exposed to songs from different cultures, songs in many different styles and languages, and songs from various historical periods. You will discover connections between music and the other arts. Guidelines for becoming a better singer and choir member include:

- Come to class prepared to learn.
- Respect the efforts of others.
- Work daily to improve your sight-singing skills.
- Sing expressively at all times.
- Have fun singing.

This book was written to provide you with a meaningful choral experience. Take advantage of the knowledge and opportunities offered here. Your exciting adventure of experiencing choral music is about to begin!

Lessons

Lessons for the Beginning of the Year

Lessons for Mid-Winter

Lessons for Concert/Festival

We Want To Sing

OVERVIEW

Composer: Roger Emerson
Text: Roger Emerson
Voicing: 2-Part
Key: C major
Meter: 4/4
Form: ABA'BA"
Style: American Pop
Accompaniment: Piano
Programming: Festival, School Assembly, Light Concert

Vocal Ranges:

Part I

Part II

OBJECTIVES

After completing this lesson, students will be able to:

• Perform expressively, from memory and notation, a varied repertoire of music representing styles from diverse cultures.

• Demonstrate appropriate small-ensemble and large-ensemble performance techniques.

VOCABULARY

Have students review vocabulary in student lesson. Introduce terms found in the music. A complete glossary of terms is found on page 246 of the student book.

We Want To Sing

Composer: Roger Emerson
Text: Roger Emerson
Voicing: 2-Part

VOCABULARY

singing posture
stage presence
two-part music
rest
tie

SPOTLIGHT

To learn more about posture, see page 11.

Focus

• Sing expressively.

• Perform two-part music.

Getting Started

Have you ever received a note or card from a friend that was so special to you that you kept it? When you have felt down, have you ever read the card again to lift your spirits? Singing has a way of making us feel good, too. "We Want To Sing" is an upbeat song with a positive message. Share this message with your audience through your enthusiasm, the excited expression on your face, and your **singing posture,** or *the way you stand when you sing.* These elements combined help to create your **stage presence,** or *your overall appearance on stage.*

◆ History and Culture

In the early 1970s while attending a choral camp in Shasta County, California, Roger Emerson, a small group of students, and a few counselors wrote "We Want To Sing." They wished to compose a piece of music that would reflect the message of goodwill to others and express the joy of singing.

"We Want To Sing" is an example of two-part music. **Two-part music** is *a type of music in which two different parts of music are sung together.* To make this song more interesting, the melody is sometimes found in Part I and other times found in Part II. As you learn "We Want To Sing," make sure that the melody line is clearly heard and not overshadowed by the other part.

RESOURCES

Beginning Sight-Singing

Sight-Singing in C major, pages 7–12, 14–17, 27–29, 116–117

Reading Rhythms in 4/4 Meter, pages 2–6

Teacher Resource Binder

Teaching Master 1, *Developing "Stage Presence"*

Teaching Master 2, *Performing "We Want to Sing" With Stage Presence*

Evaluation Master 9, *Identifying Vocal Balance*

Vocal Development 13, *Posture and Breathing*

For additional resources, see TRB Table of Contents.

Links to Learning

◆ **Vocal**

Establish your singing posture. Perform the following examples to practice singing in two parts.

◆ **Theory**

In music notation, a **rest** is *a symbol used to indicate silence.* A **tie** is *a curved line used to connect two notes of the same pitch together in order to make one longer note.* Perform the following examples to practice rhythmic patterns with rests and ties.

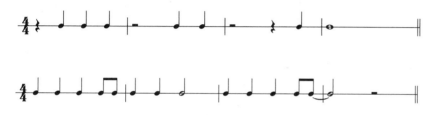

Evaluation

Demonstrate how well you have learned the skills and concepts featured in the lesson "We Want To Sing" by completing the following:

- Perform "We Want To Sing" expressively. In what ways did you show the meaning of the text through your overall stage presence?

- Select one person from Part I and one person from Part II to come forward and serve as listeners. As the choir sings measures 19–34, have the listeners decide if they can hear the two parts clearly, or if they hear one part overshadowed by the other.

LINKS TO LEARNING

Vocal

The Vocal section is designed to prepare students to sing in two-part harmony.

Have students:

- All sing Part I.
- All sing Part II.
- Divide into two groups, singing both parts together.

Theory

The Theory section is designed to prepare students to:

- Understand rests and ties.
- Read and perform rhythmic notation, including quarter and half rests and a tied rhythm pattern.

Have students:

- Tap the quarter note pulse.
- Speak the rhythms on a neutral syllable, while tapping the quarter note pulse.
- Clap the rhythms, feeling the quarter note pulse inside.

RESOURCES

Beginning Unison, 2-Part/3-Part Rehearsal/Performance CD

CD 1:1 Voices

CD 1:2 Accompaniment Only

CD 3:1 Vocal Practice Track—Part I

CD 4:1 Vocal Practice Track—Part II

National Standards

1. Singing, alone and with others, a varied repertoire of music. **(a, b)**

5. Reading music and notating music. **(e)**

9. Understanding music in relation to history and culture. **(b)**

LESSON PLAN

Suggested Teaching Sequence and Performance Tips

1. Introduce

Direct students to:

- Read and discuss the information found in the Getting Started section on page 2.
- Practice singing the two-part exercises found in the Vocal section on page 3 to establish good intonation, posture and breath support.
- Practice the rhythm patterns found in the Theory section on page 3. Pay particular attention to observing rests and holding long notes and tied notes accurately. Practice rhythmic breathing for clean precision of entrances and releases.

Progress Checkpoints

Observe students' progress in:

- ✓ Their ability to sing with pitch accuracy in two parts while using good singing posture and breath support.
- ✓ Their ability to read and perform rests and long and tied notes with rhythmic precision.
- ✓ Their ability to breathe rhythmically for accurate entrances and releases.

We Want To Sing

For 2-Part and Piano

Words and Music by
ROGER EMERSON

Copyright © 1977 HAL LEONARD CORPORATION
International Copyright Secured   All Rights Reserved

4   Beginning Unison, 2-Part/3-Part

TEACHER **2** TEACHER

An ideal song for starting off the year, "We Want To Sing" has a rock beat the students will enjoy and an inspiring text you can use to build a feeling of unity and goodwill in your classroom.

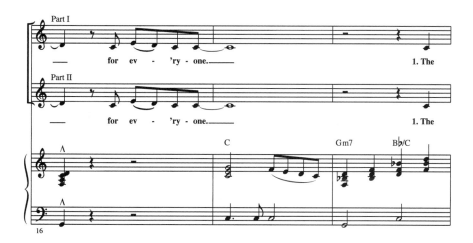

2. Rehearse

Direct students to:

- Count the rhythms for measures 2–17. Establish breathing pattern to reinforce the accuracy of each section's entrance and release. Ask the students to also use their fingers to tap the beat when counting the tied notes. Identify this section as the Chorus.

- Add solfège syllables and sing measures 2–17. Continue to tap the beat for whole notes and tied notes.

- Count the rhythms for measures 18–34. Repeat process from measures 2–17. Add solfège syllables and sing measures 18–34. Identify this section as the Verse. Note that the melody is in Part I.

- Practice moving from unison to harmony. *(measures 18–19, 21, 22–23, 26–27, 28–29, 30–32)* Remember that the unison places are focal points that will help the intonation of the parts following them. The melody should be louder than the harmony.

MORE ABOUT...

Expressive Elements of Music

In language, expression is used to communicate mood. The expressive elements of tempo, dynamics, tone color, pitch, articulation and intensity help to convey mood. These same expressive elements are available in performing music, and help the performer to establish and communicate the intended mood. It is up to the performer to understand and interpret the intentions of the composer and arranger. In a large group, the conductor frequently helps the group make these decisions, so they are all interpreting the piece in the same way. Have students interpret all music symbols and terms referring to tempo, dynamics and articulation in this piece of music.

- Count the rhythms in measures 34–42, then sing using solfège syllables. Note the imitation between voices. Continue using finger taps for rhythmic accuracy.
- Count the rhythms for measures 42–49. Note that this section is unison with the exception of measures 45–48, where Part II has the melody.
- Count the rhythms, then sing the coda using solfège syllables. Identify similarities and differences between the two parts. (*The word "make" in measures 51 and 55 is unison; measure 58 to the end is unison; the melody, in Part II, is altered in measures 52 and 54. The subito piano in measure 58 is different.*)

Progress Checkpoints

Observe students' progress in:
- ✓ Reading and performing syncopated rhythms.
- ✓ Singing in two parts.
- ✓ Locating the melody as well as unison and harmony parts in the score.
- ✓ Singing with proper breath control.

MORE ABOUT...

Practicing Singing and Reading Pitches

Solfège is a system designed to match notes on the staff with specific interval relationships, so the singer sight-sings accurately. Hand signs provide additional kinesthetic reinforcement of the pitch relationships. Sight-singing is a skill and improves through practice, building muscular and tonal memory. If interval patterns become "locked in" to the memory through repetition, the students will recall familiar patterns when they appear in the notation.

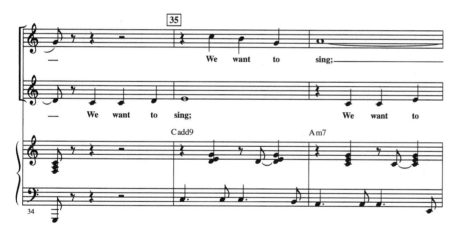

3. Refine

Direct students to:

- Sing the entire song using solfège syllables, correct rhythms and correct breaths.
- Sing musical phrasing of each melodic line. Using hands, move from left to right to draw the shape of each phrase. Use fingers to indicate consonant endings and releases.
- Use the concept of "staggered breathing" to communicate the text in the longer musical phrases. Identify the phrases that will require staggered breathing as a choir. *(measures 18–22, 26–30, 44–49)*
- Speak the words using unified vowel sounds. Analyze the words of each verse, noting how they correspond with the pitch and rhythm. Practice saying each verse with rhythmic precision. When accurate, add pitches.

Progress Checkpoints

Observe students' progress in:

✓ Singing accurate pitches, rhythms and text.

✓ Using breath support for rhythmic and staggered breathing.

✓ Performing with expressive phrasing.

✓ Singing unified vowel sounds.

MORE ABOUT...

Composer Roger Emerson

Roger Emerson is one of the most widely performed choral composers/arrangers in America today. He received his degree in music education from Southern Oregon University and served as music specialist for 12 years in the Mt. Shasta Public School system. He concluded his teaching career at the College of the Siskiyous, also in Northern California, and now devotes himself full-time to composing, arranging and consulting.

ASSESSMENT

Informal Assessment

In this lesson, students showed the ability to:

- Read and perform in two parts, as well as discriminate between the melody and the harmony throughout the song.
- Sing with good posture and proper breath support throughout.
- Read and perform tied notes, rests and syncopated rhythms in 4/4 meter.
- Sing the text expressively by understanding the meaning of the text.

Student Self-Assessment

Have students evaluate their individual performances based on the following:

- Expressive Singing
- Correct Part-Singing
- Posture
- Breath Management
- Phrasing

Have each student rate his/her performance of this song in the areas above on a scale of 1–5, 5 being the best.

MORE ABOUT...

Correct Breathing

Deep diaphragmatic breathing occurs most naturally when a person·lies on his or her back and the abdomen rises and falls. Suggest that students try this technique at home:

- Lie on your back as described above.
- With hands pressing the diaphragm, feel the muscle response when a sipping breath is taken. Exhale with a long hiss.
- Again with hands pressing the diaphragm, feel the response when a quick, surprised breath is taken. Exhale with short, accented hisses. Only the diaphragm should move visibly.

Individual and Group Performance Evaluation

To further measure growth of musical skills presented in this lesson, direct students to complete the Evaluation section on page 3.

- Videotape a performance of your choir singing "We Want To Sing." Show the videotape to the choir and ask, "Were members of the choir singing with expression that matched the lyrics?"
- Have each choir member sing measures 19–34 in a duet with one on a part. Ask the other choir members if each pair sang their part accurately and maintained their part within the ensemble.

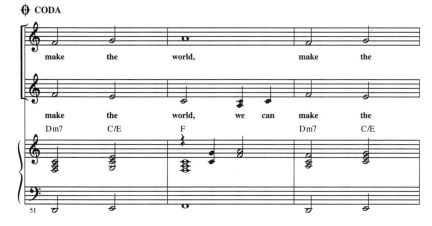

MUSIC, SOCIETY AND CULTURE

Have students perform additional songs representing diverse cultures, including American and Texas heritage. Go to **music.glencoe.com**, the Web site for Glencoe's choral music programs, for additional music selections students can perform.

EXTENSION

Creating Choreography

Create riser choreography to express the text and music of "We Want To Sing." Be sure to include a variety of steps and turns as well as hand movements. Create imitative choreography for the imitative singing sections.

Additional National Standards

The following National Standards are addressed through the Assessment, Extension, Enrichment and bottom-page activities:

7. Evaluating music and music performances. **(a, b)**

8. Understanding relationships between music, the other arts, and disciplines outside the arts. **(a)**

SPOTLIGHT

Posture

Posture is important for good singing. By having the body properly aligned, you are able to breath correctly so that you have sufficient breath support needed to sing more expressively and for longer periods of time.

To experience, explore and establish proper posture for singing, try the following:

Standing

- Pretend someone is gently pulling up on a thread attached to the top of your head.
- Let out all of your air like a deflating balloon.
- Raise your arms up over your head.
- Take in a deep breath as if you were sipping through a straw.
- Slowly lower your arms down to your sides.
- Let all your air out on a breathy "pah," keeping your chest high.
- Both feet on floor, shoulder-width apart.
- Chest high, shoulders relaxed.
- Neck relaxed, head straight.

Sitting

- Sit on the edge of a chair with your feet flat on the floor while keeping your chest lifted.
- Hold your music with one hand and turn pages with the other.
- Always hold the music up so you can easily see the director and your music.

Spotlight *Posture* **11**

POSTURE

Objectives
- Demonstrate basic performance techniques, including proper singing posture.

Suggested Teaching Sequence

Direct students to:
- Read the Spotlight On Posture on student page 11 and identify the importance of proper posture in singing.
- Perform the exercise for standing posture as presented on page 11.
- Perform the exercise for sitting posture as presented on page 11.
- Compare the concept of proper posture to basic performance techniques and the effect posture has on breath support, tone quality and overall stage presence.

Progress Checkpoints

Observe students' progress in:
- ✓ Their ability to stand in correct singing posture.
- ✓ Their ability to sit using correct singing posture.
- ✓ Their ability to explain the importance of proper posture in singing.

RESOURCES

Teacher Resource Binder

Vocal Development 13, *Posture and Breathing*

National Standards

1. Singing, alone and with others. **(b)**

My America

OVERVIEW

Composer: Based on "America," arranged by Joyce Eilers

Text: Samuel F. Smith, with new words by Joyce Eilers

Voicing: 2-Part

Key: E♭ major/F major

Meter: 3/4

Form: A A' A"

Style: Patriotic

Accompaniment: Piano

Programming: Concert, Patriotic Program

Vocal ranges:

OBJECTIVES

After completing this lesson, students will be able to:

• Read and perform music in 3/4 meter.

• Relate music to history.

• Perform music representative of American heritage.

VOCABULARY

Have students review vocabulary in student lesson. Introduce terms found in the music. A complete glossary of terms is found on page 246 of the student book.

My America

Composer: Based on "America," arranged by Joyce Eilers
Text: Samuel F. Smith, with new words by Joyce Eilers
Voicing: 2-Part

VOCABULARY

arrangement

descant

fermata

$\frac{3}{4}$ meter

Focus

• Read and perform music in $\frac{3}{4}$ meter.

• Relate music to other subjects.

• Perform music of American heritage.

Getting Started

What does America mean to you? What is your definition of patriotism? Patriotism can mean different things to different people. For some, it can be the image of the American flag or a historic monument. To others, it is the memory of those who have given their lives defending our country. Singing "My America" can help you express your feelings of patriotism and show what America means to you.

◆ **History and Culture**

The tune "My Country 'tis of Thee" can be found in many countries, including England, where it serves as the national anthem. In 1831, Samuel Smith, an American minister and author, wrote new words to this famous melody. It was first performed in Boston, Massachusetts, by a group of children at a Fourth of July celebration.

"My America" is an example of a choral arrangement. An **arrangement** is *a piece of music in which a composer takes an existing song and adds extra features or changes the song in some way.* Joyce Eilers has added new words and a **descant**, or *a special part that is usually sung higher than the other parts,* to the familiar tune "My Country 'tis of Thee" to create this arrangement.

SPOTLIGHT

To learn more about vowels, see page 75.

RESOURCES

Beginning Sight-Singing

Sight-Singing in E♭ Major, pages 147–151

Sight-Singing in F Major, pages 38–40, 60, 76–77, 118, 121–122

Reading Rhythms in 3/4 Meter, pages 15–16

Teacher Resource Binder

Vocal Development 13, *Posture and Breathing*

Teaching Master 3, *"America": My View*

Skill Builder 7, *Conducting: an Introduction*

Skill Builder 9, *Conducting in 3/4 Meter*

Teaching Master 4, *Arranging "My Country 'tis of Thee"*

For additional resources, see TRB Table of Contents.

Links to Learning

◆ Vocal

When singing in a choir, proper vowel sounds are the foundation of a good choral tone. Read and perform the following example to practice singing with uniform vowel sounds.

mee__ may__ mah__ moh__ moo   mee__ may__ mah__ moh__ moo

This symbol ⌒ is called a fermata. A **fermata** is *a symbol that instructs a musician to hold a note longer than its value.* Find a fermata in "My America."

◆ Theory

Read and perform the example below to practice reading rhythmic patterns in ¾ **meter,** *a time signature in which there are three beats per measure and the quarter note receives the beat.* Try conducting as you read.

ti ti ta ta   tam   ti ta   ti ti ta ta   ta–a–a

ta–a   ta   tam   ti ta   ta   ta   ta   ta–a–a

◆ Artistic Expression

To develop artistry through writing, write an introduction to "My America" to be read at a performance. Choose words appropriate to the patriotic style of this piece that will encourage your listeners to think of what America means to them.

Evaluation

Demonstrate how well you have learned the skills and concepts featured in the lesson "My America" by completing the following:

- Sing and conduct measures 5–20 to show your understanding of ¾ meter.
- Listen as each student reads his or her introduction to "My America." As a class, decide which introduction should be read at a performance.

RESOURCES

Beginning Unison, 2-Part/3-Part Rehearsal/Performance CD

CD 1:3 Voices
CD 1:4 Accompaniment Only
CD 3:2 Vocal Practice Track—Part I
CD 4:2 Vocal Practice Track—Part II

National Standards

1. Singing, alone and with others, a varied repertoire of music. **(a, c)**
5. Reading and notating music. **(a)**
8. Understanding relationships between music, the other arts and disciplines outside the arts. **(b)**
9. Understanding music in relation to history and culture. **(b)**

LINKS TO LEARNING

Vocal

The Vocal section is designed to prepare students to:

- Sing with uniform vowel sounds.
- Understand fermata and locate it in the score.

Have students:

- Sing the exercise, concentrating on matching the vowel sound to their neighbor.
- Continue singing the exercise, modulating up by half steps.

Theory

The Theory section is designed to prepare students to:

- Understand 3/4 meter.
- Read and perform rhythmic patterns in 3/4 meter.

Have students:

- Conduct a 3/4 pattern.
- Speak the rhythm exercise while conducting a 3/4 pattern.

Artistic Expression

The Artistic Expression section is designed to prepare students to understand the meaning of "My America." Have students write an introduction to "My America" incorporating their thoughts on what America means to them.

LESSON PLAN

Suggested Teaching Sequence and Performance Tips

1. Introduce

Direct students to:

• Read and discuss the information found in the Getting Started section on page 12.

• Read the text for "My America." Discuss the feelings of patriotism expressed in the text. Brainstorm to create a list of words to describe patriotism. Use some of these ideas as you write your introduction to "My America" as described in the Artistic Expression section on page 13.

• Practice the exercise found in the Vocal section on page 13 as a vocal warm-up. Discuss and practice observing the fermata sign.

• Sing "America" (measures 24–39) on "loo," using uniform vowel sounds. Pay particular attention to breath support and mouth shape. Relax the shoulders and breathe deeply while making a "fish face" mouth shape. Once sounds are unified, sing the text.

My America

For 2-Part and Piano

Arranged with new words by
JOYCE EILERS

Words by SAMUEL F. SMITH
Based on "America"

Pur-ple moun - tain maj - es-ties, am-ber waves of grain.

This is my A - mer - i - ca, to ___ thee we

Copyright © 1987 by HAL LEONARD CORPORATION
International Copyright Secured   All Rights Reserved

14   Beginning Unison, 2-Part/3-Part

TEACHER 2 TEACHER

Students will enjoy learning a partner song to "America." The flowing lines give a wonderful opportunity for musical phrasing and expressive singing.

- Practice the rhythmic patterns as shown in the Theory section on page 13 to increase ability to read and perform rhythms in 3/4 time. When accurate, conduct while chanting.
- Conduct and chant the rhythms for measures 24–39.

Progress Checkpoints

Observe students' progress in:

✓ Their ability to verbally express the feeling of patriotism.

✓ Their ability to sing uniform vowel sounds.

✓ Their ability to take deep, relaxed breaths.

✓ Their ability to read rhythms in 3/4 meter.

TEACHING STRATEGY

Phrases

Determining phrase length is not an accurate science. Although there are guidelines for determining phrase boundaries, there are frequent disagreements among musicians, leading to very different interpretations of the same piece. It usually is up to the conductor to make the final call, and then everyone in the ensemble must conform for a clear performance.

2. Rehearse

Direct students to:

- Chant the rhythm of measures 5–20. Isolate and practice the dotted quarter note/eighth note pattern. Locate this rhythm in the familiar song "America," as found in measures 43–58. *(measures 44, 46, 52, 56)*

- Practice singing the E♭ major scale using solfège syllables, as written on the overhead or chalkboard.

- Chant the solfège syllables for measures 5–20. Locate the large skips in the melody. *(measure 6: sol–re, measures 8–9: mi–la, measure 10: do–mi–sol, measure 18: sol–do, measures: 18–19: do–la)* Discuss and sing these intervals, reading the director's hand signs.

- Sight-sing measures 5–20 using solfège syllables, paying particular attention to tuning the intervals drilled.

- Sing the text in four-measure phrases to create an expressive musical line.

Progress Checkpoints

Observe students' progress in:

- ✓ Singing with rhythmic precision, particularly in dotted quarter note/eighth note patterns.
- ✓ Singing accurate pitches.
- ✓ Performing expressive four-measure phrases.

MORE ABOUT...

Arranger Joyce Eilers

Joyce Eilers' compositions are consistent favorites of teachers and students across the nation, and while her teaching experience spans all levels, she is particularly well known for her work with elementary and junior high singers. Her guidelines for writing in the 3-Part Mixed idiom revolutionized the middle school/junior high choral experience. Many of her compositions are standards for this age group, including "Dreamer," "Brighten My Soul With Sunshine" and "Send Down the Rain." She is the coauthor of *The Choral Approach To Sight-Singing* and *Patterns Of Sound*, both sight-singing methods for the beginning part-singer, as well as the choral text book *Essential Elements for Choir*.

sea to shin - ing sea.   My   A -

land   of   the   pil - grim's pride.   From   ev - 'ry —

mer - i - ca,   let free - dom   ring.

moun - tain side,   let — free - dom   ring.

3. Refine

Direct students to:

- Divide into two parts and chant the words at measures 24–58. Note measures where the voices move entirely in the same rhythm. *(measures 44, 46, 52, 54, 56, 58)*

- Note the key change. *(key of F major, measure 43)* Practice singing the F major scale using solfège syllables, as written on the overhead or chalkboard.

- Sing parts together using solfège syllables. Isolate and practice crossed voices. *(measures 45, 47, 51, 54, 56–57)* Add text once parts are secure.

- Sing measures 24–58 in four-measure phrases, listening for uniform vowel sounds. Pay particular attention to the dynamic markings and the *ritard.* in measure 58.

- Discuss the coda, or special ending. *(measures 59–60)* How are the two measures alike? *(same rhythm and both have a fermata)* How do they differ? *(two-part harmony with an optional second soprano written with cued notes)*

TEACHING STRATEGY

3/4 Meter and Dotted Rhythms

If students are not familiar with either the meter or dotted quarter-eighth note rhythm, have them:

- Clap a rhythm challenge in 3/4 meter that you write on the board until they are comfortable with the elements found in "My America."

- Learn the conducting pattern for 3/4 meter and conduct as they sing to feel the meter more securely.

- Sing parts separately until secure. Combine parts, making sure the forte ending carries through the fermata with no *decrescendo*.
- Add the accompaniment and perform "My America."

Progress Checkpoints

Observe students' progress in:

✓ Their ability to identify key changes.

✓ Secure part-singing with text, particularly when voices cross.

✓ Using unified vowel sounds.

✓ Identifying differences and similarities between Part I and Part II.

✓ Performing in four-measure phrases.

✓ Their ability to perform dynamic and style markings as presented in the score.

ASSESSMENT

Informal Assessment

In this lesson, students showed the ability to:

- Sing correct pitches in E♭ and F major.
- Read and perform a variety of rhythms in 3/4 meter.
- Sing accurately in two parts.
- Create audible contrasts between dynamic levels.

18   Beginning Unison, 2-Part/3-Part

MUSIC, SOCIETY AND CULTURE

Have students perform additional songs representing diverse cultures, including American and Texas heritage. Go to **music.glencoe.com**, the Web site for Glencoe's choral music programs, for additional music selections students can perform.

Student Self-Assessment

Have students evaluate their individual performances based on the following:

- Posture
- Breath Management
- Phrasing
- Expressive Singing
- Accurate Pitches

Have each student rate his/her performance of this song in the areas above on a scale of 1–5, 5 being the best.

Individual and Group Performance Evaluation

To further measure growth of musical skills presented in this lesson, direct students to complete the Evaluation section on page 13.

- After the students have sung and conducted measures 5–20, invite individuals to conduct those measures. Evaluate each conductor's performance by asking the other students, "How clear was his/her conducting? Were you able to follow the tempo and feeling of 3/4 meter?"

- After the students have written their introductions to "My America," have them read their introductions to the class. The class should evaluate each and vote on which one to use at the performance.

Additional National Standards

The following National Standards are addressed through the Assessment, Extension, Enrichment and bottom-page activities:

5. Reading and notating music. **(c)**

9. Understanding music in relation to history and culture. **(a)**

ARRANGING

Objectives

- Arrange melodic and rhythmic phrases.

Suggested Teaching Sequence

Direct students to:

- Read the Spotlight On Arranging on student page 20 and discuss the definition of an arrangement.
- Discuss the four elements used by arranger Joyce Eilers to arrange "My America."
- Study the arrangement of "My America" on pages 14–19 and locate the arranging devices used.
- Sing "My Country 'tis of Thee," then write an arrangement of "My Country 'tis of Thee" using the techniques discussed on page 20.
- Perform the arrangement for the class.
- Find other familiar songs and write arrangements for those as well.

Progress Checkpoints

Observe students' progress in:

- ✓ Their ability to identify the techniques used in arranging.
- ✓ Their ability to write a simple arrangement of "My Country 'tis of Thee."

SPOTLIGHT

Arranging

In music, an **arrangement** is *a composition in which a composer takes an existing melody and adds extra features or changes the melody in some way.* Composer Joyce Eilers wrote an arrangement of the familiar tune "My Country 'tis of Thee" by using the following techniques:

- Adding a piano accompaniment that supports the melody line.
- Writing a **descant** (*a special part that is usually sung higher than the melody*).
- Changing the key of the piece the second time the melody is sung.
- Writing a special ending sometimes referred to as a coda.

Study the music to "My America" found on pages 15–20. Identify the features mentioned above.

Other techniques that a composer may use in writing an arrangement of an existing melody is to lower or raise the pitch to make it easier to sing. A composer may take a vocal song and add instruments, or rearrange the song for instruments only. Sometimes a composer will change the time signature or meter, which may result in an arrangement that sounds quite different from the original.

In the example below, the familiar tune "My Country 'tis of Thee" has been changed from $\frac{3}{4}$ meter to $\frac{4}{4}$ meter, thus creating a new arrangement. Sing the example.

My coun-try 'tis of thee, sweet land of li - ber-ty of thee I sing.

On your own, complete this arrangement of "My Country 'tis of Thee" in $\frac{4}{4}$ meter. Think of another familiar melody and write an arrangement using some of the techniques suggested on this page.

20   Beginning Unison, 2-Part/3-Part

RESOURCES

Teacher Resource Binder

Teaching Master 4, *Arranging "My Country 'tis of Thee"*
Skill Builder 31, *Time Signatures in Music*
Reference 7, *Building a Musical Vocabulary*
Reference 15, *Exploring Careers in Music*

National Standards

4. Composing and arranging music within specific guidelines. **(b)**

SPOTLIGHT

Breath Management

Vocal sound is produced by air flowing between the vocal cords; therefore, correct breathing is important for good singing. Good breath management provides you with the support needed to sing expressively and for longer periods of time.

To experience, explore and establish proper breathing for singing, try the following:

- Put your hands on your waist at the bottom of your rib cage.

- Take in an easy breath for four counts, as if through a straw, without lifting your chest or shoulders.

- Feel your waist and rib cage expand all the way around like an inflating inner tube.

- Let your breath out slowly on "sss," feeling your "inner tube" deflating as if it has a slow leak.

- Remember to keep your chest up the entire time.

- Take in another easy breath for four counts before your "inner tube" has completely deflated, then let your air out on "sss" for eight counts.

- Repeat this step several times, taking in an easy breath for four counts and gradually increasing the number of counts to let your air out to sixteen counts.

Sometimes in singing it is necessary to take a quick or "catch" breath.

- Look out the window and imagine seeing something wonderful for the first time, like snow.

- Point your finger at the imaginary something and let in a quick, silent breath that expresses your wonderment and surprise.

- A quick breath is not a gasping breath, but rather a silent breath.

Spotlight *Breath Management* **21**

BREATH MANAGEMENT

Objectives

- Sing accurately with good breath control.

Suggested Teaching Sequence

Direct students to:

- Read the Spotlight on Breath Management on student page 21 and identify the importance of breath management when singing.

- Perform the exercise described on page 21.

- Practice a "catch" breath as described at the bottom of page 21.

- Compare the concept of proper breath management to effective performance practices.

Progress Checkpoints

Observe students' progress in:

✓ Their ability to perform the breathing exercises described on page 21.

✓ Their ability to discuss the importance of proper breath management when singing.

RESOURCES

Teacher Resource Binder

Vocal Development 13, *Posture & Breathing*

National Standards

1. Singing, alone and with others. **(b)**

Music Alone Shall Live

OVERVIEW

Composer: Shirley W. McRae
Text: Traditional
Voicing: Unison Voices/3-Part canon
Key: C major
Meter: 4/4
Form: Canon
Style: Contemporary American Round
Accompaniment: Piano
Programming: Concert Opener

Vocal Ranges:

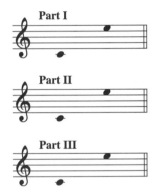

Part I

Part II

Part III

OBJECTIVES

After completing this lesson, students will be able to:

• Identify music forms presented aurally.

• Read and write music notation.

VOCABULARY

Have students review vocabulary in student lesson. Introduce terms found in the music. A complete glossary of terms is found on page 246 of the student book.

Music Alone Shall Live

Composer: Shirley W. McRae
Text: Traditional
Voicing: Unison Voices/3-Part Canon

VOCABULARY

unison

canon

a cappella

scale

trio

Focus

• Identify and perform a canon.

• Read and write music notation.

Getting Started

In a choir, there are many ways to sing. You can sing in **unison,** which means *all parts sing the same notes at the same time.* Or, you can sing a canon. A **canon** is *a form of music in which one part sings a melody and the other parts sing the same melody, but enter at different times.* Canons are sometimes called rounds. Singing in a canon is sometimes difficult because it is easy to lose track of your own part and join the others. However, when each singer can successfully stay on his or her own part, beautiful music is created.

 **SKILL BUILDERS**

To learn more about the key of C major, see Beginning Sight-Singing, pages 4 and 14.

◆ **History and Culture**

While "Music Alone Shall Live" can be sung with piano accompaniment, it can also be sung **a cappella,** or *without accompaniment.* This style of singing dates back hundreds of years, to when music was sung a cappella in the early European churches. In fact, this is where the term originated. In Latin, the word *a cappella* means "of the chapel." Today, a cappella singing encompasses a wide variety of musical styles, including barbershop, vocal jazz, gospel and others.

22   Beginning Unison, 2-Part/3-Part

RESOURCES

Beginning Sight-Singing

Sight-Singing in C major, pages 7–12, 14–17, 27–29, 116–117

Reading Dotted Notes, pages 43–45, 92, 110

Teacher Resource Binder

Evaluation Master 14, *Performance Evaluation: Part Singing*

Skill Builder 12, *Constructing Major Scales*

Skill Builder 14, *8-line Staff Paper*

Skill Builder 30 *Solfège Hand Signs*

Vocal Development 16, *Warm-up: Part Singing*

For additional resources, see TRB Table of Contents.

Links to Learning

◆ Vocal

Read and perform the melodic patterns below. Which pattern is found at the beginning of "Music Alone Shall Live?"

1   **2**

do   mi   mi   sol   do   mi   fa   sol

◆ Theory

This song is in the key of C major and is based on the C major scale. A **scale** is *a group of notes that are sung in succession and are based on a particular home tone.* The C major scale is easy to play on a piano or keyboard because this scale uses all white keys. To locate "C" on a piano, find any set of two black keys. "C" is the white key just to the left. Using the keyboard below as a guide, play the C major scale.

Sing the C major scale.

C   D   E   F   G   A   B   C   B   A   G   F   E   D   C
do   re   mi   fa   sol   la   ti   do   ti   la   sol   fa   mi   re   do

Evaluation

Demonstrate how well you have learned the skills and concepts featured in the lesson "Music Alone Shall Live" by completing the following:

- In your own words, describe a canon.
- Form a **trio**, or *a group of three singers.* Sing "Music Alone Shall Live" to show that you are able to stay on your own part.
- Based on the key of C major, write the pitches *do-mi-fa-sol* on a music staff.

LINKS TO LEARNING

Vocal

The Vocal section is designed to prepare students to:

- Sing ascending intervals with accurate pitch and intonation.
- Locate melodic patterns in their choral score.

Have students:

- Sing exercise 1 on solfège.
- Sing exercise 2 on solfège.
- Determine which pattern is found at the beginning of "Music Alone Shall Live."

Theory

The Theory section is designed to prepare students to:

- Understand the meaning of *scale*.
- Sing the C major scale with accuracy.

Have students:

- Play the C major scale on the keyboard. If selected students will play the scale on the keyboard, others should follow closely on the keyboard printed on page 23.
- Sing the C major scale on note names.
- Sing the C major scale on solfège.

RESOURCES

Beginning Unison, 2-Part/3-Part Rehearsal/Performance CD

CD 1:5 Voices

CD 1:6 Accompaniment Only

CD 3:3 Vocal Practice Track—Part I

CD 4:3 Vocal Practice Track—Part II

CD 4:4 Vocal Practice Track—Part III

National Standards

5. Reading and notating music. **(a, d)**

6. Listening to, analyzing, and describing music. **(a)**

LESSON PLAN

Suggested Teaching Sequence and Performance Tips

1. Introduce

Direct students to:

- Read and discuss the information found in the Getting Started section on page 22.
- Practice singing the intervals in the Vocal section on page 23.
- Practice singing the C major scale in the Theory section on page 23.

Progress Checkpoints

Observe students' progress in:

✓ Singing the ascending intervals in tune.

✓ Singing the pitches of a C major scale.

2. Rehearse

Direct students to:

- Rehearse the piece, encouraging them to shape beautiful phrases.
- Sing with good agogic stress. Two-syllable words like "mu-sic" normally have a strong first syllable and weak second syllable.

Progress Checkpoints

Observe students' progress in:

✓ Singing phrases as one musical thought.

✓ Their ability to place correct emphasis on appropriate syllables.

Music Alone Shall Live

For Unison Voices/3-Part Canon and Piano

Traditional

Music by SHIRLEY W. McRAE

Copyright © 1995 Plymouth Music Co., Inc., 170 N.E. 33rd St., Ft. Lauderdale, FL 33334
International Copyright Secured   Made in U.S.A.   All Rights Reserved

24 Beginning Unison, 2-Part/3-Part

TEACHER 2 TEACHER

The canon form in "Music Alone Shall Live" is an excellent method for introducing part-singing. Make sure all of the students can sing the melody with confidence before dividing into parts.

*May be performed with or without piano accompaniment.

3. Refine

Direct students to:

- Sing the music in unison, then divide them into two groups and sing a two-part canon.
- Sing the canon in three parts as soon as the two-part canon is solid.
- Sing the three-part canon without accompaniment once all parts are strong.

Progress Checkpoints

Observe students' progress in:

✓ Their ability to sing each part independently.

✓ Their ability to sing without accompaniment.

MORE ABOUT...

Canons

Music composition known as *canon music* dates back to England in the thirteenth century. The word *canon* evolved from the Greek word meaning "standard." The music is written for several vocal parts. One voice begins the song, and soon after, another voice either repeats or answers. When the song concludes, or begins again, it is called a circular canon. We imitate the canon tradition of music when we sing songs in "rounds."

ASSESSMENT

Informal Assessment

In this lesson, students showed the ability to:

- Sing independently.
- Sing without help from the piano part.

Student Self-Assessment

Have students evaluate their individual performances based on the following:

- Posture
- Breath Management
- Accurate Pitches
- Accurate Rhythms
- Correct Part-Singing

Have each student rate his/her performance of this song in the areas above on a scale of 1–5, 5 being the best.

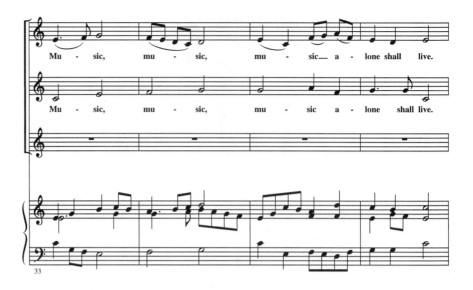

TEACHING STRATEGY

Vocal Development

Have students:

- Support a full tone with breath and open-throated, resonant singing.
- Sing legato with long phrases and tall vowels. Feel a forward movement to the peak of each phrase, usually the highest or longest tone in a phrase.
- Shape each phrase expressively by articulating the two note phrases; that is, lean into the first note and give it a slight stress. The second note is not stressed.
- Feel the phrasing by making a large horizontal circle counter-clockwise, in front of the body, while singing loud and soft. The soft is located close to the body, and the hand turns from palm up to a conducting position.

Individual and Group Performance Evaluation

To further measure growth of musical skills presented in this lesson, direct students to complete the Evaluation section on page 23:

- After singing "Music Alone Shall Live," have students describe a canon in their own words. Assess their answers.
- After singing "Music Alone Shall Live" in trios with one singer on each part, have the class evaluate each group. Was each singer able to stay on his/her own part?
- After students have written the pitches for *do-mi-fa-sol* in C major on a music staff (C, E, F, G), collect them and play each on the keyboard. Are all pitches correct?

Additional National Standards

The following National Standards are addressed through the Assessment, Extension, Enrichment and bottom-page activities:

1. Singing, alone and with others, a varied repertoire of music. **(a, b, d)**

7. Evaluating music and music performances. **(b)**

Singabahambayo

OVERVIEW

Composer: South African Folk Song

Text: Traditional Nguni

Voicing: Unison Voices with Optional 2-Part/3-Part

Key: G major

Meter: 4/4

Form: ABABAB'

Style: South African Folk Song

Accompaniment: Piano

Programming: Multicultural Concert

Vocal Ranges:

Objectives

After completing this lesson, students will be able to:

- Relate music to society.
- Read and perform with accurate rhythm.
- Perform a varied repertoire of music representing styles from diverse cultures.

VOCABULARY

Have students review vocabulary in student lesson. Introduce terms found in the music. A complete glossary of terms is found on page 246 of the student book.

Singabahambayo

Composer: South African Folk Song

Text: Traditional Nguni

Voicing: Unison Voices with Optional 2-Part/3-Part

VOCABULARY

interval

syncopation

Focus

- Relate music to society.
- Read and perform syncopation.
- Perform music representing South African culture.

Getting Started

This is an imaginary story that takes place not so long ago. It is a story about a young person of color named Mary who is a native inhabitant of the country of South Africa. She lives with her mother in a rural area, but her father must live and work in the city. When Mary and her family go into the city, her mother must have a special pass to go shopping or to visit Mary's father. As a woman, Mary's mother is not allowed to work in the city, to vote, or to socialize with anyone outside her race.

Then, the situation changes in South Africa, and Mary and her family are offered a lifestyle of equality and freedom. In what ways might Mary express this new freedom? She could sing "Singabahambayo," which is a song of celebration—a celebration of freedom.

◆ History and Culture

For many decades, South Africa was a place of social and political turmoil. This struggle affected men, women and children. As outsiders moved into the area, apartheid, or the separation of people by race, developed. Soon the native inhabitants were deprived of their land, their jobs and their rights. Men were used as inexpensive labor to work in the gold and diamond mines. Finally, after much struggle and violent protest, all South Africans gained freedom and equal rights on April 27, 2001.

SKILL BUILDERS

To learn more about syncopation, see Beginning Sight-Singing, *page 132.*

RESOURCES

Beginning Sight-Singing

Sight-Singing in G Major, pages 84–89, 93

Reading Syncopation, pages 160–161

Teacher Resource Binder

Teaching Master 5, *Pronunciation Guide for "Singabahambayo"*

Teaching Master 6, *Struggle for Freedom Here and There*

Evaluation Master 3, *Assessing Performing Syncopated Rhythms*

Skill Builder 24, *Rhythm Challenge Using Syncopation*

For additional resources, see TRB Table of Contents.

Links to Learning

◆ Vocal

An **interval** is *the distance between two notes*. Read and perform the following melodic patterns to practice singing intervals in tune.

◆ Theory

Read and perform the following example to practice rhythmic patterns that contain syncopation. **Syncopation** is *the placement of accents on a weak beat or a weak portion of the beat.*

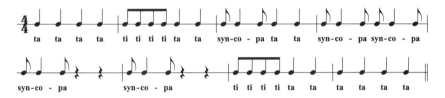

◆ Artistic Expression

Movement can enhance the interpretation or character of a song. Form two or three circles in the room. Walk to the beat of a drum. Once you are secure in walking the beat, begin singing "Singabahambayo." Notice the words that occur on the first beat of each measure. Stress these words as you sing and walk.

Evaluation

Demonstrate how well you have learned the skills and concepts featured in the lesson "Singabahambayo" by completing the following:

- Individually perform the rhythmic patterns found in the Theory section above to test your ability to read syncopated rhythms.
- South African music is known for its strong sense of the beat and its overall rhythmic excitement. Apply what you have learned about this style of music by indicating the words or syllables that occur on the strong beats. Check your choices with your teacher. How accurate were you?

RESOURCES

Beginning Unison, 2-Part/3-Part Rehearsal/Performance CD

CD 1:7 Voices

CD 1:8 Accompaniment Only

CD 3:4 Vocal Practice Track—Part I

CD 4:5 Vocal Practice Track—Part II

CD 4:6 Vocal Practice Track—Part III

National Standards

1. Singing, alone and with others, a varied repertoire of music. **(c)**
5. Reading and notating music. **(a)**
9. Understanding music in relation to history and culture. **(b)**

LINKS TO LEARNING

Vocal

The Vocal section is designed to prepare students to:

- Understand the meaning of an interval.
- Sing and tune melodic patterns.

Have students:

- Sing exercise 1 and name the intervals between the pitches.
- Repeat this procedure for exercises 2 and 3.

Theory

The Theory section is designed to prepare students to:

- Understand the meaning of syncopation.
- Establish rhythmic accuracy in reading syncopated rhythms in 4/4 meter.

Have students:

- Tap or clap the quarter note pulse.
- Speak the rhythms while tapping the quarter note pulse.
- Speak the rhythms while feeling the quarter note pulse inside.

Artistic Expression

The Artistic Expression section is designed to prepare students to add movement to enhance the interpretation of the song.

Have students:

- Form circles and walk to the beat of a drum.
- Sing "Singabahambayo" while walking, noticing the words that are stressed.

LESSON PLAN

Suggested Teaching Sequence and Performance Tips

1. Introduce

Direct students to:

- Read and discuss the information found in the Getting Started section on page 28.
- Sing, tune and practice the intervals found in the Vocal section on page 29.
- Practice and chant the rhythms found in the Theory section on page 29.
- Locate, discuss and practice the repeated melodic patterns and passages.
- Describe the form of the piece as ABABAB'.
  (Section A is measures 4–12. Section B is measures 13–20)
- Chant the solfège syllables for all pitches.

Progress Checkpoints

Observe students' progress in:

- ✓ Their ability to read syncopated rhythms.
- ✓ Their ability to sing melodic passages accurately.
- ✓ Their ability to identify AB form.

2. Rehearse

Direct students to:

- Chant the rhythm or text on a steady beat. Breathe in marked places to establish consistency and precision.
- Sight-sing the melody in measures 4–12.
- Sight-sing the melody in measures 12–16.

Singabahambayo

For Unison Voices with Optional 2-Part/3-Part and Piano

Piano arrangement by
MICHAEL SPRESSER

South African Folk Song
English words by JOHN HIGGINS

With joy (♩ = 108)

1. Sin - ga - ba - ham - ba - yo thi - na, ku -
march - ing for free - dom, we're

lom - hla - ba.___ Ke - pha si - ne - kha - ya,___ e -
go - ing home. Our hearts are filled with song,___ so

Zul - wi - ni.___ Sin - ga - ba - ham - ba - yo thi - na, ku -
sing out strong. Oh, we are march - ing for free - dom, we're

*Accompaniment CD has two measures fill before downbeat of measure 1.

Copyright © 2001 by MUSIC EXPRESS LLC
International Copyright Secured   All Rights Reserved

30   Beginning Unison, 2-Part/3-Part

TEACHER 2 TEACHER

"Singabahambayo" is a wonderful piece to use to introduce multicultural literature to your students and audience. It has a limited vocal range and the repeated syncopation has a natural feeling. What a wonderful piece for building team spirit in your group!

lom - hla - ba.___ Ke - pha si - ne - kha - ya,___ e -
go - ing home. *Our hearts are filled with song,___ so*

Zul - wi - ni.___ Ha - le - lu - ya!___ Ha -
sing out strong.___

le - lu - ya!___ Ha - le - lu - ya! Ha - le - lu - ya! Ha -

le - lu - ya!___ Ha - le - lu - ya!___ Ha -

*May be sung in unison or with optional harmony.

Lesson 4 *Singabahambayo* **31**

Progress Checkpoints

Observe students' progress in:

✓ Their ability to breathe with rhythmic accuracy.

✓ Singing accurate pitches and rhythms in all voice parts.

✓ Their ability to identify repeated patterns.

✓ Using the proper vocal tone in the Alto part.

3. Refine

Direct students to:

• Speak the Nguni diction in echo-style with the director. The pronunciation guide can be found in the Teacher Resource Binder, Teaching Master 5, *Pronunciation Guide for "Singabahambayo."*

• Divide the song into smaller sections. Practice each section with the correct Nguni diction and word stress. Use the physical movement from the Artistic Expression section on page 29 to reinforce appropriate style and expression.

Progress Checkpoints

Observe students' progress in:

✓ Singing with rhythmic and pitch accuracy.

✓ Using proper Nguni diction and word stress.

CULTURAL CONNECTIONS

Nelson Mandela (b. 1918)

Nelson Mandela, the first democratically elected State President of South Africa from 1994–1999, spent his entire life fighting for human rights and the abolishment of racism and apartheid (a policy of racial segregation practiced in the Republic of South Africa). In 1993, after spending thirty years in prison for his political views, Mandela accepted the Nobel Peace Prize on behalf of all South Africans who suffered and sacrificed so much to bring peace and equality to their land. The song "Singabahambayo" was often sung at gatherings led by Mandela and by others who were relentless in their fight for equality and freedom for all people.

ASSESSMENT

Informal Assessment

In this lesson, students showed the ability to:

- Read and perform syncopated rhythms.
- Sing a traditional Nguni text with appropriate word stress and style while marching and singing at the same time.
- Sing in three-part harmony.

Student Self-Assessment

Have students evaluate their individual performances based on the following:

- Diction
- Foreign Language
- Intonation
- Accurate Pitches
- Accurate Rhythms

Have each student rate his/her performance of this song in the areas above on a scale of 1–5, 5 being the best.

Individual and Group Performance Evaluation

To further measure growth of musical skills presented in this lesson, direct students to complete the Evaluation section on page 29.

- After performing the rhythm patterns in the Theory section, evaluate each student's ability to perform syncopated rhythms.
- Direct students to underline each stressed syllable in the choral score. Review as a class. Ask students how accurate they were.

32 Beginning Unison, 2-Part/3-Part

Additional National Standards

The following National Standards are addressed through the Assessment, Extension, Enrichment and bottom-page activities:

3. Improvising melodies, variations and accompaniments. **(c)**

9. Understanding music in relation to history and culture. **(c)**

SPOTLIGHT

Diction

Singing is a form of communication. To communicate well while singing, you must not only form your vowels correctly, but also say your consonants as clearly and cleanly as possible.

There are two kinds of consonants: voiced and unvoiced. Consonants that require the use of the voice along with the **articulators** (*lips, teeth, tongue, and other parts of the mouth and throat*) are called voiced consonants. If you place your hand on your throat, you can actually feel your voice box vibrate while producing them. Unvoiced consonant sounds are made with the articulators only.

In each pair below, the first word contains a voiced consonant while the second word contains an unvoiced consonant. Speak the following word pairs, then sing them on any pitch. When singing, make sure the voiced consonant is on the same pitch as the vowel.

Voiced:	Unvoiced Consonants:	More Voiced Consonants:
[b] bay	[p] pay	[l] lip
[d] den	[t] ten	[m] mice
[g] goat	[k] coat	[n] nice
[ʤ] jeer	[ʧ] cheer	[j] yell
[z] zero	[s] scenic	[r] red
[ʒ] fusion	[ʃ] shun	
[ð] there	[θ] therapy	More Unvoiced Consonants:
[v] vine	[f] fine	[h] have
[w] wince	[hw] whim	

The American "r" requires special treatment in classical choral singing. To sing an American "r" at the end of a syllable following a vowel, sing the vowel with your teeth apart and jaw open. In some formal sacred music and English texts, you may need to flip or roll the "r." For most other instances, sing the "r" on pitch, then open to the following vowel quickly.

Spotlight *Diction* **33**

RESOURCES

Teacher Resource Binder

Vocal Development 8, *Articulation*
Vocal Development 9, *Diction*
Reference 7, *Building a Musical Vocabulary*

National Standards

1. Singing, alone and with others, a varied repertoire of music. **(b)**
8. Understanding relationships between music, the other arts, and disciplines outside the arts. **(b)**

DICTION

Objectives

- Demonstrate basic performance techniques using proper diction.

Suggested Teaching Sequence

Direct students to:

- Read the Spotlight On Diction on student page 33 and identify the importance of diction in singing.
- Define articulators.
- Describe the difference between voiced and unvoiced consonants.
- Speak the voiced and unvoiced consonants out loud and find examples in music.
- Compare the concept of proper diction to effective performance practices.
- Discuss the proper use of the "r" consonant when singing.

Progress Checkpoints

Observe students' progress in:

✓ Their ability to speak voiced and unvoiced consonants properly.
✓ Their ability to name the parts of the body that are the articulators.
✓ Their ability to recognize voiced and unvoiced consonants in other music they are studying.
✓ Their ability to relate the importance of proper diction in other areas such as drama, speech and public speaking.

Good Cheer

OVERVIEW

Composer: Late Medieval English Song, arranged by Audrey Snyder

Text: Audrey Snyder

Voicing: 2-Part, Any Combination

Key: A♭ major/F major

Meter: 6/8

Form: AA'A''

Style: Medieval English Song

Accompaniment: Optional brass, hand percussion (finger cymbals, hand drum), instrumental pack available for C, B♭ and F instruments.

Programming: Concert Opener

Vocal Ranges:

Part I

Part II

OBJECTIVES

After completing this lesson, students will be able to:

• Perform a varied repertoire of music representing styles from diverse cultures.

• Read, write and perform music in 6/8 meter.

• Relate the other fine arts to music concepts.

VOCABULARY

Have students review vocabulary in student lesson. Introduce terms found in the music. A complete glossary of terms is found on page 246 of the student book.

LESSON 5

Good Cheer

Composer: Late Medieval English Song, arranged by Audrey Snyder

Text: Audrey Snyder

Voicing: 2-Part, Any Combination

VOCABULARY

Medieval period

a cappella

lute

intonation

$^6_8$ meter

MUSIC HISTORY

To learn more about the Medieval and Renaissance periods, see page 106.

Focus

• Describe and perform music from the Medieval period.

• Read, write and perform music in $^6_8$ meter.

• Interpret musical content through drama.

Getting Started

Imagine you are living in 14th century England. His Lordship, the Duke of Gloucester, is having a banquet, and you have been invited! The parchment invitation, secured with the Duke's own sealing wax, was delivered yesterday by a steward. What will you wear? What will you bring? What will you say? What kind of music will be performed? No doubt you would sing and dance to a song similar to "Good Cheer."

◆ History and Culture

This joyful piece is based upon a song entitled "Edi Be Thu," which was written in Gloucestershire, England during the **Medieval period** *(400–1430)*. Vocal music of this period was sometimes performed **a cappella**, or *without instrumental accompaniment*. At other times, it would not have been uncommon for a wooden flute or a **lute**, *an early form of the guitar*, to double the vocal parts. A drum would have been used to maintain the steady beat. When you perform "Good Cheer," try singing it a cappella and then again with instrumental accompaniment. Discuss which way you like the best.

34 Beginning Unison, 2-Part/3-Part

RESOURCES

Beginning Sight-Singing

Sight-Singing in F Major, pages 38–40, 60, 76–77, 118, 121–122

Reading 6/8 Meter, pages 119–121

Teacher Resource Binder

Teaching Master 7, *Creating Rhythmic Patterns in 6/8 Meter*

Teaching Master 8, *Let's Imagine: Medieval Moments*

Music and History 1, *Characteristics of Medieval and Renaissance Music: 1430–1600*

For additional resources, see TRB Table of Contents.

Links to Learning

◆ **Vocal**

"Good Cheer" is in the key of F major and is based on the F major scale. To locate "F" on a piano, find any set of three black keys. "F" is the white key just to the left. This scale uses the notes F, G, A, B♭, C, D, E, F. Using the keyboard below as a guide, play the F major scale.

Sing the following scale, paying attention to **intonation**, or *in-tune singing*.

| F | G | A | B♭ | C | D | E | F | E | D | C | B♭ | A | G | F |
| do | re | mi | fa | sol | la | ti | do | ti | la | sol | fa | mi | re | do |

◆ **Theory**

Read and perform the following rhythmic pattern to practice reading music in ⁶⁄₈ **meter,** *a time signature in which there are six beats per measure and the dotted quarter note receives the beat.*

| tam | tam | ti ti ti tam | ta ti ti ti ti | tik-um ti tam |

Evaluation

Demonstrate how well you have learned the skills and concepts featured in the lesson "Good Cheer" by completing the following:

- Discuss the musical characteristics of the Medieval period.

- Write four measures of rhythmic patterns in ⁶⁄₈ meter. Use the music as a guide. Perform your composition for the class.

- With four to six friends, create a short skit about life in medieval Gloucester that ends with singing the first verse of "Good Cheer." Your characters might include the Duke, a weaver, a goldsmith, a blacksmith or a friar.

RESOURCES

Beginning Unison, 2-Part/3-Part Rehearsal/Performance CD

CD 1:9 Voices

CD 1:10 Accompaniment Only

CD 3:5 Vocal Practice Track—Part I

CD 4:7 Vocal Practice Track—Part II

National Standards

1. Singing, alone and with others, a varied repertoire of music. **(c)**

5. Reading and notating music. **(a)**

8. Understanding relationships between music, the other arts, and disciplines outside the arts. **(b)**

Vocal

The Vocal section is designed to prepare students to:

- Recognize and play the F major scale.

- Sing the F major scale with accuracy.

Have students:

- Play the F major scale on the keyboard. If selected students will play the scale on the keyboard, others should follow closely on the keyboard printed on page 35.

- Sing the F major scale on note names.

- Sing the F major scale on solfège.

Theory

The Theory section is designed to prepare students to:

- Understand 6/8 meter.

- Read and perform rhythmic patterns in 6/8 meter.

Have students:

- Tap or clap the eighth note pulse in 6/8 meter, emphasizing beats 1 and 4.

- Speak the rhythm exercise while tapping the eighth note pulse.

- Speak the rhythm exercise while the director conducts, feeling the eighth note pulse inside.

LESSON PLAN

Suggested Teaching Sequence and Performance Tips

1. Introduce

Direct students to:

- Read and discuss the information found in the Getting Started section on page 34.

- Practice reading rhythmic patterns in 6/8 meter as found in the Theory section on page 35.

- Find examples of each of these rhythmic patterns in the choral score. *(measure 1 in example in measure 61; measure 2 in example in measures 14, 18, 26, 46, 50; measure 3 in example in measures 11, 15, 19, 21, 23, 43, 47, 51, 53, 55; measure 4 in example in measures 22, 54)*

- Count the rhythms in measures 11–18, noting the repetition. *(measures 11–14 repeated in measures 15–18)* Point out the cued note in measure 17 and relate it to the text.

- Count the rhythms in measures 19–22, noting the repetition. *(measures 19–20 repeated similarly in measures 21–22)*

- Count the rhythms in measures 23–26, noting they are the same as those in measures 11–14.

Good Cheer
(Festival Procession)

For 2-Part, Any Combination, with Piano* and Optional Hand Percussion**

Arranged by
AUDREY SNYDER

Words by AUDREY SNYDER
Based on a Late Medieval English Song

*May be sung a cappella.
**Hand Percussion parts found on page 41.

Copyright © 1999 by HAL LEONARD CORPORATION
International Copyright Secured   All Rights Reserved

36   Beginning Unison, 2-Part/3-Part

TEACHER 2 TEACHER

Students' imaginations will soar as they sing this Medieval English Song. Here is a wonderful opportunity to use sight-singing skills by learning the piece without piano.

The music above includes lyrics:

Line (measures 17–19):
mer - ry hearts___ and spir - its bright. Sing we now___ most
glad___ some in - stru - ments then___ re - ply. Sing we now___ most

Lower line:
mer - ry hearts and spir - its bright. Sing we now most
glad - some in - stru - ments then___ re - ply. Sing we now most

Line (measure 20):
joy - ful - ly, de - light - ing in___ your com - pa - ny,
joy - ful - ly, de - light - ing in___ your com - pa - ny,

Lower line:
joy - ful - ly, de - light - ing in your com - pa - ny,
joy - ful - ly, de - light - ing in your com - pa - ny,

Line (measure 23):
Wel - come, wel - come from far and near, we wel - come you___ with
Wish - ing peace and good will to all who cel - e - brate___ with -

Lower line:
Wel - come, wel - come from far and near, we wel - come you with
Wish - ing peace and good will to all who cel - e - brate with -

Play treble staff both times

Lesson 5 *Good Cheer* **37**

- Compare the rhythms in measures 11–26 to those in measures 43–62. Note the repetition throughout, with the exception of measures 59–62, which is the Coda. Chant the Coda and discuss the rhythmic differences. *(tied notes in measure 60 and successive dotted quarter notes in measures 61–62)*

Progress Checkpoints

Observe students' progress in:
- ✓ Their ability to read rhythms in 6/8 meter.
- ✓ Their ability to find specific rhythmic figures in the score.
- ✓ Their ability to locate repeated rhythmic patterns.

TEACHING STRATEGY

Reading Rhythms in 6/8 Meter

If students are not familiar with the rhythmic notation for 6/8 meter, return to the introductory pages and find the rhythms in 6/8 chart. Have students:

- Construct a rhythm challenge together, beginning with just one or two of the rhythms, and gradually adding more challenging combinations.
- Keep track of how well they are doing on the rhythm challenge by graphing the measure on which they made their first mistake.
- Track and graph this information over 15 trials. By the end of these trials, the students should be ready to work in 6/8 meter.

2. Rehearse

Direct students to:

- Practice singing the F major scale as found in the Vocal section on page 35.

- Sing the following melodic patterns found in Part I as the director signs them: *do–mi–sol, do–re–la–sol, do–re–fa.* Locate these skips in the music.

- Sight-sing Part I without the piano when the scale and melodic patterns are secure. Divide the verses into the same sections used when chanting rhythms.

- Repeat the process for Part II. Note that this part moves mostly in step-wise motion, making it easier to sight-sing.

- Combine Parts I and II using solfège syllables. Follow the dynamics and make certain to follow the breath marks in the score.

Progress Checkpoints

Observe students' progress in:

- ✓ Their ability to read and perform the F major scale with good intonation.

- ✓ Their ability to sing melodic patterns as signed by the director.

- ✓ Their ability to identify patterns moving in step-wise and skipping motion.

- ✓ Their ability to read and perform dynamic and breath marks as presented in the score.

38   Beginning Unison, 2-Part/3-Part

TEACHING STRATEGY

Describing Musical Instruments

- Have the students listen to the accompaniment of "Good Cheer" as found on the CD in the Teacher Resource Binder. As they listen, have them list the instruments they hear. If this is too difficult, have them name the instrument families from which they come. *(Two recorders (woodwind family), Viola, Cello (string family), Hand Drum, Finger Cymbals (percussion family)*

- Have students describe and classify the sound of this instrumentation in the following categories: genre *(chamber music)*; style *(joyful)*; period *(Medieval)*; culture *(English).*

3. Refine

Direct students to:

- Listen to and follow the music for the introduction and interlude. Sing the piece with piano accompaniment and discuss ways in which the accompaniment changes the feel of the piece.

- Sing the piece with a feeling of two pulses per measure. Accent the first note in a slur except in measures 20 and 22, where both notes are stressed.

- Articulate the text with clean, crisp diction.

- Assume the role of a medieval character in the King's court and perform the piece "in character."

Progress Checkpoints

Observe students' progress in:

✓ Their ability to follow the accompaniment score.

✓ Their ability to sing 6/8 meter with a feeling of two.

✓ Using energetic presentation of the text with understandable diction.

✓ Their ability to sing expressively in an assumed role.

TEACHING STRATEGY

Musical Elements of Style

The combination of musical elements determines the style of a piece. Have students:

- Compile a list of musical elements that might affect style.

- Share the lists to compile one master list.

- Sing known songs, trying out different styles, and then try to describe the musical elements that are characteristic of that style. (Try salsa, operatic, Broadway, rock, military and lullaby styles to start; then take suggestions.)

ASSESSMENT

Informal Assessment

In this lesson, students showed the ability to:

- Sight-sing music in F major with accurate pitches.
- Read and perform music in 6/8 meter with a feeling of two pulses per measure.
- Create an expressive performance based upon the style of the Medieval period.

Student Self-Assessment

Have students evaluate their individual performances based on the following:

- Diction
- Expressive Singing
- Intonation
- Accurate Pitches
- Accurate Rhythms

Have each student rate his/her performance of this song in the areas above on a scale of 1–5, 5 being the best.

40   Beginning Unison, 2-Part/3-Part

TEACHING STRATEGY

Guiding Composition

Guiding student composition is a delicate balance. On one hand, you want to build self-esteem through praise and encouragement. On the other hand, you want to encourage growth and push students beyond the obvious to the interesting and creative. The writing process used in Language Arts offers a series of steps that can become a process for musical composition as well. The first step is planning; then a first draft. Next is a peer consultation and a first revision. This process continues until students feel they are close to a finished work. At this point, a conference is scheduled with you. There is more revision until a final product is achieved, which is written and performed.

Good Cheer
(Festival Procession)

HAND PERCUSSION
(Hand Drum, Finger Cymbals)

Words by AUDREY SNYDER
Based on a Late Medieval English Song
Arranged by AUDREY SYNDER

Copyright © 1999 by HAL LEONARD CORPORATION
International Copyright Secured   All Rights Reserved

Lesson 5 *Good Cheer*   **41**

Additional National Standards

The following National Standards are addressed through the Assessment, Extension, Enrichment and bottom-page activities:

4. Composing and arranging music within specific guidelines. **(a)**

9. Understanding music in relation to history and culture. **(a)**

Individual and Group Performance Evaluation

To further measure growth of musical skills presented in this lesson, direct students to complete the Evaluation section on page 35.

- After discussing the musical characteristics of the Medieval period, create a poster or bulletin board listing these characteristics to serve as a reminder for future Medieval pieces.

- After each student writes a four-measure composition in 6/8 meter and performs it for the class, ask the class, "Were the rhythms in 6/8 meter? Was the composition four measures long?"

- After the small groups have created a short skit about life in medieval times, perform the skits for the class and ask for constructive criticism of the musical and dramatic elements.

EXTENSION

Creating a Drama

The Duke of Gloucester is holding court. Choose several guests to attend and stage the drama to occur during the singing of "Good Cheer." Choose different sections of the piece to be sung as solos or duets. During instrumental interludes have the medieval characters presented to the court. Add costumes (or at least hats!) and sing expressively as you create the drama.

Winter's Night

OVERVIEW

Composer: Frode Fjellheim
Text: Frode Fjellheim
Voicing: 2-Part
Key: D minor/G minor
Meter: 3/4
Form: Intro ABA'
Style: Norwegian Folk Style
Accompaniment: Piano and
B♭ Soprano Saxophone,
Triangle
Programming: Winter,
Multicultural Concert

Vocal Ranges:

OBJECTIVES

After completing this lesson,
students will be able to:

- Relate music to culture.
- Demonstrate fundamental
  skills while performing,
  including good diction.
- Perform a varied repertoire
  of music representing styles
  from diverse cultures.

VOCABULARY

Have students review
vocabulary in student lesson.
Introduce terms found in the
music. A complete glossary
of terms is found on page
246 of the student book.

Winter's Night

Composer: Frode Fjellheim
Text: Frode Fjellheim
Voicing: 2-Part

VOCABULARY

yoik
diction
perfect fifth

Focus

- Relate music to culture.
- Sing with good diction.
- Perform music from the Arctic region of Sampi.

Getting Started

In the month of December, how many hours of daylight does your location receive? What time is light visible? What time does darkness return? Imagine living in the Arctic Circle, where for two months during the winter, the sun barely rises above the horizon, leaving the daytime in darkness. Winter begins in October and extends through May. Temperatures may get as cold as 60° F *below* zero. Lakes and rivers are frozen, and the snow that covers the landscape mutes sound. According to the composer, "Winter's Night" musically paints a picture of the silence and darkness during such a winter.

◆ History and Culture

"Winter's Night" loosely models the style of a **yoik**, *a vocal tradition of the Sami people.* The Sami are some of the original inhabitants of the Arctic region called Sampi (formerly referred to as Lapland), which includes the northernmost sections of Norway, Sweden and Finland, as well as Russia's Kola Peninsula. The yoik vocal tradition typically features short melodic phrases that are repeated with slight variations. The text of "Winter's Night" uses syllables that have no meaning, but are designed to sound like the Norwegian language.

SKILL BUILDERS

To learn more about the key of D minor, see Beginning Sight-Singing, *page 50.*

RESOURCES

Beginning Sight-Singing

Sight-Singing in D Minor, pages 50–54, 61–63, 78–81
Reading 3/4 Meter, pages 15–16

Teacher Resource Binder

Evaluation Master 6, *Diction Checkup*
Teaching Master 9, *The Colors of Sound*
Skill Builder 13, *Constructing Minor Scales*
Skill Builder 18, *Major and Minor Scales*
Vocal Development 9, *Diction*

For additional resources, see TRB Table of Contents.

Links to Learning

◆ Vocal

In vocal music, **diction** is *the pronunciation of words while singing.* Read and perform the following examples to practice singing with good diction.

◆ Theory

"Winter's Night" is in the key of D minor and is based on the D minor scale. Read and perform the first example to establish the key of D minor. **A perfect fifth** is *the interval of two pitches that are five notes apart on the staff.* Read and perform the second example to practice singing perfect fifths in tune.

Evaluation

Demonstrate how well you have learned the skills and concepts featured in the lesson "Winter's Night" by completing the following:

- Discuss ways in which the music paints a picture of the silence and darkness of the long, harsh winters of Sampi.
- Perform your part in measures 48–64 to show you can sing with good diction.

Lesson 6 *Winter's Night* **43**

Vocal

The Vocal section is designed to prepare students to:

- Understand diction.
- Sing using proper diction.

Have students:

- Sing example 1, following the pronunciation guide under the lyrics and concentrating on good diction.
- Follow the same procedure for exercises 2–4.

Theory

The Theory section is designed to prepare students to:

- Read music in the key of D minor.
- Understand and practice singing the interval of a fifth.

Have students:

- Listen as you play the D minor scale on the keyboard.
- Sing the D minor scale on note names.
- Sing the D minor scale on solfège syllables.
- Sing exercise 2 on solfège, carefully tuning each interval, especially the interval of a fifth.

RESOURCES

Beginning Unison, 2-Part/3-Part Rehearsal/Performance CD

CD 1:11 Voices

CD 1:12 Accompaniment Only

CD 3:6 Vocal Practice Track—Part I

CD 4:8 Vocal Practice Track—Part II

National Standards

1. Singing, alone and with others, a varied repertoire of music. **(b, c)**
9. Understanding music in relation to history and culture. **(a)**

LESSON PLAN

Suggested Teaching Sequence and Performance Tips

1. Introduce

Direct students to:

- Read and discuss the information found in the Getting Started section on page 42.
- Practice chanting and singing the text as found in the Vocal section on page 43.
- Practice singing the D minor scale and perfect fifths as directed in the Theory section on page 43.

From NORWEGIAN SAMI SONGS

Winter's Night
(Vinternatt)

For 2-Part and Piano with Optional B♭ Soprano Saxophone and Triangle*

Words and Music by
FRODE FJELLHEIM

* Instrument parts found on pages 53–55.

© Copyright 2001 by Boosey & Hawkes, Inc.
Copyright for all countries.   All rights reserved.

44   Beginning Unison, 2-Part/3-Part

TEACHER 2 TEACHER

"Winter's Night" is a stunning composition! Frode Fjellheim has taken a very old vocal tradition—"yoik"—and placed it in a contemporary setting. Encourage the choir to imagine themselves placed in the dark, still, wintry scene.

Progress Checkpoints

Observe students' progress in:

✓ Their ability to pronounce the text.

✓ Their ability to sing the D minor scale and perfect fifths in tune.

TEACHING STRATEGY

Diction

Clear pronunciation requires attention to both vowels and consonants. Have students:

- Identify the need for clear diction so the audience will know what the piece is about.
- Discuss what choral techniques will produce clear diction. (*unified vowels, crisp beginning and ending consonants, quick mouth movement to shape sounds*)
- Sing through slowly with only vowels, keeping the jaw lowered and blending the vowels.
- Add the consonants, keeping the vowels blended.
- Sing through the piece attending to clear diction.

2. Rehearse

Direct students to:

- Count the rhythms in measures 22–30. Notice that Part I repeats a two-measure rhythmic pattern, while Part II repeats a four-measure pattern.
- Add pitches to measures 22–30.
- Count the rhythms in Section A, measures 31–47. Chant the lyrics before adding pitches.
- Count rhythms for Part I at Section B (measure 48), noticing that the melody is identical to that in Section A, though transposed.
- Count rhythms at measure 48 for Part II. Keep the pulse steady so that the quarter note following two tied notes (measure 49, beat 3, for example) is placed accurately. Add pitches and text after rhythms are correct.

TEACHING STRATEGY

Minor Sound

If students seem interested in the minor sound, place a staff on the board and write both the F major scale and the D minor scale. They both have the same key signature. Minor scales have three possibilities: natural, melodic and harmonic. There are also minor modes. Have the students find out more about minor scales and modes in a theory text, then learn to play each one. They might improvise or compose short minor melodies using mostly stepwise motion.

- Sing all of Section B with both parts together.
- Have Part I sing the melody for the return of Section A (measure 74), while Part II sight-sings their line.

Progress Checkpoints

Observe students' progress in:

✓ Their ability to perform accurate rhythms and pitches. Give particular attention to the initial vertical major second, D–E. *(measures 22, 24, 26, and 28)*

✓ Their ability to sing with proper intonation on vertical perfect fifths between Parts I and II in measures 22–30.

✓ Their ability to sing correct pronunciation with tall, rounded vowels.

✓ Their ability to recognize repeated melodic patterns.

TEACHING STRATEGY

Sight-Singing in D Minor

Have students:

- Write the D minor scale on a staff.
- Select one partner to point to the pitches randomly, first in stepwise order, then using some skips, creating melodic fragments or phrases. The other partner will sing the pitches that are pointed to as accurately as possible, with both correcting mistakes using a pitched instrument for reference. Switch roles.
- Both listen for melodic fragments of phrases that might become part of a melody they could write for others to sight-sing.

3. Refine

Direct students to:

- Sing the entire song using solfège syllables and correct rhythms.
- Sing the entire song with the lyrics using proper diction.
- In Sections A and B, sing four-measure phrases.
- Voice the "v" in the syllable "vai."
- Keep sustained notes active by mentally counting the eighth notes often present in the piano accompaniment.
- Apply the dynamic markings provided by the composer to create a large-scale arch.

CURRICULUM CONNECTIONS

Sampi

The Sampi southern border is approximately the Arctic Circle, which is near the latitude 66.5° N. (As a reference, the U.S.-Canadian border is the 49th latitude). The Arctic Circle is the line where the sun remains in the sky for 24 hours in the summer and disappears for 24 hours in the winter.

Progress Checkpoints

Observe students' progress in:

✓ Singing accurate rhythms and pitches, as well as executing precise cut-offs.

✓ Performing fluid four-measure phrases.

✓ Enunciating proper diction with understandable consonants.

✓ Using dynamic contrast between sections.

TEACHING STRATEGY

Performance Techniques

1. Identify appropriate performance techniques to be used in the performance of this song.

2. Either in small-ensembles or with the entire choir (large-ensemble), perform the song exhibiting these performance techniques.

3. Describe the performance techniques experienced during the performance.

4. Critique the performance based on the observed performance techniques.

5. Repeat this process often in both informal and formal concert settings.

ASSESSMENT

Informal assessment

In this lesson, the students showed the ability to:

- Read rhythms correctly throughout the song.
- Sing perfect fifths in tune in the key of D minor.
- Sing four-measure phrases in 3/4 meter.

Student Self-Assessment

Have students evaluate their individual performances based on the following:

- Phrasing
- Diction
- Foreign Language
- Tall Vowels
- Intonation

Have each student rate his/her performance of this song in the areas above on a scale of 1–5, 5 being the best.

50   Beginning Unison, 2-Part/3-Part

MORE ABOUT...

Careers in Music

There are many career opportunities in the field of music. Discuss the following options with the students and perhaps bring in a guest speaker from each field:

- Performer
- Composer
- Manager
- Music Technician
- Teacher
- Conductor
- Music Sales
- Music Publisher

To further measure growth of musical skills presented in this lesson, direct students to complete the Evaluation section on page 43:

- After singing "Winter's Night," find specific musical passages that remind you of a harsh winter landscape.

- After singing measures 48–64 in pairs with one singer on each part, evaluate the performance by asking, "How understandable was the text as it was sung?"

MORE ABOUT...

Composer Frode Fjellheim

Born in 1959, Norwegian Frode Fjellheim is a freelance musician and composer who studied classical piano at the Music Conservatory in Trondheim between 1980 and 1984. With his band TRANSJOIK, he has toured extensively playing modern techno/ambient-influenced music based on traditional Sami yoik. "Winter's Night" is one of six movements from a set titled "Norwegian Sami Songs."

EXTENSION

Compose

Have students compose a sound portrait of one scene with which they are familiar. The possibilities include lunchtime in the school cafeteria, school hallways between classes, and a class taking a test. To begin, describe the mood or feeling the music is to communicate (for example, frenetic, calm or busy). List any specific elements of the scene that the music is to portray in the composition (for example, a ringing bell or shuffling feet). Place the elements in order. Generate musical motives that capture the mood of the scene and notate them. Include instrumental accompaniment as appropriate. In class, video-tape a performance of the composition. Evaluate both the composition and the perform-ance. Rewrite as necessary and repeat the video-and-evalua-tion process before performing in front of an audience.

Additional National Standards

The following National Standards are addressed through the Assessment, Extension, Enrichment and bottom-page activities:

3. Improvising melodies, variations and accompaniments. **(c)**

4. Composing and arranging music within specific guidelines. **(a)**

From NORWEGIAN SAMI SONGS

Winter's Night
(Vinternatt)

Bb Soprano Saxophone (Bb Clarinet)

Music by
FRODE FJELLHEIM

Music, Society and Culture

Have students perform additional songs representing diverse cultures, including American and Texas heritage. Go to **music.glencoe.com**, the Web site for Glencoe's choral music programs, for additional music selections students can perform.

© Copyright 2001 by Boosey & Hawkes, Inc.
Copyright for all countries.   All rights reserved.

Lesson 6 *Winter's Night*   **53**

From NORWEGIAN SAMI SONGS

Winter's Night
(Vinternatt)

Instrumental Part in C

Music by
FRODE FJELLHEIM

© Copyright 2001 by Boosey & Hawkes, Inc.
Copyright for all countries.   All rights reserved.

From NORWEGIAN SAMI SONGS

Winter's Night
(Vinternatt)

Triangle

Music by
FRODE FJELLHEIM

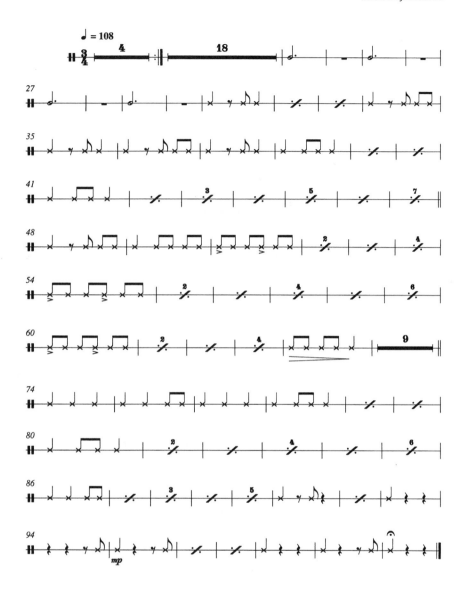

© Copyright 2001 by Boosey & Hawkes, Inc.
Copyright for all countries. All rights reserved.

Lesson 6 *Winter's Night*   **55**

Radiator Lions

OVERVIEW

Composer: Michael Jothen
Text: Dorothy Aldis
Voicing: Unison Voices
Key: G minor
Meter: 2/4, 4/4, 3/4, 3/8
Form: Rondo/ABACA'
Style: Contemporary
American Song
Accompaniment: Piano
Programming: Concert,
Festival

Vocal Ranges:

Objectives

After completing this lesson, students will be able to:

- Sing individually and in groups a varied repertoire of music, including music from the Contemporary period.
- Identify music forms presented aurally and through music notation.
- Read, write and perform with nontraditional notation.

VOCABULARY

Have students review vocabulary in student lesson. Introduce terms found in the music. A complete glossary of terms is found on page 246 of the student book.

Radiator Lions

Composer: Michael Jothen (b. 1944)
Text: Dorothy Aldis
Voicing: Unison Voices

VOCABULARY

Contemporary
period
rondo form
music notation

Focus

- Describe and perform music from the Contemporary period.
- Identify rondo form.
- Use nontraditional notation to read, write and perform music.

Getting Started

Some common ways to express yourself with your voice are whispering, speaking, singing, and shouting. But if you imitate the sound of an airplane, a school bell or a siren, you use your voice in a different way. Try making these sounds with your voice.

The word *traditional* describes characteristics common to a specific time or concept, whereas *nontraditional* describes characteristics that are uncommon. For example, two houses may have the same number of rooms, but may look different due to the style used to create them. In the traditional house, you might find walls, a roof and windows, while the nontraditional house might be built into the side of a hill or underground.

MUSIC & HISTORY

To learn more about the Contemporary period, see page 122.

◆ History and Culture

"Radiator Lions" is a musical composition from the **Contemporary period** *(1900–present)*. A common practice in this period is to combine traditional and nontraditional elements in the same piece of music. This song is written in a traditional form known as rondo form. **Rondo form** is *a musical form in which a repeated section is separated by several contrasting sections.* If you were to divide this song into sections, it might look something like this: A, B, A, C, A. Through the use of nontraditional **music notation**, or *a means of writing down music*, you will see how to produce a variety of sounds with your voice. Find examples of this notation in the music.

RESOURCES

Beginning Sight-Singing

Sight-Singing in G Minor, pages 140–145
Reading Mixed Meter, page 108

Teacher Resource Binder

Teaching Master 10, *Composing in Rondo Form*
Teaching Master 11, *Creating Nontraditional Notation*
Teaching Master 12, *Analyzing the Form of "Radiator Lions"*
Music and History 13, *Characteristics of Contemporary Music*
For additional resources, see TRB Table of Contents.

Links to Learning

◆ **Theory**

Read and perform the following example to develop rhythmic precision.

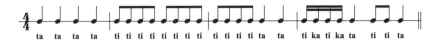

ta   ta   ta   ta   ti ti ti ti ti ti ti ti   ti ti ti ti ta   ta   ti ka ti ka ta   ti   ti   ta

◆ **Artistic Expression**

Study the following definitions to help you interpret nontraditional music notation.

1 ▮ = Speak

2 = Get louder and softer according to the rise and fall of the line

3 ～～～～ = Continue making the sound until instructed to stop

4 = Speak with inflection

Read and perform the following example to practice speaking with inflection. Make your voice sound higher and lower based on the rise and fall of the notes.

ta–a   ta–a   ti ti ti ti ta   ta   ti ti ti ti ti ti ti ti   tam   ti ti ti ta

Evaluation

Demonstrate how well you have learned the skills and concepts featured in the lesson "Radiator Lions" by completing the following:

- Discuss the musical characteristics of the Contemporary period.

- Look in the music to find sections that are repeated and sections that are different. Label the sections that make up the rondo form in this piece.

- On a piece of staff paper, create nontraditional music notation for the sounds of an airplane, a school bell and a siren. Share your notation with other members of the class.

LINKS TO LEARNING

Theory

The Theory section is designed to prepare students to develop rhythmic precision in 4/4 meter.

Have students:

- Tap or clap the quarter note pulse.
- Speak the rhythm exercise while tapping the quarter note pulse.
- Speak the rhythm exercise while feeling the quarter note pulse inside.

Artistic Expression

The Artistic Expression section is designed to prepare students to:

- Interpret and perform nontraditional music notation.
- Speak using voice inflection.

Have students:

- Learn symbols and definitions of the nontraditional music notation.
- Locate these symbols in "Radiator Lions."
- Perform the spoken exercise with voice inflection following the rise and fall on the notes.

RESOURCES

Beginning Unison, 2-Part/3-Part Rehearsal/Performance CD

CD 1:13 Voices
CD 1:14 Accompaniment Only
CD 3:7 Vocal Practice Track—Unison

National Standards

1. Singing, alone and with others, a varied repertoire of music. **(a, b, c)**
5. Reading and notating music. **(a, b, c)**
6. Listening to, analyzing, and describing music. **(c)**

LESSON PLAN

Suggested Teaching Sequence and Performance Tips

1. Introduce

Direct students to:

- Read and discuss the information found in the Getting Started section on student page 56.
- Practice reading the rhythms used in this song as shown in the Theory section on page 57.
- Offer various versions for performing the first measure of the song.
- Identify the first section of the rondo form and label it A. *(measures 4–11)*

Progress Checkpoints

Observe students' progress in:

✓ Their ability to perform rhythms accurately.

✓ Their ability to read nontraditional music notation and perform with voice inflections.

✓ Their ability to study the score and find the first A section.

Radiator Lions

For Unison Voices and Piano

Words by DOROTHY ALDIS   Music by MICHAEL JOTHEN

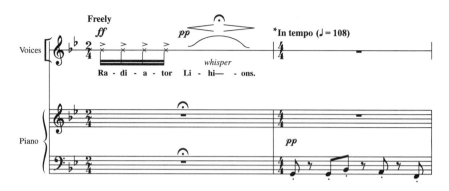

* CD accompaniment starts here.

Copyright © 2003 by HAL LEONARD CORPORATION
International Copyright Secured   All Rights Reserved

58   Beginning Unison, 2-Part/3-Part

TEACHER 2 TEACHER

This exciting piece provides a means for the students to use their voices as instruments in unusual ways. They sing of everyday life with a wide palette of sounds!

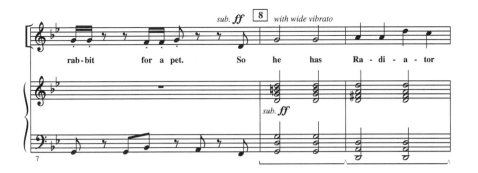

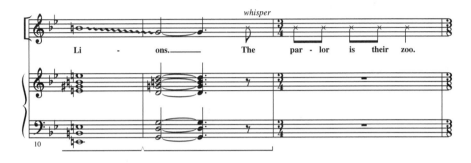

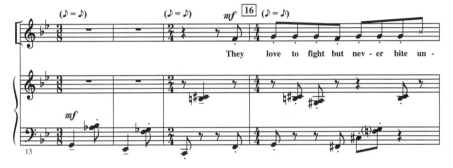

2. Rehearse

Direct students to:

- Sing measures 4–7 and then 8–12. Note the contrasts of the music. (*The first measures are very soft using staccato articulations and short note durations; the second measures are loud and then soft and have notes with longer values.*)

- Sing measures 4–11 and then measures 21–28. Compare these two sections. (*They are the same, the A section of the rondo form.*)

- Sing measures 44 to the end and compare that with the first A section (*It is similar but shorter and has different lyrics.*)

Progress Checkpoints

Observe students' progress in:

✓ Singing various dynamics and articulations with precision.

✓ Singing pitches with accuracy.

✓ Identifying the form.

Lesson 7 *Radiator Lions* **59**

CONNECTING THE ARTS

Visual Arts

Have students create their own "Radiator Lions" in any art form they choose. They may draw or paint their idea of the lion, or they may choose to sculpt it from clay or dough. The lion could also be created from paper bags, cloth, yarn, etc. Encourage them to use their creativity. Display your "Radiator Lions" at your performance.

3. Refine

Direct students to:

- Sing the entire song using crisp, clear diction. Pay attention to all dynamics and articulations.
- Perform the spoken sections as solos, asking for volunteers. Select students with much expression in their voice. Allow them to perform those sections as solos for demonstration purposes.
- Sing measures 31–34 using legato phrases while gradually getting faster and louder.
- Divide the choir into two groups. Allow each group to stand in different areas of the room and perform this section. Each group should be dramatic with their parts.

Progress Checkpoints

Observe students' progress in:

- ✓ Their accuracy of pitches and rhythms.
- ✓ Their crisp, clear diction.
- ✓ Their energetic presentation of text, be it sung or spoken.

*Forearm thrusts on black notes on keyboard; actual note ranges are approximate.

60   Beginning Unison, 2-Part/3-Part

EXTENSION

Composing Contrasting Sections

Have students create an original rhythmic composition based on rondo form. In small groups have students create and notate a four-measure rhythm pattern to represent Section A. Then direct students to create and notate three other rhythm patterns to represent Sections B, C and D. Be sure they notate the meter rhythm, pitch (if necessary) and dynamics of each pattern. Perform the composition in rondo form (A-B-A-C-A-D-A). Have other students interpret the dynamics, tempo and articulations, as well as evaluate the form. Did it follow a rondo form?

† Pause CD track at this point.

* Divide choir into two parts. Group II should double the size of Group I. Members of Group II should perform as many of the sounds, as many times as possible, before being stopped. These should be as loud as possible.

Lesson 7 *Radiator Lions* **61**

ASSESSMENT

Informal Assessment

In this lesson, students showed the ability to:

- Locate and perform traditional and nontraditional notation.
- Locate differences and similarities between sections and perform appropriately.
- Perform with energy using crisp, clear diction and expressive, dramatic readings of text.

Student Self-Assessment

Have students evaluate their individual performances based on the following:

- Posture
- Diction
- Expressive Singing
- Accurate Pitch
- Accurate Rhythms

Have each student rate his/her performance of this song in the areas above on a scale of 1–5, 5 being the best.

ENRICHMENT

Nontraditional Music Notation

Have students research music, performances and recordings that use nontraditional music notation. They may bring their sample to class and share it with others, or they may write an evaluation of the piece in which they explain what meaning the piece expressed to them.

Individual and Group Performance Evaluation

To further measure growth of musical skills presented in this lesson, direct students to complete the Evaluation section on page 57.

- After discussing the musical characteristics of the Contemporary period, create a poster or bulletin board listing these characteristics to serve as a reminder for future Contemporary pieces.
- After labeling the sections of the music that make up the rondo form, see if you can locate other pieces of music in rondo form.
- After each student has created nontraditional music notation for various sounds, exchange their piece with another student. Each student should perform the other's composition. By their performances, can you tell what sound was being notated?

EXTENSION

Lyrics

Research the background of Dorothy Aldis and the text for "Radiator Lions." Look for similar types of poems that could be used as a text for a new composition. Defend your selection and write an opening passage of music based on your found poem.

† Start CD here to continue.

Additional National Standards

The following National Standards are addressed through the Assessment, Extension, Enrichment and bottom-page activities:

4. Composing and arranging music within specific guidelines. **(a)**

6. Listening to, analyzing, and describing music. **(a)**

7. Evaluating music and music performances. **(b)**

SPOTLIGHT

Vocal Production

There are many ways we can use our voices to communicate. We can speak, shout, laugh, whisper, sigh and sing. This lesson will focus on your singing voice. It is best to think of singing as extended speech so you do not put too much physical effort into it.

Perform the following exercises to experience, explore and establish singing as extended speech.

- Say the phrase "Hello, my name is _____" as if you were greeting someone enthusiastically.

- Say the phrase again, but speak all of it on the same pitch as the first syllable.

- Repeat the phrase, making sure you take a singer's breath before you start.

- Feel the flow of the breath as it smoothly connects each word to the next.

- Try the phrase several times, starting on different pitches, seeing how long you can hold out your name.

- Remember to keep your chest high and your "inner tube" inflated for as long as you can. (It will feel like a belt is tightening around your waist the longer you hold it.)

Explore your **head voice** *(the singer's higher singing voice)* and your **chest voice** *(the singer's lower singing voice)* by performing the following exercises.

- Place your upper teeth on your lower lip as if you were going to say the letter "v."

- Make a singing tone on a lower pitch for a few seconds, keeping your teeth on your lower lip.

- Now, take a singer's breath and start the "v" sound on a lower pitch, but immediately move the pitch upward as high as you can go.

- Repeat the last step, this time bringing the voice back down low again.

- Notice the stretching feeling you have in your throat as you go higher and lower.

Objectives
- Demonstrate proper fundamental skills.

Suggested Teaching Sequence
Direct students to:
- Read the Spotlight On Vocal Production on student page 63.
- Perform the exercises in the order listed to establish singing as extended speech. Check for proper posture.
- Discuss the difference between head voice and chest voice. Demonstrate the difference with their voices.
- Perform the exercises in the order listed to explore their head voices and chest voices.

Progress Checkpoints
Observe students' progress in:
- ✓ Their ability to establish singing as extended speech.
- ✓ Their ability to sing with proper posture.
- ✓ Their ability to know and demonstrate the difference between head voice and chest voice.

RESOURCES

Teacher Resource Binder
Vocal Development 1-6, *Developing the Voice*

National Standards
1. Singing, alone and with others, a varied repertoire of music. **(b)**

Jesu, Joy Of Man's Desiring

OVERVIEW

Composer: Johann Sebastian Bach (1685–1750), arranged by Henry Leck

Text: Verse 6 of *Jesu, meiner Seelen Wonne* by Martin Jahn (1661)

Voicing: Unison Voices/2-Part

Key: E♭ major

Meter: 3/4

Form: Chorale AABA'

Style: German Baroque Chorale

Accompaniment: Piano or organ, brass available

Programming: Contest, Seasonal Concerts

Vocal Ranges:

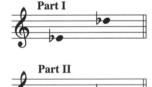

Objectives

After completing this lesson, students will be able to:

• Perform and describe a varied repertoire of music representing styles from diverse cultures and periods.

• Read and write standard music notation, including triplets.

• Perform expressively, demonstrating basic performance techniques.

VOCABULARY

Have students review vocabulary in student lesson. Introduce terms found in the music. A complete glossary of terms is found on page 246 of the student book.

64

Jesu, Joy of Man's Desiring

Composer: Johann Sebastian Bach (1685–1750), arranged by Henry Leck
Text: Verse 6 of *Jesu, meiner Seelen Wonne* by Martin Jahn (1661)
Voicing: Unison Voices/2-Part

VOCABULARY

cantata

Baroque period

legato

triplet

phrase

Focus

• Describe and perform music from the Baroque period.

• Read and write triplets.

• Sing phrases expressively.

Getting Started

What do the following activities have in common?

• Taking out the garbage
• Going to a piano lesson
• Reading the Sunday comics

If you guessed "things you do once a week," you're right. What other activities would you personally add to the list?

MUSIC & HISTORY

To learn more about the Baroque period, see page 110.

◆ **History and Culture**

If you were Johann Sebastian Bach (1685–1750), you could include "composing a cantata" on your list. Now this may not seem too difficult for one of the world's greatest composers, but a **cantata** is *a musical piece made up of several movements for singers and instrumentalists* that can last over 20 minutes. While working as a church musician in Germany, Bach's job included writing a cantata for every church service. He also wrote cantatas for other special occasions. Over 200 of his cantatas are still in publication. "Jesu, Joy of Man's Desiring" is a part of Bach's *Cantata 147*.

Bach lived during the **Baroque period** *(1600–1750)*. Music of the Baroque period frequently features a simple melody, supported by a fancy accompaniment with a continuously moving bass line. Many large works, including cantatas, were developed during this period.

64 Beginning Unison, 2-Part/3-Part

RESOURCES

Beginning Sight-Singing

Sight-Singing in E♭ Major, pages 147–151

Reading 3/4 Meter, pages 15–16

Reading Triplet Rhythms, page 143

Teacher Resource Binder

Teaching Master 13, *Composing Rhythm Patterns With Triplets*

Skill Builder 26, *Rhythm Challenge in 3/4 Meter*

Music and History 4, *Characteristics of Baroque Music: 1600–1750*

Music and History 5, *Johann Sebastian Bach, a "Baroque" Composer*

For additional resources, see TRB Table of Contents.

Links to Learning

◆ Vocal

Perform the following example to practice singing in a **legato** (*connected and sustained*) style.

noo   noo   noo   noo   noo   noo   noo   noo

◆ Theory

Perform the following examples to practice rhythmic patterns found in "Jesu, Joy of Man's Desiring," which include **triplets** (*three eighth notes per beat*). Form two groups. At the same time, one group taps the steady beat while the other group claps the rhythms. Switch roles.

◆ Artistic Expression

A **phrase** is *a musical idea with a beginning and an end*. Sing the phrase in measures 9–12 of "Jesu, Joy of Man's Desiring" while drawing an arch in the air above your head. Shape your phrase by beginning softly at measure 9. Your phrase should be loudest at the highest point of your arch and softest at its lowest point.

Evaluation

Demonstrate how well you have learned the skills and concepts featured in the lesson "Jesu, Joy of Man's Desiring" by completing the following:

- Discuss the musical characteristics of the Baroque period.
- Write a four-measure rhythmic phrase in $\frac{3}{4}$ meter that includes two to four triplets. Perform your phrase for others in the class.
- Find other phrases in the music. Select one person to come forward and serve as a "phrase leader." Sing each phrase while following the arch shown by the phrase leader. How expressively were you able to sing the phrases?

Lesson 8 Jesu, Joy of Man's Desiring **65**

RESOURCES

Beginning Unison, 2-Part/3-Part Rehearsal/Performance CD

CD 1:15 Voices
CD 1:16 Accompaniment Only
CD 3:8 Vocal Practice Track—Part I
CD 4:9 Vocal Practice Track—Part II

National Standards

1. Singing, alone and with others, a varied repertoire of music. **(b, c, d)**
5. Reading and notating music. **(a, c, f)**
6. Listening to, analyzing, and describing music. **(a)**

LINKS TO LEARNING

Vocal

The Vocal section is designed to prepare students to:

- Understand the meaning of *legato*.
- Sing in a legato style.

Have students:

- Sing the example connecting each note.
- Locate this melodic phrase in the choral score.

Theory

The Theory section is designed to prepare students to understand and perform triplet rhythms.

Have students:

- Divide into two groups.
- One group taps the quarter note pulse as indicated by stems down, the other groups claps the rhythms indicated by stems up.
- Switch roles and repeat.

Artistic Expression

The Artistic Expression section is designed to prepare students to:

- Understand the meaning of a phrase.
- Sing an expressive, arch-shaped phrase.

Have students:

- Sing measures 9–12 while drawing an arch in the air with your arm.
- Shape the phrase by beginning softly and *crescendo* to the high point of the phrase at the highest note. Their arms should be at the highest point at the same time. Then they should *decrescendo* to the end of the phrase.

65

LESSON PLAN

Suggested Teaching Sequence and Performance Tips

1. Introduce

Direct students to:

- Read and discuss the information found in the Getting Started section on student page 64.

- Practice singing a musical phrase with the exercise in the Vocal section on page 65.

- Locate this melodic phrase in Part I of the score. *(measures 9–12, 24–27, 52–55)*

- Watch the score and listen to the recording of measures 1–32. Have them sign the solfège syllables and internally sing or hum measures 9–12 and 24–27.

- Practice measures 1–32 again with the recording and have singers add the text to the phrases previously rehearsed and sight-sing on rhythmic syllables measures 14–17 and 29–32.

- Compare and contrast measures 57–60 to measures 14–17 and 29–32. *(measures 57–60 have the same rhythm and melody as measures 14–17 and measures 29–23)*

- Count-sing or use rhythmic syllables to practice measures 14–17.

- Practice measures 8–32 and 52–60 with text.

- Sing Part II in measures 14–17 and 29–32 on neutral syllable "loo," then using solfège syllables.

As Recorded by THE CANADIAN BRASS *and* THE INDIANAPOLIS CHILDREN'S CHOIR
Henry Leck, Conductor

Jesu, Joy Of Man's Desiring
from *CANTATA 147*
For Unison/2-Part and Piano

Arranged by HENRY LECK
Piano Arrangement by DEAN CROCKER

JOHANN SEBASTIAN BACH (1685–1750)
Brass Accompaniment by FREDERICK MILLS

Copyright © 1975 Brassworks Music, Inc.
This arrangement Copyright © 1995 Brassworks Music, Inc.
International Copyright Secured   All Rights Reserved

66   Beginning Unison, 2-Part/3-Part

TEACHER 2 TEACHER

"Jesu, Joy of Man's Desiring" is one of Bach's best known and most accessible works. Students will enjoy the driving basso continuo and triplet accompaniment contrasting the smooth, legato melodic line.

- Practice measures 9–32 with Part I and Part II singing as written with accompaniment. Strive to sing an expressive legato line over the rhythmically active accompaniment.
- Listen to measures 40–49 and compare this section with the previously learned sections. (Measures 40–49 use similar rhythms as the previously learned phrase, but have completely different pitches.)
- Sight-sing measures 40–49, Part I and Part II separately, using rhythmic syllables. When accurate, add text and sing in harmony.
- Practice measures 40 to the end.

Progress Checkpoints

Observe students' progress in:
- ✓ Their ability to read and perform with pitch accuracy.
- ✓ Their ability to sing and maintain two parts.
- ✓ Their ability to maintain an expressive legato line over the rhythmically active accompaniment.

CONNECTING THE ARTS

Enhancing Your Rehearsal with Movement

Listen to the recording of "Jesu, Joy of Man's Desiring" and explore ways to move to the three rhythmic components that create the counterpoint of this piece: basso continuo, triplet rhythms of the accompaniment, and the stately pace of the melody's rhythm. Explore a variety of actions for each rhythmic element and then divide the group in thirds. Have each group choose a separate motion for each of the three textural rhythms and the order in which to demonstrate each rhythmic component. Have them practice within their group and then demonstrate and describe their ideas for the other groups. Sing the entire song with accompaniment and creative movement of all groups.

2. Rehearse

Direct students to:

- Read and discuss the information found in the Theory section on page 65. Practice the rhythmic exercises.

- Review measure 3 of Theory exercise 1 on page 65 and then locate this pattern in the score wherever it occurs. *(Part I measures 16, 31, and 59)*

- Practice exercise 2 in the Theory section on page 65.

- Locate the triplet rhythmic patterns in the score. *(found in the accompaniment)*

- Practice using duplet and triplet patterns during the introduction. Listen to measures 1–4, then lightly clap/tap Theory exercise 1 during measures 4–8. Repeat this exercise using Theory exercise 2.

- Establish the steady beat of the basso continuo line by lightly tapping the back of one hand. Sing the entire song while tapping a continuous light steady beat.

- Repeat measures 40–end, tapping the beat while singing and tapping triplet eighth notes during the interludes.

Progress Checkpoints

Observe students' progress in:

✓ Their rhythmic precision, particularly in the sixteenth-note patterns.

✓ Their ability to read voice parts and accompaniment.

✓ Correctly indicating steady beat versus triplet eighth notes.

68 Beginning Unison, 2-Part/3-Part

ENRICHMENT

Baroque Art

The Baroque period (1600–1750) is most noted as an artistic style highlighted by extravagant forms in art and architecture. Highly ornamented visual arts with brilliant colors, flourishes, gilding and curves are a feature of this period. Baroque churches, palaces and public spaces are a flurry of the artisan's elaborate work. Musicians of this historical period painted their music with the same flamboyant ornamentations of the other arts through improvisation, tonal color and polyphony.

Have students research visual examples of Baroque art, architecture and dancers. Share their findings with the group and describe why these pictures are good examples of the Baroque period.

3. Refine

Direct students to:

- Read and practice the concepts found in the Artistic Expression section on page 65.
- Locate the phrase marking in the Vocal section. Sing the example, drawing an arch in the air while creating a beautiful legato phrase that is loud at the peak of the arch and soft at the end of the phrase.
- Sing entire song drawing the phrase arch for each line of music. Have students determine if every phrase of the song should be sung with arched phrasing, or if sometimes the text, dynamic markings or some other character of the music indicates a need for a different type of phrase.
- Sing entire song with clear diction, using all dynamic markings as indicated.
- Repeat various sections, using the students' ideas for phrasing.
- Repeat the entire song, focusing on the teacher's and arranger's signals and symbols for phrasing.

Progress Checkpoints

Observe students' progress in:

✓ Their artistic and appropriate phrasing.

✓ Singing accurate pitches and rhythms.

✓ Their effective use of dynamics.

✓ Their clear diction within the context of a legato phrase.

TEACHING STRATEGY

Describing Musical Instruments

- Have the students listen to the accompaniment of "Jesu, Joy of Man's Desiring" as found on the CD in the Teacher Resource Binder. As they listen, have them list the instruments they hear. If this is too difficult, have them name the instrument family from which they come. (*Brass Quintet featuring two Trumpets, Trombone, French Horn, Tuba all members of the Brass family*)
- Have students describe and classify the sound of this instrumentation in the following categories: genre (*Brass Choir or quintet*); style (*flowing*); period (*Baroque*); culture (*German*).

ASSESSMENT

Informal Assessment

In this lesson, students showed the ability to:

- Read and perform duplet and triplet eighth note rhythmic patterns in 3/4 meter.
- Sing two-part harmony with good intonation.
- Create an artistic vocal phrase within four measures.
- Evaluate and interpret conducting signals.
- Audibly contrast dynamic levels.

Student Self-Assessment

Have students evaluate their individual performances based on the following:

- Posture
- Phrasing
- Expressive Singing
- Accurate Rhythms
- Correct Part-Singing

Have each student rate his/her performance of this song in the areas above on a scale of 1–5, 5 being the best.

CURRICULUM CONNECTIONS

Social Studies

Leipzig is located south of Berlin in the Northeast sector of Germany. Its settlements date to the seventh century as the first Slav village near the Elster and Parthe rivers. Leipzig developed as a fortified city on the intersection of major eleventh-century trade routes. It has been famous for its printing industry since 1470. Locate Leipzig, Germany, on a world map.

Individual and Group Performance Evaluation

To further measure growth of musical skills presented in this lesson, direct students to complete the Evaluation section on page 65.

- After discussing the musical characteristics of the Baroque period, create a poster or bulletin board listing these characteristics to serve as a reminder for future Baroque pieces.

- After each student has written a four-measure rhythmic phrase in 3/4 meter that includes triplets, have them perform their phrase for the rest of the class. Have the class evaluate by asking, "Did this student meet all of the qualifications of the assignment?"

- After the choir has sung several phrases following the arch of the "phrase leader," evaluate the expressiveness of the phrase. Is it more expressive than before or less?

EXTENSION

Baroque Dance

Though dance and movement would never have been a part of a Baroque cantata, dance was an important part of Baroque society. Have students investigate the popular dances of Bach's day, such as courante, saraband, gigue and minuet. Have the students learn to dance a minuet.

Additional National Standards

The following National Standards are addressed through the Assessment, Extension, Enrichment and bottom-page activities:

7. Evaluating music and music performances. **(b)**

8. Understanding the relationships between music, the other arts, and disciplines outside the arts. **(a)**

9. Understanding music in relation to history and culture. **(b)**

Da pacem Domine

OVERVIEW

Composer: Melchior Franck (c. 1579–1639), arranged by Emily Crocker

Text: Traditional Latin

Voicing: 2, 3 or 4-Part, Any Combination

Key: F major

Meter: 4/4

Form: Canon at a fourth and unison

Style: Renaissance Canon

Accompaniment: a cappella

Programming: Concert opener, Special services

Vocal Ranges:

OBJECTIVES

After completing this lesson, students will be able to:

• Perform expressively a varied repertoire of music including canon.

• Identify music forms presented aurally and through music notation.

• Use standard terminology to explain intervals.

• Demonstrate fundamental skills while performing.

VOCABULARY

Have students review vocabulary in student lesson. Introduce terms found in the music. A complete glossary of terms is found on page 246 of the student book.

Da pacem Domine

Composer: Melchior Franck (c. 1579–1639), arranged by Emily Crocker
Text: Traditional Latin
Voicing: For 2, 3 or 4-Part, Any Combination

VOCABULARY

harmony

canon

Baroque period

step-wise motion

skip-wise motion

SPOTLIGHT

To learn more about careers in music, see page 175.

Focus

• Identify and perform a canon.

• Explain and demonstrate step-wise and skip-wise motion.

Getting Started

There are many ways to sing in harmony. **Harmony** is *a musical sound that is formed when two or more different pitches are sung at the same time.* A canon, sometimes known as a round, is a great way to sing in harmony. In a **canon,** *one part sings a melody. Then, another part sings the same melody, entering a short time after the first part has begun.*

"Da pacem Domine" is an excellent example of a canon. Written in Latin, it was composed almost 500 years ago. Translated, the text means, "Give us peace, O Lord, in our days." How do these words still hold meaning for us today?

◆ History and Culture

Melchior Franck (c. 1579–1639) was a well-known German composer who lived during the early **Baroque period** *(1600–1750).* He wrote over 600 pieces of choral music. Franck served at the court of Coburg as Kapellmeister (master of the chapel or director of music) for the majority of his life.

Latin is sometimes used in choral music because of its pure vowel sounds. Vowels are the foundation of a good choral tone. Singing vowels properly will help you blend well with others in your choir to create a pleasing sound.

72   Beginning Unison, 2-Part/3-Part

RESOURCES

Beginning Sight-Singing

Sight-Singing in F Major, pages 38–40, 60, 76–77, 118, 121–122

Reading 4/4 Meter, pages 2–6

Reading Quarter Notes/Rests, Half Notes/Rests, pages 1–6

Reading Dotted Notes, pages 43–45, 92, 110

Teacher Resource Binder

Teaching Master 14, *Pronunciation Guide for "Da pacem Domine"*

Skill Builder 3, *Composing with Steps and Skips*

Skill Builders 20, *Naming Intervals*

Vocal Development 15, *Vowels*

For additional resources, see TRB Table of Contents.

Links to Learning

◆ **Vocal**

Perform the following example to practice singing vowels in Latin.

Da pa - cem   Do - mi - ne,   da pa - cem   Do - mi - ne in di - e - bus   no - stris.
dah pah-chem   daw - mee - neh,   dah pah-chem   daw-mee-neh een dee - eh - boos   naw - strees

◆ **Theory**

Step-wise motion is *the movement from a given note to the next note above or below it on the staff.* Look at the example below. Notice that the notes move from a space to the next line or from a line to the next space. Read and perform the following example to practice singing in step-wise motion.

do   re   mi   fa   sol   fa   mi   re   do

Skip-wise motion is *the movement from a given note to another note that is two or more notes above or below it on the staff.* Look at the example below. Notice that most of the notes do not move from a space to the next line or from a line to the next space. Read and perform the following example to practice singing in skip-wise motion.

do   mi   sol   mi   sol   fa   re   mi   do   re   do

Evaluation

Demonstrate how well you have learned the skills and concepts featured in the lesson "Da pacem Domine" by completing the following:

• Select a canon that you already know. With a group of your friends, perform the canon for the class.

• Locate in "Da pacem Domine" examples of step-wise and skip-wise motion. Sing one example of each.

RESOURCES

Beginning Unison, 2-Part/3-Part Rehearsal/Performance CD

CD 1:17 Voices

CD 1:18 Accompaniment Only

CD 3:9 Vocal Practice Track—Part I

CD 4:10 Vocal Practice Track—Part II

National Standards

1. Singing, alone and with others, a varied repertoire of music. **(c, d)**

5. Reading and notating music. **(a, d)**

6. Listening to, analyzing, and describing music. **(c)**

LINKS TO LEARNING

Vocal

The Vocal section is designed to prepare students to practice singing vowels in Latin.

Have students:

• Echo the teacher's pronunciation of the Latin text, speaking it in rhythm until comfortable.

• Sing the example concentrating on tall, pure vowels.

• Locate this passage in their choral score.

Theory

The Theory section is designed to prepare students to:

• Understand skip-wise and step-wise motion.

• Sing skip-wise and step-wise motion with good intonation.

Have students:

• Examine example 1 and determine if the intervals are step-wise or skip-wise. *(stepwise)*

• Sing example 1 on solfège, listening carefully for good intonation.

• Examine example 2 and determine if the intervals are step-wise or skip-wise. *(skipwise)*

• Sing example 2 on solfège, listening carefully for good intonation.

LESSON PLAN

Suggested Teaching Sequence and Performance Tips

Direct students to:

- Read the information in the Getting Started section on page 72 and practice the exercises on page 73.

- All sing Part I until the Latin text and all intervals are secure and comfortable. A Latin pronunciation guide may be found in the Teacher Resource Binder, Teaching Master 14.

- Divide into two equal groups. Sing the piece as a two-part canon with each part following the phrasing and breath marks for their part.

- Divide into three and four parts when comfortable. Sing as a three- or four-part canon.

Progress Checkpoints

Observe students' progress in:

✓ Using pure Latin vowels to develop vocal blend.

✓ Their ability to maintain two-, three- and four-part harmony.

ASSESSMENT

Informal Assessment

In this lesson, students showed the ability to:

- Read and identify step-wise and skip-wise motion.

- Sing with good intonation and phrasing.

- Sing in two-, three- and four-part harmony in a group.

Da pacem Domine

For 2, 3 or 4-Part, Any Combination, a cappella

Arranged by EMILY CROCKER

MELCHIOR FRANCK (c. 1579–1639)

Copyright © 2003 by HAL LEONARD CORPORATION
International Copyright Secured All Rights Reserved

74   Beginning Unison, 2-Part/3-Part

Student Self-Assessment

Have students evaluate their individual performances based on the following:

- Phrasing
- Latin Pronunciation
- Tall Vowels
- Intonation

Have each student rate his/her performance of this song in the areas above on a scale of 1–5, 5 being the best.

Individual and Group Performance Evaluation

To further measure growth of musical skills presented in this lesson, direct students to complete the Evaluation on page 73.

- After small groups have performed familiar canons for the class, ask about the similarities and differences between theirs and "Da pacem Domine."

SPOTLIGHT

Vowels

The style of a given piece of music dictates how we should pronounce the words. If we are singing a more formal, classical piece, then we need to form taller vowels as in very proper English. If we are singing in a jazz or pop style, then we should pronounce the words in a more relaxed, conversational way. To get the feeling of taller vowels for classical singing, do the following:

- Let your jaw gently drop down and back as if it were on a hinge.
- Place your hands on your cheeks beside the corners of your mouth.
- Sigh on an *ah* [ɑ] vowel sound, but do not spread the corners of your mouth.
- Now sigh on other vowel sounds—*eh* [ɛ], *ee* [i], *oh* [o] and *oo* [u]—keeping the back of the tongue relaxed.
- As your voice goes from higher notes to lower notes, think of gently opening a tiny umbrella inside your mouth.

ee	eh or ā*	ah	oh	oo
[i]	[ɛ] [e]	[a]	[o]	[u]

Other vowel sounds used in singing are diphthongs. A **diphthong** is *a combination of two vowel sounds*. For example, the vowel *ay* consists of two sounds: *eh* [E] and *ee* [i]. To sing a diphthong correctly, stay on the first vowel sound for the entire length of the note, only lightly adding the second vowel sound as you move to another note or lift off the note.

I = *ah*_____(ee) [ɑi]

boy = *oh*_____(ee) [oi]

down = *ah*_____(oo) [ɑu]

*Note: This is an Italian "ā," which is one sound, and not an American "ā," which is a diphthong, or two sounds.

RESOURCES

Teacher Resource Binder

Vocal Development 10, *Diphthongs*
Vocal Development 15, *Vowels*
Reference 29, *Zeroing in on IPA*

National Standards

1. Singing, alone and with others. **(b)**

VOWELS

Objectives

- Demonstrate basic performance techniques through proper use of vowels.

Suggested Teaching Sequence

Direct students to:

- Read the Spotlight on Vowels on student page 75 and identify the importance of uniform vowels in singing.
- Practice the exercise as presented on page 75.
- Identify the five basic vowels. Practice speaking and singing each.
- Define diphthong and demonstrate the proper and improper way to sing a diphthong.
- Find examples of each of the five basic vowels and diphthongs in music they are currently studying.
- Compare the concept of uniform vowels to appropriate large- and small-ensemble performance techniques.

Progress Checkpoints

Observe students' progress in:

✓ Their ability to speak the five basic vowels properly and uniformly.
✓ Their ability to define *diphthong*, find examples in the music, and sing them properly.
✓ Their ability to relate the importance of uniform vowels in ensemble singing.

Sanctus

OVERVIEW

Composer: Franz Schubert
(1797–1828), arranged by
Donald Moore

Text: Traditional Latin

Voicing: 2-Part

Key: F major

Meter: 3/4

Form: Canonic

Style: German Classical
Anthem

Accompaniment: Piano,
optional flute or C instrument

Programming: Contest,
Festival, appropriate for
small or large ensemble

Vocal Ranges:

OBJECTIVES

After completing this lesson,
students will be able to:

- Describe and perform a
  varied repertoire of music
  representing styles from
  diverse periods, including
  the Romantic period.

- Demonstrate basic performance
  techniques while performing.

- Identify music terms,
  including *melodic contour.*

- Demonstrate appropriate
  small-ensemble performance
  techniques.

VOCABULARY

Have students review
vocabulary in student lesson.
Introduce terms found in the
music. A complete glossary
of terms is found on page
246 of the student book.

76

Sanctus

Composer: Franz Schubert (1797–1828), arranged by Donald Moore
Text: Traditional Latin
Voicing: 2-Part

VOCABULARY

Romantic period

mass

sequence

melodic contour

duet

MUSIC & HISTORY

*To learn more about the
Romantic period, see
page 118.*

Focus

- Describe and perform music from the Romantic period.

- Identify and demonstrate melodic contour.

- Sing independently in duets.

Getting Started

If you like…   *You could thank …*

To ride your bicycle   Baron Karl von Drais
To work with computers   Mr. Alan Turing
To eat chocolate   Mr. Milton Hershey

And if you like to sing, you could thank Mr. Franz Schubert!

◆ History and Culture

Born in Vienna, Austria, Franz Schubert (1797–1828) can be
considered one of the best songwriters of all time. Schubert
wrote over 600 songs with harmonies and rhythms that perfectly
capture the mood and meaning of the words. His music is also
filled with spinning, lyrical melodies. With its expressiveness,
complex harmonies and rich sound, Schubert's music is an
important part of the early **Romantic period** *(1820–1900).*

The Sanctus is the text from one section of the **mass,** *a
religious service of prayers and ceremonies.* A common language of
the mass is Latin. Although Latin is not a modern spoken
language, its pure vowels make it a favorite of singers.
Composers throughout the centuries have set the words of the
Sanctus to music. So, if you find yourself singing the beautiful
melody of this "Sanctus," don't forget to thank Franz Schubert!

RESOURCES

Beginning Sight-Singing

Sight-Singing in F Major, pages 38–40,
60, 76–77, 118, 121–122

Reading 3/4 Meter, pages 15–16

Teacher Resource Binder

Teaching Master 15, *Pronunciation
Guide for "Sanctus"*

Evaluation Master 7, *Evaluating
Musical Expression*

Music and History 10, *Characteristics of
Romantic Music: 1820–1900*

Music and History 11, *Franz Schubert,
a "Romantic" Composer*

For additional resources, see TRB
Table of Contents.

Links to Learning

◆ Vocal

Read and perform the following examples to practice singing two of the melodic patterns found in "Sanctus." Find these patterns in the music.

do sol mi do sol mi do re mi

◆ Theory

A **sequence** is *a successive musical pattern that begins on a higher or lower pitch each time it is repeated.* Perform the following example to practice singing a sequence. Find the sequences in "Sanctus."

loo loo loo loo loo loo loo loo loo loo loo loo loo loo loo loo loo loo loo loo loo loo

◆ Artistic Expression

Be choir directors! While your teacher sings measures 7–12, show the **melodic contour**, or *the overall shape of the melody*, by using conducting motions. Then, as a choir, continue to conduct while you sing this passage, expressing the melodic contour of the piece through your voices.

Evaluation

Demonstrate how well you have learned the skills and concepts featured in the lesson "Sanctus" by completing the following:

- Discuss the musical characteristics of the Romantic period.
- Create a dance or movement performance that shows the melodic contour of "Sanctus."
- Expressively sing "Sanctus" as a **duet** *(two singers with one singer on each of two parts).*

Lesson 10 *Sanctus* **77**

RESOURCES

Beginning Unison, 2-Part/3-Part Rehearsal/Performance CD

CD 1:19 Voices
CD 1:20 Accompaniment Only
CD 3:10 Vocal Practice Track—Part I
CD 4:11 Vocal Practice Track—Part II

National Standards

1. Singing, alone and with others, a varied repertoire of music. **(a, b, c, d)**
5. Reading and notating music. **(c)**
6. Listening to, analyzing, and describing music. **(b)**

LINKS TO LEARNING

Vocal

The Vocal section is designed to prepare students to sing two of the melodic patterns in "Sanctus."

Have students:

- Sing example 1 on solfège, concentrating on accurate intervals and good intonation.
- Sing example 2 on solfège the same way.
- Locate these two melodic passages in their choral score.

Theory

The Theory section is designed to prepare students to understand and perform a sequence.

Have students:

- Sing the example on "loo," concentrating on accurate intervals and good intonation.
- Locate this musical sequence in their choral score.

Artistic Expression

The Artistic Expression section is designed to prepare students to:

- Understand melodic contour.
- Demonstrate melodic contour in their conducting patterns and singing.

Have students:

- Conduct the melodic contour of measures 7–12, while the teacher sings.
- Continue to conduct while they sing the same phrase expressing the melodic contour of the piece.

LESSON PLAN

Suggested Teaching Sequence and Performance Tips

1. Introduce

Direct students to:

- Read and discuss the information found in the Getting Started section on page 76.

- Practice singing the melodic patterns found in the Vocal section on page 77.

- Follow as Part I, measures 7–18, is played. Sing through the melody. The first time through, sing only the F's *(do)* at the correct time. Repeat, singing only the C's *(sol)* and A's *(mi)*. Continue this pattern to increase the ability to read pitches. Repeat again, singing only two pitches (such as F and C, F and G, *do* and *sol*, *do* and *re*). Continue until all combinations of pitches have been sung.

- Identify this as the A section.

- Work with a partner and choose a way to sing measures 7–18 without using the text (e.g., note names, solfège, rhythm values, descriptive words, neutral syllables). Sing this version for the choir.

Progress Checkpoints

Observe students' progress in:

✓ Their accuracy of pitches and rhythms.

✓ Their ability to identify notes using pitch names.

✓ Identifying the AB form.

Sanctus

For 2-Part and Piano and Optional Flute or C Instrument*

Arranged with additional music
by DONALD MOORE

Traditional Latin
Based on a canon by FRANZ SCHUBERT (1797–1828)

*Flute part found on page 82.

Copyright © 1999 Heritage Music Press (a division of The Lorenz Corporation)
International Copyright Secured All Rights Reserved

78   Beginning Unison, 2-Part/3-Part

TEACHER 2 TEACHER

With its simple Latin text and lovely sequential melody, Schubert's "Sanctus" provides an opportunity for your students to develop a free, healthy tone with pure, blended vowels.

2. Rehearse

Direct students to:

- Identify measures 25–32 as the B section. What is the same about these measures? *(rhythm and melodic contour – measures 25, 27, 29, and measures 26, 28)* Define and discuss the compositional technique of sequence.

- Learn measures 25–32, using solfège syllables.

- Look at their entire vocal part as a section and list the measures they don't yet know. *(Part I: measures 20–24, 38–40, Coda; Part II: measures 33–40, Coda)* In groups of three or four, choose one of these sections to independently learn. Allow time for students to perform for each other.

- Rehearse both Parts I and II with the entire group. Divide the choir into two groups and sing both parts together. Switch parts and sing again.

- Chant, then sing the piece on the Latin text. The Latin pronunciation guide may be found in the Teacher Resource Binder, Teaching Master 15.

Progress Checkpoints

Observe students' progress in:

- ✓ Their ability to read notation for both voice parts.

- ✓ Their ability to work and contribute in small groups setting.

- ✓ Their ability to sing both parts using correct Latin pronunciation.

EXTENSION

Compare and Contrast

Listen to settings of "Sanctus" from different historical periods and in different styles (e.g., Palestrina, Mozart, Rutter, David Fanshaw's African Sanctus). Discuss and compare.

3. Refine

Direct students to:

- Work in groups of two to six and prepare a performance of "Sanctus" with both parts. Allow groups to sing for each other.
- Prepare a "silent" version of "Sanctus" in the same small groups, in which the audience would see the flowing legato style of the melodic line rather than hear it. Students could use hands, arms or conventional dance movements. As they practice their performance, the sequence in measures 25–32 should be visible. Does the choreography look like a sequence? Allow groups to perform for each other.
- Sing "Sanctus" as a choir while watching one of the "moving scores," responding to the style, tempo and dynamics of the "dancers." Discuss how the singers can make their voices sound more like the appearance of the movements.

Progress Checkpoints

Observe students' progress in:

✓ Their ability to express the style of the piece through movement.

✓ Their ability to sing the melodic line in a legato style.

80   Beginning Unison, 2-Part/3-Part

ENRICHMENT

Franz Schubert lived from 1797 to 1828. Prepare a time line for his lifetime. Include his birth and death on the time line as well as major historical events, inventions and other composers and artists who lived during this time.

ASSESSMENT

Informal Assessment

In this lesson, students showed the ability to:

- Locate, read and perform sequences in F major.
- Work independently in small groups to read and perform the melodic and rhythmic notation in 3/4 meter.
- Create a "moving score," illustrating sequences and a legato style.

Student Self-Assessment

Have students evaluate their individual performances based on the following:

- Phrasing
- Melodic Contour
- Latin Pronunciation
- Tall Vowels
- Expressive Singing

Have each student rate his/her performance of this song in the areas above on a scale of 1–5, 5 being the best.

MORE ABOUT...

Franz Schubert

Franz Schubert (1797–1828) was born into a family with modest means in Vienna, Austria. He received an excellent music education as a chorister at the Imperial Court Chapel (the Vienna Choir Boys). Although he wrote operas, church music, orchestral music and chamber music, he is best known as a songwriter. He composed more than 500 songs with verse settings from Shakespeare to his friends and contemporaries. After suffering from a long illness, he died at the young age of 31.

Sanctus

Individual Performance Assessment

To further measure growth of musical skills presented in this lesson, direct students to complete the Evaluation on page 77.

- After discussing the musical characteristics of the Romantic period, create a poster or bulletin board listing these characteristics to serve as a reminder for future Romantic pieces.

- After creating a dance or movement that shows the melodic contour of "Sanctus," have individuals perform their dance for the class. Do their movements represent the melodic contour of the piece?

- After several small groups have rehearsed "Sanctus" as a duet with one singer on each part, have a mini-recital with all duets singing the piece. Have the class evaluate each small group.

FLUTE (C INSTRUMENT)

Traditional Latin
Based on a canon by FRANZ SCHUBERT (1797– 1828)
Arranged with additional music by DONALD MOORE

Copyright © 1999 Heritage Music Press (a division of The Lorenz Corporation)
International Copyright Secured   All Rights Reserved

82   Beginning Unison, 2-Part/3-Part

Additional National Standards

The following National Standards are addressed through the Assessment, Extension, Enrichment and bottom-page activities:

7. Evaluating music and music performances. **(b)**

9. Understanding music in relation to history and culture. **(a, b)**

SPOTLIGHT

Pitch Matching

As you begin to learn how to read music, you must learn not only how to identify the notes on the printed page, but also how to sing the notes you read in tune. Accurate pitch matching requires that you hear the note in your head before you sing it instead of trying to find the note with your voice. Learning to sing from one note to another in scale patterns will help you hear the notes in your head before you sing them. Perform the scale below first using note names, then numbers, and finally solfège syllables.

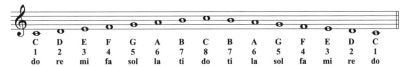

To help you sing the following examples on the correct pitch, hear the notes in your head before you sing them. If you cannot hear the interval skip in your head before you sing it, mentally sing the first note followed by all the notes in between until you come to the right note. Then, begin again and sing the pattern as written.

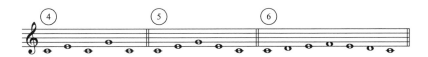

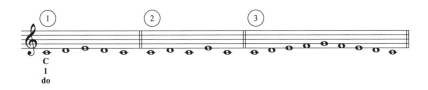

Spotlight *Pitch Matching* **83**

PITCH MATCHING

Objectives

- Perform independently with accurate intonation.

Suggested Teaching Sequence

Direct students to:

- Read the Spotlight On Pitch Matching on student page 83 and identify the importance of hearing a pitch in their heads before singing it.
- Sing the C major scale as presented on page 83.
- Chant the pitch names for exercise 1, then sing the exercise, repeating as many times as necessary to sing in tune securely.
- Repeat the same process for each exercise.
- Sing exercises 1–9 straight through. Check constantly for accurate intonation.

Progress Checkpoints

Observe students' progress in:

- ✓ Their ability to sing the C major scale in tune.
- ✓ Their ability to sing intervals found in the C major scale in tune.
- ✓ Their ability to read and sing simple melodic passages on solfège syllables.

RESOURCES

Teacher Resource Binder

Skill Builder 20, *Naming Intervals*
Skill Builder 21, *Pitch and Kodály*
Skill Builder 30, *Solfège Hand Signs*
Kodály 5, *Music Reading: Pitch*
Reference 7, *Building a Musical Vocabulary*
Reference 19, *Pitch Tone Ladder*

National Standards

1. Singing, alone and with others. **(b)**

Alleluia

OVERVIEW

Composer: Wolfgang Amadeus Mozart (1756–1791), arranged by Henry Leck
Text: Traditional Latin
Voicing: 2-Part
Key: D major
Meter: 2/4
Form: ABA'CDA''
Style: Classical Art Song
Accompaniment: Piano
Programming: Concert, Festival

Vocal Ranges:

OBJECTIVES

After completing this lesson, students will be able to:

- Describe aurally presented music representing diverse periods.
- Perform a varied repertoire of music representing styles from diverse periods.
- Demonstrate fundamental skills while performing.
- Identify, read and perform sixteenth notes.

VOCABULARY

Have students review vocabulary in student lesson. Introduce terms found in the music. A complete glossary of terms is found on page 246 of the student book.

Alleluia

Composer: Wolfgang Amadeus Mozart (1756–1791), arranged by Henry Leck
Text: Traditional Latin
Voicing: 2-Part

VOCABULARY

Classical period
melisma

Focus

- Describe and perform music from the Classical period.
- Sing melismas correctly.
- Identify, read and perform sixteenth notes.

Getting Started

Imagine singing a song that uses only one word. How interesting do you think that would be? In "Alleluia," Wolfgang Amadeus Mozart—using only one word—created a masterpiece.

Many qualities of the **Classical period** *(1750–1820)* are found in the music of Mozart. One of these qualities is music that is light in character. Sometimes, this music contains melismas. A **melisma** is *many notes that are sung on one syllable or word.* Often, these fast-moving passages make this music challenging to sing. The use of melismas in the Classical period is shown in Mozart's "Alleluia."

MUSIC & HISTORY

To learn more about the Classical period, see page 114.

◆ History and Culture

Wolfgang Amadeus Mozart (1756–1791) is one of the most famous composers in Western music. He lived in Vienna, Austria, and worked as a professional musician during the late 1700s. He began composing music at the age of five. Mozart also wrote a wide variety of music for instruments and singers.

"Alleluia" is from Mozart's larger work, *Exsultate, jubilate.* He wrote this piece when he was just sixteen years old. Written in 1773, "Alleluia" is one of Mozart's most well-known pieces of vocal music.

84 Beginning Unison, 2-Part/3-Part

RESOURCES

Beginning Sight-Singing

Sight-Singing in D Major, pages 102–109

Reading 2/4 Meter, page 59

Reading Sixteenth Notes, pages 58–59, 74–75, 82–83

Teacher Resource Binder

Teaching Master 16, *Rhythmic Patterns With Sixteenth Notes*

Teaching Master 17, *Identifying Syllabic and Melismatic Passages in "Alleluia"*

Music and History 7, *Characteristics of Classical Music: 1750–1820*

Music and History 8, *Wolfgang Amadeus Mozart, a "Classical" Composer*

For additional resources, see TRB Table of Contents.

Links to Learning

◆ Vocal

Read and perform the D major scale below to practice singing melismas. Begin slowly, then increase the speed as you are able.

This arrangement of "Alleluia" is in the key of D major and is based on the D major scale. To locate "D" on the piano, find any set of two black keys. "D" is the white key between these two keys. This scale uses the notes D, E, F♯, G, A, B, C♯, D. Using the keyboard below as a guide, play the D major scale.

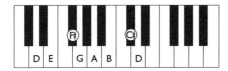

◆ Theory

Read and perform the following example to practice rhythmic patterns with sixteenth notes.

Evaluation

Demonstrate how well you have learned the skills and concepts featured in the lesson "Alleluia" by completing the following:

* Discuss the musical characteristics of the Classical period.
* Sing the D major scale ascending and descending on "ah" to show that you can sing melismas with a light tone.
* Find the page in the music that contains the most sixteenth notes. Perform two measures to show that you can read rhythmic patterns with sixteenth notes.

Lesson 11 *Alleluia* **85**

RESOURCES

Beginning Unison, 2-Part/3-Part Rehearsal/Performance CD

CD 1:21 Voices

CD 1:22 Accompaniment Only

CD 3:11 Vocal Practice Track - Part I

CD 4:12 Vocal Practice Track - Part II

National Standards

1. Singing, alone and with others, a varied repertoire of music. **(a, b, c, d)**

5. Reading and notating music. **(a, c)**

9. Understanding music in relation to history and culture. **(a, b)**

LINKS TO LEARNING

Vocal

The Vocal section is designed to prepare students to:

* Read and perform melismas in D Major.
* Play the D major scale on a keyboard.

Have students:

* Sing the exercise on "tah" as indicated, increasing speed as they are able.
* Continue with verse 2 and verse 3, increasing the number of notes per syllable.
* Play the D major scale on the keyboard. If selected students will play the scale on the keyboard, others should follow closely on the keyboard printed on page 85.

Theory

The Theory section is designed to prepare students to read and perform rhythmic patterns with sixteenth notes.

Have students:

* Tap or clap the quarter note pulse.
* Speak the exercise while tapping the quarter note pulse.
* Speak the exercise while feeling the quarter note pulse inside.

LESSON PLAN

Suggested Teaching Sequence and Performance Tips

1. Introduce

Direct students to:

- Read and discuss the information found in the Getting Started section on student page 84.

- Practice the Vocal section examples, beginning slowly using "tah," "pah" and "lah." Gradually increase the speed, always remembering to sing lightly. Reinforce the use of breath support and a relaxed throat.

- Practice the rhythmic patterns with sixteenth notes as found in the Theory section on page 85.

From EXSULTATE, JUBILATE
Alleluia
For 2-Part and Piano

Arranged by
HENRY LECK

WOLFGANG AMADEUS MOZART
(1756–1791)

Copyright © 2003 by HAL LEONARD CORPORATION
International Copyright Secured   All Rights Reserved

86   Beginning Unison, 2-Part/3-Part

TEACHER 2 TEACHER

Mozart's "Alleluia" will both charm and challenge your singers! This giant step into the Classical period presents many opportunities to develop vocal technique.

- Chant the rhythm of the text in measures 9–24. Locate and practice the melisma in measure 21.
- Sing each part separately in measures 9–24 using solfège syllables and then sing on the text. When comfortable, combine parts. Practice shortening or releasing all notes (even quarters) to establish the style of Mozart.
- Sing measures 26–48 in the same manner, noting dynamic contrasts.
- Sing measures 49–67 in the same manner, noting dynamic contrasts and unison parts. Use very little weight in the voice. Make certain to tune the *re-fa-mi* in measures 52–53.

Lesson 11 *Alleluia* **87**

TEACHING STRATEGY

Performance Techniques

1. Identify appropriate performance techniques to be used in the performance of this song.
2. Either in small-ensembles or with the entire choir (large-ensemble), perform the song exhibiting these performance techniques.
3. Describe the performance techniques experienced during the performance.
4. Critique the performance based on the observed performance techniques.
5. Repeat this process often in both informal and formal concert settings.

- Sing measures 72–85, making sure to point out the contrasting rhythms of melismas on eighth notes and the eighth note/sixteenth note patterns in measure 77.
- Sing melismas on the neutral syllables as given in the Vocal section on page 85. Use variety to maintain focus and secure the pitch and rhythm.
- Sing measures 95–101, making note of the imitation. *(measures 95–97 and measures 99–101)*
- Study measures 102–105, making note of the imitation. *(measures 102–103 and 104–105)* Note that while the pattern in measure 106 begins in imitation, a new idea is introduced in measure 107.

88   Beginning Unison, 2-Part/3-Part

TEACHING STRATEGY

Exploring Syllabic, Melismatic and Imitative Treatment of Text

The strategy used to help students discover and identify syllabic, melismatic and imitative text treatment allows students to use their own knowledge to construct meaning. This exploration is sometimes a bit noisy, but allows the students to take control of their own learning and is highly motivating and engaging. Have students:

- Choose a proverb or short line of text from the newspaper.
- Compose short pieces using one treatment or combinations of these three treatments of the text. Be sure they notate the meter, rhythm, pitch and dynamics of their piece.

- Study measures 107–112, noting that while measures 107 and 109 are the same, measure 111 has the same rhythm, but different pitches. Sing slowly on solfège.
- Chant the solfège for measures 112–117 while pulsing the eighth note. How many eighth note pulses occur during the half note tied to the eighth note in measures 112–113? *(five eighth note pulses)*

Progress Checkpoints

Observe students' progress in:

✓ Using proper vocal tone.

✓ Using proper style.

✓ Their ability to identify unison sections.

✓ Their ability to read and tune melismatic passages.

✓ Their ability to locate imitative passages in the score.

ASSESSMENT

Evaluating the Quality of a Performance

Have students:

1. Listen to a video or audio recording of this piece as performed by the choir.

2. Compare this performance to exemplary models such as other recordings or other live performances of the piece.

3. Develop constructive suggestions for improvement based on the comparison.

2. Rehearse

Direct students to:

- Listen to the piano at measures 119–122. Sing measures 123–126, noting that the piano part asks the question and the voice parts give the musical answer. Listen for the same compositional technique at measures 60–67.
- Sight-sing measures 135 to the end. Note the repetition. *(measures 135–140 and measures 143–149)* Be especially aware of the change in the repetition at measure 150. A Mozart surprise!
- Perform measures 119 to the end, singing all dynamics and accents as marked in the score.

90   Beginning Unison, 2-Part/3-Part

ASSESSMENT
Creating an Assessment Rubric

Have students:

1. Discuss the characteristics of a desirable performance of this piece, using all their knowledge of the performance techniques.
2. Design and identify the criteria by which they think an adjudicator might assess the performance, quality and effectiveness of this piece.
3. For each criterion, decided what characteristics will comprise an adequate, good, very good and excellent performance.
4. Create a rubric chart.
5. Use the rubric to assess quartets or small ensembles performing all or part of this song.

Progress Checkpoints

Observe students' progress in:

✓ Their ability to locate and describe compositional techniques.

✓ Their ability to locate and perform repetitions.

✓ Their ability to perform the dynamics and style markings in the score.

TEACHING STRATEGY

Register

Because of the style and ranges of this piece, it is a good time to introduce heavy versus light registration, and their stylistic appropriateness. Explore the difference between the heavier, chestier feeling and a lighter head-tone quality. Listen for examples of each on the radio or in concerts. Discuss the necessity to maintain in-tune singing and diction regardless of registration. The Mozart "Alleluia" should be sung in lighter registration, or with a blended sound, giving a very different feeling from the heavy registration sound.

3. Refine

Direct students to:

- Practice singing with the piano accompaniment, noting sections where the vocal parts are included in the piano accompaniment. *(measures 9–24, 37–48, 64–67, 72–74, 112–117, 123–138, 143–146)* These contrast the sections where the accompaniment does not include the vocal part. *(measures 30–32, 49–59, 75–85, 95–111, 139–142, 147–154)*

- Sing with a light, articulated style.

- Line up the three vowels in this song (*ah*, *eh* and *oo*) so they have the same brightness and character.

- Emphasize the light staccato character of the rhythms.

- Practice using head voice while forming and shaping pure vowel sounds to aid in the blending of voices and tuning of the vocal line.

- Keep a silent, steady beat to aid in rhythmic precision. Count the interludes and practice entering at the appropriate time.

EXTENSION

Exsultate, Jubilate

Have students research the origin of the Mozart "Alleluia." Listed above the title on student page 86 is the piece from which this song is lifted. *Exsultate Jubilate* is a famous piece by Mozart. Have students find and listen to the complete work and write an evaluation of the piece.

Progress Checkpoints

Observe students' progress in:

✓ Their ability to perform the entire song with a light, articulated style and piano accompaniment.

✓ Their ability to sing in the head voice, producing the vowel sounds with same brightness and character.

✓ Their ability to tune the unison and two-part sections.

✓ Their ability to sing expressively in the Classical style.

✓ Their ability to sing melismas with agility and accuracy of pitch and rhythm.

CURRICULUM CONNECTIONS

Technology in Music

Have students:

1. Identify technology used in music (computer, midi, mp3, CD, audio/video recordings, synthesizer, sound equipment, electronic sounds, and so forth.

2. Discuss what effect technology has on music.

3. Create a musical composition using a form of technology.

4. Perform a solo or small ensemble for the class incorporating technology.

ASSESSMENT

Informal Assessment

In this lesson, students showed the ability to:

- Sing stylistically correctly for the Classical style.
- Sing melismas correctly in 2/4 meter.
- Read and perform music in the key of D major.
- Apply dynamic and style markings as indicated in the score.
- Locate in the score repetitions in both the accompaniment and voice parts.
- Count the piano introduction and interludes and enter at the appropriate time.

Student Self-Assessment

Have students evaluate their individual performances based on the following:

- Breath Management
- Phrasing
- Tall Vowels
- Accurate Rhythms
- Correct Part-Singing

Have each student rate his/her performance of this song in the areas above on a scale of 1–5, 5 being the best.

94   Beginning Unison, 2-Part/3-Part

MUSIC, SOCIETY AND CULTURE

Have students perform additional songs representing diverse cultures, including American and Texas heritage. Go to **music.glencoe.com**, the Web site for Glencoe's choral music programs, for additional music selections students can perform.

Individual and Group Performance Evaluation

To further measure growth of musical skills presented in this lesson, direct students to complete the Evaluation section on page 85.

- After discussing the musical characteristics of the Classical period, create a poster or bulletin board listing these characteristics to serve as a reminder for future Classical pieces.
- After students have sung the D major scale ascending and descending on "ah," evaluate their ability to sing melismas with a light tone.
- Divide into small groups to perform the two measures of sixteenth note patterns. Have each group perform for the class. Ask the class, "Did this group demonstrate the ability to perform sixteenth note rhythms?"

MORE ABOUT...

Wolfgang Amadeus Mozart (1756–1791)

As a representative composer of the Classical period, Mozart embodied the spirit of the classical style: crisp harmonies, exuberant melodies, formal balance and symmetry. He composed in virtually all forms of the time, including symphonies, operas, string quartets, art songs and masses. Now a household word, due to the immense popularity of the movie *Amadeus*, Mozart died at the early age of 35, cutting short the career of one of the most prolific composers of all time.

Al - le - lu - ia,

Al - le - lu - ia,

al - le - lu - ia.

al - le - lu - ia.

Additional National Standards

The following National Standards are addressed through the Assessment, Extension, Enrichment and bottom-page activities:

4. Composing and arranging music within specific guidelines. **(a)**

6. Listening to, analyzing, and describing music. **(a, b)**

7. Evaluating music and music performances. **(b)**

SPOTLIGHT

Melismas

Sing the first phrase of "My Country 'tis of Thee" as shown below. Notice that every syllable of the text receives exactly one note.

My coun-try 'tis of thee, sweet land of li-ber-ty of thee I sing.

This style of text setting is known as **syllabic** (*one syllable for every note*). Can you think of other songs with syllabic text settings?

When one syllable is given many pitches, this is referred to as melismatic singing. A **melisma** is *a group of notes sung to a single syllable*. Melismatic singing became popular in the Middle Ages (c. 400–1450), when as many as several dozen notes would have been sung on the final syllable of a Gregorian chant. The example below shows a melisma on the word "alleluia" similar to those found in Mozart's "Alleluia" on page 87.

Al - le - lu - ia.

When learning to sing a melisma, the key is to begin slowly. First, learn the pitches on syllables or numbers, and then, count-sing the rhythm of the melisma. Once your pitches and rhythms are secure, sing the melisma on a neutral syllable, such as "doo." Start at a slow tempo, gradually increasing your speed over several weeks. With each repetition, make sure every note is distinct, yet smoothly connected to one another. When you are able to sing the melisma clearly on "doo," switch to the syllable "ah." Once again, begin slowly, then gradually increase your speed to the performance tempo.

Singing a melisma is a vocal skill that may take time to master. With diligent practice, you will soon sing them musically and beautifully!

RESOURCES

Teacher Resource Binder
Vocal Development 11, *Flexibility and Range*
Reference 7, *Building a Musical Vocabulary*

National Standards
1. Singing, alone and with others. **(b)**

MELISMAS

Objectives
- Perform melismas with accurate intonation and rhythm.

Suggested Teaching Sequence
Direct students to:
- Read the Spotlight on Melismas on student page 97 and discuss the definitions of *syllabic* and *melisma*.
- Sing "My Country 'tis of Thee" to demonstrate an example of syllabic text setting.
- Sing the example from Mozart's "Alleluia" to demonstrate an example of a melisma.
- Practice this melisma by first slowly singing the pitches on solfège syllables.
- Count-sing the rhythm of the melisma.
- Sing the melisma on a neutral syllable such as "doo" on every note, slowly at first and then gradually increasing the tempo.
- Sing the melisma on the text when comfortable, singing many notes on one syllable as indicated.

Progress Checkpoints
Observe students' progress in:
- ✓ Their ability to recognize the difference between syllabic text setting and melismas.
- ✓ Their ability to sing an example of a syllabic text setting.
- ✓ Their ability to properly practice and sing a melisma.

Waters Ripple and Flow

OVERVIEW

Composer: Slovakian Folk Song, arranged by Ruth Boshkoff

Text: Traditional

Voicing: 2-Part

Key: F major/G major

Meter: 3/4

Form: AA'A"

Style: Slovakian Folk Song

Accompaniment: Piano

Programming: Appropriate for large or small ensemble, Festival, Multicultural concert, Thematic programming on songs of the sea (international folk song)

Vocal ranges:

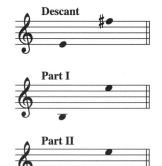

Objectives

After completing this lesson, students will be able to:

• Read music notation including triplets and sixteenth notes.

• Create music within specific guidelines.

• Perform a varied repertoire of music representing styles from diverse cultures.

VOCABULARY

Have students review vocabulary in student lesson. Introduce terms found in the music. A complete glossary of terms is found on page 246 of the student book.

98

LESSON 12

Waters Ripple and Flow

Composer: Slovakian Folk Song, arranged by Ruth Boshkoff

Text: Traditional

Voicing: 2-Part

VOCABULARY

folk song

descant

Focus

• Read rhythmic patterns with triplets and sixteenth notes

• Compose rhythmic phrases

• Perform music from different cultures

Getting Started

Have you ever played the "Telephone Game"? One person whispers a phrase into another's ear, and then that person whispers it to the next, and so forth. The last person to hear the phrase states what he or she has heard. It is fun to see how the phrase changes as it passes from one person to another.

Folk songs develop in a similar way. Throughout history, people have created songs about their everyday lives. **Folk songs** are *songs that have been passed down by word of mouth from generation to generation.* Parents would teach a song to their children, and their children would teach it to their children. As you can imagine, some folk songs have stayed very much the same, while others, just like the whispered phrases in the "Telephone Game," have changed as they have been passed from person to person.

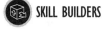 **SKILL BUILDERS**

To learn more about sixteenth notes and triplets, see Beginning Sight-Singing, *pages 58 and 143.*

◆ History and Culture

"Waters Ripple and Flow" is a folk song that came from Slovakia, in central Europe. In an attempt to keep the traditions and customs of their country alive, the people of Slovakia have developed a rich tradition of folk art, music, and dance. The melody of this beautiful song flows like the river that will bring the lonesome singer's true love back home.

RESOURCES

Beginning Sight-Singing

Sight-Singing in F Major, pages 38–40, 60, 76–77, 118, 121–122

Sight-Singing in G Major, pages 84–89, 93

Reading Triplets, page 143

Reading Sixteenth Notes, pages 58–59, 74–75, 82–83

Teacher Resource Binder

Teaching Master 18, *Compose and Perform Rhythmic Patterns*

Evaluation Master 8, *Evaluating Rhythmic Accuracy*

Skill Builder 26, *Rhythm Challenge in 3/4 Meter*

Dalcroze 12, *Moving to the Beat and Beat Subdivision*

For additional resources, see TRB Table of Contents.

Links to Learning

◆ **Theory**

Read and perform the following examples to get a feel for how the division of the beat moves from quarter notes to eighth notes, triplets and sixteenth notes. Step the beat as you perform.

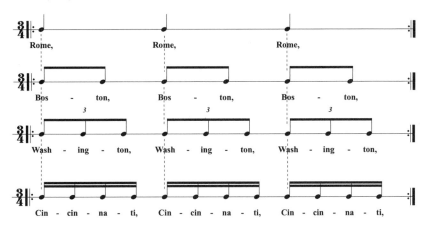

◆ **Artistic Expression**

To develop artistry through rhythmic chanting, organize into groups of four students. Within your group, select two different rhythmic patterns from the Vocal section above. Have half of your group chant one city name, while the other half claps another. Through this exercise, you will be able to get a feel for the complex rhythms found in "Waters Ripple and Flow."

Evaluation

Demonstrate how well you have learned the skills and concepts featured in the lesson "Waters Ripple and Flow" by completing the following:

• To show that you can read the rhythms used in this song, clap the rhythm of the **descant** (*a special part that is often higher than the other parts*) in measures 29–40.

• Think of some animals or foods whose syllables can represent different notes. For example, "corn" (quarter notes), "green beans" (eighth notes), "cantaloupe" (triplets), and "watermelon" (sixteenth notes). Write and perform two of these rhythmic patterns using the Vocal section above as a guide. How did you do?

LINKS TO LEARNING

Theory

The Theory section is designed to prepare students to:

• Read and perform quarter notes, eighth notes, triplets and sixteenth notes.

• Feel the division of the beat through movement.

Have students:

• Step the quarter note pulse.

• Speak the first line while stepping the quarter note pulse.

• Continue with the other exercise, moving to eighth notes, triplets and sixteenth notes.

Artistic Expression

The Artistic Expression section is designed to prepare students to feel complex rhythms.

Have students:

• Divide into groups of four and have each group select two rhythm patterns from the Vocal section.

• Divide their groups in half, having half of their group chant one city name, while the other half claps another.

• Switch roles and repeat.

RESOURCES

Beginning Unison, 2-Part/3-Part Rehearsal/Performance CD

CD 1:23 Voices

CD 1:24 Accompaniment Only

CD 3:12 Vocal Practice Track - Part I

CD 4:13 Vocal Practice Track - Part II

National Standards

1. Singing, alone and with others, a varied repertoire of music. **(a, b, c, d)**

4. Composing and arranging music within specific guidelines. **(a)**

5. Reading and notating music. **(a, c, d)**

LESSON PLAN

Suggested Teaching Sequence and Performance Tips

1. Introduce

Direct students to:

- Listen to a recording of the music and discuss the character of the music. Discuss life in Slovakia and the people's pride in their traditions, love for their country and longing for freedom.
- Read and discuss the information found in the Getting Started section on student page 98.
- Practice the rhythm patterns found in the Theory section on page 99.
- Read the Artistic Expression section on page 99. Divide into groups and practice combining rhythm patterns.

Progress Checkpoints

Observe students' progress in:

✓ Their ability to describe aurally presented music.

✓ Their ability to read and perform complex rhythms in 3/4 time.

For Deb Shearer

Waters Ripple and Flow

For 2-Part and Piano

Arranged by
RUTH BOSHKOFF

Slovakian Folk Song

Copyright © 2001 by HAL LEONARD CORPORATION
International Copyright Secured All Rights Reserved

TEACHER**2**TEACHER

This lovely Slovakian folk song is sure to inspire your group through its lilting melody, poignant words and expansive rhythms.

2. Rehearse

Direct students to:

- Analyze the musical score, locating measures containing the rhythms identical to those given in the Theory section on page 99. Note that the triplet rhythm is in every measure of vocal score in Section A *(measures 4–9)* and is alternated with the sixteenth note pattern in the B Section. *(measures 10–23)* In the C Section, Part II continues with the alternating rhythm. For the first time, the eighth-note pattern occurs *(measures 34, 37, 40)* in Part I.

- Rehearse by clapping and/or stepping each of the measures in the Theory section on page 99. It is vital at this time that the rhythm becomes eurhythmic; that is, flowing and expressive in movement. Use tiny steps when crowding many motions into one beat.

CURRICULUM CONNECTION

Geography

Locate Slovakia on a world map. Have students research this country and make a list of special characteristics of the area. Perhaps they can determine what body of water this song refers to.

- Study measures 11–22, noticing the rhythmic subdivisions on the last beat of the measure, leading to a strong downbeat in the following measure. Step the rhythm for measures 11–22, feeling this strong downbeat. The eighth note after each dotted quarter acts as a springboard, providing the impetus to perform the swiftness of the third beat in a flowing manner.

- Practice singing parts separately, then together. Encourage students to use clean, crisp diction while maintaining the legato style.

Progress Checkpoints

Observe students' progress in:

- ✓ Their ability to read and perform complex rhythmic patterns in 3/4 meter.
- ✓ Their ability to create flowing movements to a variety of rhythmic patterns.
- ✓ Their ability to sing two-part harmony.
- ✓ Pronouncing the text with clear, crisp diction.

102 Beginning Unison, 2-Part/3-Part

CONNECTING THE ARTS

Visual Arts

Have students:

- Read the text of "Waters Ripple and Flow" out loud as a class.
- Discuss images that come to mind when reading this text.
- Create or gather artwork that would depict the images that reflect this text.
- Plan a slide show to accompany your performance of this piece at concert time.

Lesson 12 *Waters Ripple and Flow* **103**

3. Refine

Direct students to:

- Sing the entire song one part at a time while moving rhythmically in a flowing manner. Try singing the entire piece while first stepping the underlying quarter note pulse and then stepping the rhythm of the text. Both movements should be dancelike.
- Divide each section in half and perform both, stepping the pulse and stepping the rhythm of the text simultaneously. Form two circles, an inside circle for the "pulse" steppers and an outside circle for the "rhythm" steppers.
- Select a small group of students to perform the circle dance while the rest of the class performs the song.

Progress Checkpoints

Observe students' progress in:

- ✓ Performing the rhythms with precision.
- ✓ Their ability to maintain their voice part.
- ✓ Their ability to experience the mood of the music while stepping either the pulse or the rhythm.

MORE ABOUT...

Correct Breathing

Deep, diaphragmatic breathing occurs most naturally when a person lies on his or her back and the abdomen rises and falls. Suggest that students try this technique at home:

- Lie on your back as described above.
- With hands pressing the diaphragm, feel the muscle response when a sipping breath is taken. Exhale with a long hiss.
- Again with hands pressing the diaphragm, feel the response when a quick, surprised breath is taken. Exhale with short, accented hisses. Only the diaphragm should move visibly.

ASSESSMENT

Informal Assessment

In this lesson, students showed the ability to:

- Maintain a steady and eurhythmic beat in 3/4 meter.
- Move independently while singing their own voice part within the ensemble.
- Internalize and communicate the kinesthetic-eurhythmic grace of this folk song.

Student Self-Assessment

Have students evaluate their individual performances based on the following:

- Breath Management
- Phrasing
- Expressive Singing
- Accurate Rhythms
- Correct Part-Singing

Have each student rate his/her performance of this song in the areas above on a scale of 1–5, 5 being the best.

Individual and Group Performance Evaluation

To further demonstrate musical growth, direct students to complete the Evaluation section on page 99.

- Have students divide into small groups and have each group clap the descant rhythms in measures 29–40 for the rest of the class. The class should evaluate. Did this group clap these rhythms correctly?
- After each student has written a rhythm pattern using animal or food names with different note values, have each perform them for the class. The class should identify which rhythm pattern was performed.

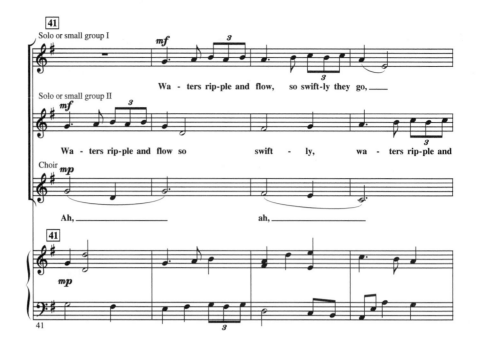

104   Beginning Unison, 2-Part/3-Part

Additional National Standards

The following National Standards are addressed through the Assessment, Extension, Enrichment and bottom-page activities:

4. Composing and arranging music within specific guidelines. **(a)**

7. Evaluating music and music performances. **(b)**

8. Understanding relationships between music, the other arts, and disciplines outside the arts. **(a)**

Music & History

Links to Music

RENAISSANCE

OVERVIEW

Objectives

After completing this lesson, students will be able to:

• Describe characteristics of Renaissance music.
• Relate music to history.

VOCABULARY

Have students review vocabulary in student lesson. A complete glossary of terms is found on page 246 of the student book.

Introduce the Renaissance period through visual art. Analyze the painting by Leonardo da Vinci on page 106. Direct students to discuss the costume of the day as depicted in the painting. Review background information of da Vinci's *Portrait of Cecilia Gallerani (Lady with an Ermine)* as found on page 106.

 Leonardo da Vinci (1452–1519) was an Italian painter who lived in Florence and Milan during the Renaissance. In *Portrait of Cecilia Gallerani (Lady with an Ermine)*, da Vinci shows opposing motion as the upper body is turned to the viewer's left and the head faces the right. The small ermine is a symbol of purity and modesty. According to legend, ermines did not get dirty, and they ate only once a day. Notice the costume of the day, about 1490 A.D.

Leonardo da Vinci. *Portrait of Cecila Gallerani (Lady with an Ermine)*. c. 1490. Oil on wood. 54.8 x 40.3 cm (21 1/2 x 15 13/16"). Czartorychi Muzeum, Cracow, Poland.

106   Beginning Unison, 2-Part/3-Part

RESOURCES

Teacher Resource Binder

Music and History 1, *Renaissance Music*

Music and History 2, *Josquin de Prez*

Transparency 1, *Portrait of Cecilia Gallerani (Lady with an Ermine)*, Leonardo da Vinci

Music and History 3, *Fine Art Teaching Strategy*

For additional resources, see Music and History section.

Listening Selections CD

(found in the Teacher Resource Binder)

Track 1 "El Grillo"

Track 2 "Canzon in echo Duodecimi Toni a 10"

Focus

- Describe characteristics of Renaissance music.
- Relate music to history.

The Renaissance— A Time of Great Awakening

Can you imagine sailing across unexplored waters or creating a new invention? During the **Renaissance period** (*c. 1430–1600*), the world experienced a time of rapid development in exploration, science, and the arts.

In 1425, Johann Gutenberg of Germany invented the printing press. Previously, to make a book, someone had to write it all by hand. It may have taken two months to produce one book. With the new printing press, books were mass-produced and became accessible to many people. The development of the compass made it possible for explorers to travel to new continents. In the early 1500s, Martin Luther led the Protestant Reformation, which caused important changes in religion, politics and music.

Among the famous people from the Renaissance who still influence our lives today are:

- Andrea Gabrieli—Italian composer
- Michelangelo and Leonardo da Vinci—Italian artists
- William Shakespeare—English playwright
- Nicolas Copernicus—Polish astronomer
- Ferdinand Magellan—Portuguese explorer

Looking Back— The Medieval Period

During the Medieval period (400–1430), also known as the Middle Ages, people in Western Europe thought of the Catholic church as the center of their lives. Much of the music written at this time was related to the church. One common form of music, the Gregorian chant, was a unison chant that was sung in Latin and performed **a cappella** (*with voices only; no accompaniment*).

Outside the church, the music was often lively and sometimes accompanied by a drum, a wooden flute or a **lute** (*an early form of the guitar*).

COMPOSERS

Josquin des Prez
(c. 1450–1521)

Andrea Gabrieli
(c. 1510–1586)

Michael Praetorius
(1571–1621)

Thomas Weelkes
(1575–1623)

ARTISTS

Gentile Bellini
(1429–1507)

Sandro Botticelli
(1445–1510)

Leonardo da Vinci
(1452–1519)

Michelangelo
(1475–1564)

Raphael
(1483–1520)

AUTHORS

Martin Luther
(1483–1546)

William Shakespeare
(1565–1616)

VOCABULARY

Renaissance period

a cappella

lute

sacred music

secular music

madrigal

polyphony

canzona

Music History *Renaissance* **107**

LESSON PLAN
Suggested Teaching Sequence

1. Examine the Renaissance period in a historical perspective.

Direct students to:

- Read and discuss the information found on student page 107.
- Turn to the time line on pages 108–109 and read the citations.
- Discuss why these are considered important dates during the Renaissance period.
- Identify specific accomplishments that were made during the Renaissance period and the people associated with those accomplishments.

2. Define the musical aspects of Renaissance music.

Direct students to:

- Discuss characteristics of Medieval (Middle Ages) music that preceded music of the Renaissance.
- Read and discuss information on Renaissance music found on student page 108.
- Describe the difference between sacred and secular music.
- Define the musical style of the madrigal.

3. Discuss the performance guidelines of Renaissance music.

Direct students to:

- Read the Performance Links found on student page 108.
- Discuss the performance guidelines.

National Standards

6. Listening to, analyzing, and describing music. **(a, b, c, e, f)**
8. Understanding relationships between music, the other arts, and disciplines outside the arts. **(a, b, c, d, e)**
9. Understanding music in relation to history and culture. **(a, c, d, e)**

This feature is designed to expand students' appreciation of choral and instrumental music of the Renaissance period.

1. Choral Selection:
"El Grillo" by
Josquin des Prez

Direct students to:

• Read the information on student page 109 to learn more about Josquin des Prez and "El Grillo."

• Review the meaning of the musical style of the madrigal.

• Define ABA form.

• Analyze the form of the piece based on hearing it several times.

• While listening to the recorded performance, identify in which section the imitation of the sound of the crickets can be heard.

2. Instrumental Selection:
"Canzon in echo Duodecimi Toni a 10"
by Giovanni Gabrieli

Direct students to:

• Read the information on student page 109 to learn more about Giovanni Gabrieli and "Canzon in echo Duodecimi Toni a 10."

• After listening to it once, discuss the ancient instruments that are heard.

• Listen to it a second time and have students raise their hands when a section that is an echo is heard.

Renaissance Music

The music of the Renaissance falls into two categories: **sacred music**, or *music associated with religious services or themes*, and **secular music**, or *music not associated with religious services or themes*. Sacred music was very important during the Renaissance. Instruments such as organs, strings (lutes, viols, harps), and winds (recorders, sackbuts) began to accompany voices in church services. In Germany, Martin Luther introduced the use of the German language during the worship service, which had previously been exclusively in Latin. He also composed sacred songs in German so that the local people could sing and understand them.

Secular music also thrived during the Renaissance. A significant new type of music was the **madrigal**, *a poem that has been set to music in the language of the composer.* With the development of the madrigal, a new style of writing emerged. This style is known as **polyphony**, *a style of music in which there are two or more melodic lines being sung or played at the same time.* Each part begins at a different place and acts independently. This style of writing was very popular; as a result, the Renaissance period is often referred to as the "golden age of polyphony."

Performance Links

When performing music of the Renaissance period, it is important to apply the following guidelines:

• Sing with clarity and purity of tone.
• Balance the vocal lines with equal importance.
• In polyphonic music, sing the rhythms accurately and with precision.
• Perform a cappella, when written.

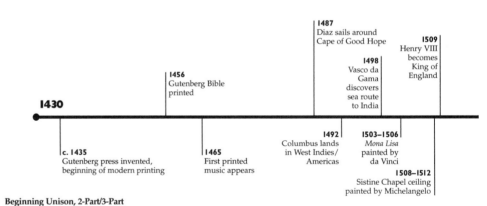

1487
Diaz sails around Cape of Good Hope

1509
Henry VIII becomes King of England

1498
Vasco da Gama discovers sea route to India

1456
Gutenberg Bible printed

1430

c. 1435
Gutenberg press invented, beginning of modern printing

1465
First printed music appears

1492
Columbus lands in West Indies/ Americas

1503–1506
Mona Lisa painted by da Vinci

1508–1512
Sistine Chapel ceiling painted by Michelangelo

108   Beginning Unison, 2-Part/3-Part

MORE ABOUT...
Renaissance Painting

Explain that while much of the visual art was still commissioned by the Catholic Church, secular paintings also began to appear as well. Artists throughout Europe painted portraits of royal personages, military heroes and wealthy merchants, as well as landscapes and scenes of everyday life.

Listening Links

CHORAL SELECTION

"El Grillo" by Josquin des Prez (c. 1450–1521)

Josquin des Prez was born in France, but worked in Italy, the Netherlands, and France as both a church and court musician. In his compositions, des Prez often used the music and text to imitate the sounds of nature. In "El Grillo," or "The Cricket," the music imitates the sound of crickets.

Published in 1504, "El Grillo" is an example of an early madrigal. It is performed a cappella. The text is in Italian, while the form is ABA. Can you hear the imitation of the crickets in this music? When does it occur?

INSTRUMENTAL SELECTION

"Canzon in Echo Duodecimi Toni a 10" by Giovanni Gabrieli (c. 1553–1612)

Giovanni Gabrieli was an important musician in Venice, Italy. He composed both sacred and secular music. Although much of his work is written for voice, he also wrote instrumental music. During the sixteenth century, the **canzona** (*a rhythmic instrumental composition that is light and fast-moving*) emerged. Canzonas are usually sectional in form and use imitation. The repetition of the opening section at the end is common. They are among the best of Gabrieli's music. Can you hear the repetition of the opening section at the end?

Check Your Understanding

1. Describe polyphony.

2. Analyze the Renaissance characteristics as heard in "El Grillo."

3. Compare the influence of the printing press during the Renaissance to the use of computers today.

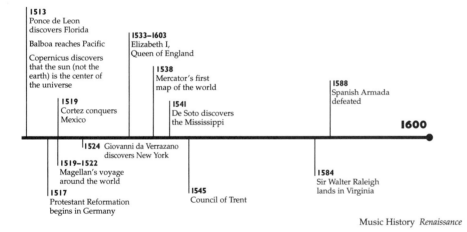

1513
Ponce de Leon discovers Florida

Balboa reaches Pacific

Copernicus discovers that the sun (not the earth) is the center of the universe

1519
Cortez conquers Mexico

1524 Giovanni da Verrazano discovers New York

1519–1522
Magellan's voyage around the world

1517
Protestant Reformation begins in Germany

1533–1603
Elizabeth I, Queen of England

1538
Mercator's first map of the world

1541
De Soto discovers the Mississippi

1545
Council of Trent

1588
Spanish Armada defeated

1584
Sir Walter Raleigh lands in Virginia

1600

Answers to Check Your Understanding.

1. Polyphony is a style of writing that developed during the Renaissance period. It is when two or more melodic lines begin at different places and act independently of each other.

2. The Renaissance musical characteristics found in "El Grillo" are: polyphony; a cappella; sounds that imitate nature; it is a madrigal.

3. Answers may vary. The printing press made it possible for books to be produced much faster, cheaper, and in greater quantity. Computers have made vast amounts of information accessible at a very fast rate. Both mass-produced books and computers have made a major impact on society.

ASSESSMENT

Informal Assessment

In this lesson, students showed the ability to:

- Share what they know about the Renaissance period.
- Describe musical characteristics, styles and forms found in Renaissance music.
- Describe some characteristics of Renaissance art.

Student Self-Assessment

Direct students to:

- Review the questions in Check Your Understanding on page 109.
- Write a paragraph answering each of the three questions about music during the Renaissance period.

ENRICHMENT

Research Project

As a small group activity, assign each group one of the following important figures of the Renaissance period: Giovanni Gabrieli, Leonardo da Vinci, William Shakespeare, Nicholas Copernicus, and Ferdinand Magellan. Have each group do research on the contributions of each, and then present findings to the rest of the class.

BAROQUE

OVERVIEW

Objectives

After completing this lesson, students will be able to:

- Describe characteristics of Baroque music.
- Identify major influences of the time that still impact our lives today.

VOCABULARY

Have students review vocabulary in student lesson. A complete glossary of terms is found on page 246 of the student book.

MUSIC&ART

Introduce the Baroque period through visual art. Analyze the painting by Jan Molenaer on page 110. Direct students to discuss the instruments being played by the children. Review background information of Molenaer's *Two Boys and a Girl Making Music* as found on page 110.

MUSIC&ART | Jan Molenaer (c. 1610–1668) was a Dutch painter who was married to artist Judith Leyster (1609–1660). In this painting, the subject of children making music celebrates the carefree pleasures of youth. The boy on the left is playing a violin, while the one on the right plays a "rommelpot" (rumbling pot). The girl is playing an accompaniment by beating spoons on a soldier's helmet.

Jan Molenaer. *Two Boys and a Girl Making Music.* 1629. Oil on canvas. 68.3 x 84.5 cm (26 15/16 x 33 1/4) National Gallery, London, United Kingdom.

110   Beginning Unison, 2-Part/3-Part

RESOURCES

Teacher Resource Binder

Music and History 4, *Baroque Music*

Music and History 5, *Johann Sebastian Bach*

Transparency 2, *Two Boys and a Girl Making Music,* Jan Molenaer

Music and History 6, *Fine Art Teaching Strategy*

For additional resources, see Music and History section.

Listening Selections CD

(found in the Teacher Resource Binder)

Track 3 "Hallelujah Chorus" from *Messiah*

Track 4 *Brandenburg Concerto No. 2,* Third Movement

Focus

- Describe the characteristics of Baroque music.
- Identify major influences of the time that still impact our lives today.

The Baroque Period— A Time of Elaboration

The **Baroque period** *(1600–1750)* was a time of great wealth and luxury for the royal and noble families of Europe. In the royal courts of the European kings, especially Louis XIV of France, life was a very fancy affair. Elaborate decoration was the rule in music, art, architecture, and fashion. Men and women of royalty wore wigs, high-heeled shoes, and colorful clothes decorated with costly lace. The term *baroque* comes from a French word meaning "imperfect or irregular pearls," which were used quite often as decorations on clothing of this period.

One of the reasons for the great wealth was the colonization of new lands with vast natural resources in the Americas and the Caribbean. In the early 1600s, groups from England, Germany and the Netherlands lived on the Eastern coast of what is today the United States. French and Spanish explorers were busily exploring and settling other parts of the New World.

With the new wealth came an interest in the arts and architecture. Royal and wealthy noble families sought to have the same level of access to art, music, and architecture that had been previously available primarily through the church.

A few of the great personalities of the Baroque period include:

- Johann Sebastian Bach—German composer
- Rembrandt van Rijn—Dutch painter
- John Milton—English writer
- William Harvey—English scientist who explained blood circulation
- Sir Isaac Newton—English scientist who formulated the theory of gravity

COMPOSERS

Johann Pachelbel
(1653–1706)

Antonio Vivaldi
(1678–1741)

Johann Sebastian Bach
(1685–1750)

George Frideric Handel
(1685–1759)

ARTISTS

El Greco
(1541–1614)

Peter Paul Rubens
(1577–1640)

Anthony van Dyck
(1599–1641)

Rembrandt van Rijn
(1606–1669)

Jan Vermeer
(1632–1675)

AUTHORS

Ben Jonson
(1572–1637)

René Descartes
(1596–1650)

John Milton
(1608–1674)

Molière
(1622–1673)

Samuel Johnson
(1709–1784)

VOCABULARY

Baroque period

oratorio

opera

concerto grosso

chorale

Music History *Baroque* **111**

LESSON PLAN
Suggested Teaching Sequence

1. Examine the Baroque period in a historical perspective.

Direct students to:

- Read and discuss the information found on student page 111.
- Turn to the time line on pages 112–113 and read the citations.
- Discuss why these are considered important dates during the Baroque period.
- Identify specific accomplishments that were made during the Baroque period and the people associated with those accomplishments.
- Compare each of these events to what occurred before and after the Baroque period.

2. Define the musical aspects of Baroque music.

Direct students to:

- Read and discuss information on Baroque music found on student page 112.
- Define *oratorio*, *opera* and *concerto grosso*.

3. Discuss the performance guidelines of Baroque music.

Direct students to:

- Read the Performance Links found on student page 112.
- Discuss the performance guidelines.

National Standards

6. Listening to, analyzing, and describing music. **(a, b, c, e, f)**
8. Understanding relationships between music, the other arts, and disciplines outside the arts. **(a, b, c, d, e)**
9. Understanding music in relation to history and culture. **(a, c, d, e)**

LISTENING LESSONS

This feature is designed to expand students' appreciation of choral and instrumental music of the Baroque period.

1. Choral Selection:

"Hallelujah Chorus" from *Messiah* by George Frideric Handel

Direct students to:

- Read the information on student page 113 to learn more about George Frideric Handel and "Hallelujah Chorus" from *Messiah*.
- Listen to the recorded performance to identify the middle imitative section of the piece.
- While listening again, write down the words that are used during this section.

2. Instrumental Selection:

Brandenburg Concerto No. 2, **Third Movement by Johann Sebastian Bach**

Direct students to:

- Read the information on student page 113 to learn more about Johann Sebastian Bach and *Brandenburg Concerto No. 2,* Third Movement.
- Listen to the recorded performance to identify the solo instruments and the instruments performing the continuo.
- Listen again, and then discuss the use of ornamentation in the soloists' improvisations.

Baroque Music

The music of the Baroque period reflected the elaborate lifestyle of the time. Baroque composers wrote music that had great dramatic flair and a strong sense of movement. The melodies were often fancy and showy, but underneath them remained a clear and carefully planned musical structure.

Many new forms of vocal music were developed during the Baroque period. One new form was the **oratorio**, *a dramatic work for solo voices, chorus, and orchestra presented without theatrical action.* George Frideric Handel's (1685–1759) *Messiah* is an example of this form. Another form was the opera. An **opera** is *a combination of singing, instrumental music, dancing, and drama that tells a story.*

There was also a dramatic rise in importance of instrumental music. In earlier times, vocal music held dominance over instrumental music. Orchestras came into being with new forms of orchestral music. Composers created an independent instrumental style with dance suites, solo sonatas, solo concertos, overtures and fugues. A **concerto grosso** is *a multi-movement baroque piece for a group of soloists and an orchestra.* Two famous concertos grosso written during this time were Antonio Vivaldi's (1678–1741) *The Four Seasons* and Johann Sebastian Bach's (1685–1750) *Brandenburg Concertos.*

A number of instruments were developed during this time, including the clavichord, harpsichord, organ and clarinet.

Performance Links

When performing music of the Baroque period, it is important to apply the following guidelines:

- Sing with pitch accuracy, especially in chromatic sections.
- Identify which part has the dominant theme. Make sure that is heard over the accompaniment.
- When in the style of the piece, keep a steady, unrelenting pulse. Precision of dotted rhythms is especially important.
- Make any changes in dynamics at the same time in all parts.

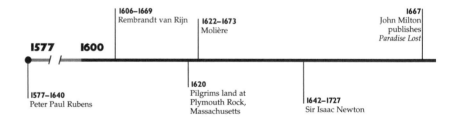

1606–1669
Rembrandt van Rijn

1622–1673
Molière

1667
John Milton publishes *Paradise Lost*

1577   **1600**

1577–1640
Peter Paul Rubens

1620
Pilgrims land at Plymouth Rock, Massachusetts

1642–1727
Sir Isaac Newton

MORE ABOUT...

Baroque Painting

The Baroque period was a time of opulence and ornamentation. Using similar art forms as the Renaissance, Baroque artists decorated each element. The distinction between the aristocracy and the common people was highly defined during this period, with the wealthy involved in the arts for their own pleasure, and in an effort to represent their status in society. Point out the details in *Two Boys and a Girl Making Music.* How do we know these children come from a wealthy family? *(clothing)*

Listening Links

CHORAL SELECTION

"Hallelujah Chorus" from *Messiah* by George Frideric Handel (1685–1759)

English composer George Frideric Handel was a musical genius. He often wrote music for special occasions for the nobility of England. Although Handel wrote operas, it was his oratorios that brought him lasting recognition. He wrote his most famous oratorio, *Messiah,* in twenty-four days.

The story has been told that King George I stood up during the first performance of "Hallelujah Chorus" to show his approval of the music. At that time, it was necessary for everyone to stand when the king was standing. Today, it is still customary to stand during the performance of this piece. The "Hallelujah Chorus" uses very few words. Identify the middle imitative section. Listen, and then write down the words that are used during this section.

INSTRUMENTAL SELECTION

Brandenburg Concerto No. 2, Third Movement by Johann Sebastian Bach (1685–1750)

German composer Johann Sebastian Bach was one of the greatest composers who ever lived. He came from a family of musicians, and learned to play the organ and the clavichord at an early age. A devout man of the Lutheran faith, Bach used **chorales**, or *hymn tunes,* in much of his sacred music. The quantity and quality of his music staggers the imagination.

Bach dedicated his six *Brandenburg Concertos* to the Margrave of Brandenburg in 1721. This selection features solo sections for trumpet, oboe, violin, and recorder. Describe what you hear during the solo sections.

Check Your Understanding

1. Compare and contrast oratorios and operas. Name one famous oratorio and its composer.

2. Describe characteristics of instrumental music during the Baroque period based on the *Brandenburg Concerto No. 2,* Third Movement.

3. Sir Isaac Newton discovered the law of gravity in the late 1600s. Discuss ways in which this discovery has influenced your life today.

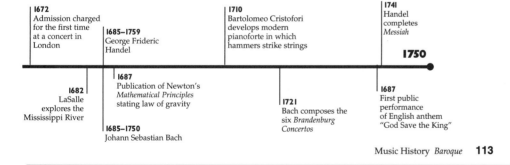

1672 Admission charged for the first time at a concert in London	**1710** Bartolomeo Cristofori develops modern pianoforte in which hammers strike strings	**1741** Handel completes *Messiah*

1685–1759 George Frideric Handel

1750

1682 LaSalle explores the Mississippi River

1687 Publication of Newton's *Mathematical Principles* stating law of gravity

1721 Bach composes the six *Brandenburg Concertos*

1687 First public performance of English anthem "God Save the King"

1685–1750 Johann Sebastian Bach

Music History *Baroque* **113**

Answers to Check Your Understanding.

1. Operas and oratorios are both written for solo voices, chorus and orchestra. They both tell a story. Operas, however, are designed to be performed on a stage with dancing, costuming and scenery. Oratorios are composed to be sung in a church or concert setting. *The Messiah* by Handel is a famous oratorio.

2. The Baroque musical characteristics found in the *Brandenburg Concerto No. 2,* Third Movement are: use of continuo, ornamentation, and improvisation; it is a concerto grosso.

3. Answers may vary. One example would be NASA. The scientists there have to use Newton's Law to determine how much energy it takes to blast the space shuttle out of the earth's gravity field in order to get into space.

ASSESSMENT

Informal Assessment

In this lesson, students showed the ability to:

- Share what they know about the Baroque period.
- Describe musical characteristics, styles and forms found in Baroque music.
- Describe some characteristics of Baroque art.

Student Self-Assessment

Direct students to:

- Review the questions in Check Your Understanding on page 113.
- Write a paragraph answering each of the three questions about the Baroque period.

ENRICHMENT

Research Project

As a small group activity, assign each group one of the following important figures of the Baroque period: J. S. Bach, Jan Molenaer, John Milton, William Harvey, Sir Isaac Newton, and Henry Hudson. Have each group do research on the contributions of each, and then present findings to the rest of the class.

CLASSICAL

OVERVIEW

Objectives

After completing this lesson, students will be able to:

• Identify two major composers from the Classical period.

• Describe characteristics of Classical music.

Have students review vocabulary in student lesson. A complete glossary of terms is found on page 246 of the student book.

Introduce the Classical period through visual art. Analyze the painting by Louis Carmontelle on page 114. Direct students to discuss what they know about W.A. Mozart. Review background information of Carmontelle's *Leopold Mozart Making Music with Wolfgang and Nannerl* as found on page 114.

Louis Carmontelle (1717–1806) was a French architect, draftsman, painter, and printmaker. Although self-taught, Carmontelle drew hundreds of portraits that chronicle court life in France prior to the French Revolution. In this painting, Wolfgang Amadeus Mozart is seated at the piano performing music with his father, Leopold, and his sister, Nannerl. They are wearing the formal dress of the Classical period.

Louis Carmontelle. *Leopold Mozart Making Music with Wolfgang and Nannerl.* c. 1763. Watercolor. Museé Conde, Chantilly, Paris, France.

114   Beginning Unison, 2-Part/3-Part

RESOURCES

Teacher Resource Binder

Music and History 7, *Classical Music*

Music and History 8, *Wolfgang Amadeus Mozart*

Transparency 3, *Leopold Mozart Making Music with Wolfgang and Nannerl,* Louis Carmontelle

Music and History 9, *Fine Art Teaching Strategy*

For additional resources, see Music and History section.

Listening Selections CD

(found in the Teacher Resource Binder)

Track 5 "Confutatis" from *Requiem*

Track 6 *Trumpet Concerto in E♭ Major,* Third Movement

Focus

- Identify two major composers from the Classical period.
- Describe characteristics of Classical music.

The Classical Period— A Time of Balance, Clarity, and Simplicity

The **Classical period** *(1750–1820)* was a time when people began looking to the early Greeks and Romans for order and structure in their lives. Artists and architects took note of the Greek and Roman objects being dug up in Athens, Pompeii, and other archeological sites. For example, the Arc de Triomphe in Paris, commissioned in 1806, was inspired by the Arch of Septiomus Severus in Rome.

The calm beauty and simplicity of this art from the past inspired artists and musicians to move away from the overly decorated styles of the Baroque period. The music, art, and architecture reflected a new emphasis on emotional restraint and simplicity.

The Classical period was witness to a rise in a democratic spirit in the lower and middle classes. Revolutions that took place in France and America abolished the rule by kings and queens, and established a more representative type of government. The main events in America during this period include the American Revolution (1775–1783), the signing of the Declaration of Independence (1776), the election of George Washington as the first President of the United States (1783), and the ratification of the National Constitution (1788).

Publishing increased dramatically, giving people other than the wealthy access to books and printed music. Among the famous books written during this period was Voltaire's *Candide*, which later served as the basis for a Broadway musical with music by Leonard Bernstein (1918–1990).

COMPOSERS

Carl Philipp Emanuel Bach
(1714–1788)

Johann Christian Bach
(1735–1762)

Franz Joseph Haydn
(1732–1809)

Wolfgang Amadeus Mozart
(1756–1791)

Ludwig van Beethoven
(1770–1827)

ARTISTS

Louis de Carmontelle
(1717–1806)

Thomas Gainsborough
(1727–1788)

Francisco Goya
(1746–1828)

Jacques-Louis David
(1748–1825)

Elisabeth Vigée-Lebrun
(1755–1842)

AUTHORS

Voltaire
(1694–1778)

William Wordsworth
(1770–1850)

Jane Austen
(1775–1817)

VOCABULARY

Classical period

secular music

homophony

crescendo

decrescendo

LESSON PLAN

Suggested Teaching Sequence

1. Examine the Classical period in a historical perspective.

Direct students to:

- Read and discuss the information found on student page 115.
- Turn to the time line on pages 116–117 and read the citations.
- Discuss why these are considered important dates during the Classical period.
- Identify specific accomplishments that were made during the Classical period and the people associated with those accomplishments.
- Compare each of these events to what occurred before and after the Classical period.

2. Define the musical aspects of Classical music.

Direct students to:

- Read and discuss information on Classical music found on student page 116.
- Define *homophony*.

3. Discuss the performance guidelines of Classical music.

Direct students to:

- Read the Performance Links found on student page 116.
- Discuss the performance guidelines.

National Standards

6. Listening to, analyzing, and describing music. **(a, b, c, e, f)**
8. Understanding relationships between music, the other arts, and disciplines outside the arts. **(a, b, c, d, e)**
9. Understanding music in relation to history and culture. **(a, c, d, e)**

This feature is designed to expand students' appreciation of choral and instrumental music of the Classical period.

1. Choral Selection:

"Confutatis" from *Requiem* by Wolfgang Amadeus Mozart

Direct students to:

- Read the information on student page 117 to learn more about Wolfgang Amadeus Mozart and "Confutatis" from *Requiem*.

- Define *requiem*.

- Listen to the recorded performance to identify and describe the sections sung by men's voices. (*energetic, forceful, agitated, strong*)

- After listening again, describe the "interruptions." (*calm, beautiful, pleading sections sung by the women's voices*)

- Describe the ending of the piece. (*full SATB choir sings together in a very quiet ending section*)

2. Instrumental Selection:

***Trumpet Concerto in E♭ Major*, Third Movement by Franz Joseph Haydn**

Direct students to:

- Read the information on student page 117 to learn more about Franz Joseph Haydn and *Trumpet Concerto in E♭ Major*, Third Movement.

- Read the definition of *concerto*.

- Listen to the recorded performance to identify the solo trumpet and the main theme, first performed by the orchestra, then by the trumpet. Count how many times it is heard.

Music of the Classical Period

During the Classical period, people developed an interest in knowing more about the cultural aspects of life, such as art and music. One of the most important advances in the Classical period was the development of public concerts. Music was now written and performed for the general public, as well as for the royal courts and churches. The increasing popularity of public concerts led to a growth in the number of professional musicians and composers. For the first time, **secular music** (*music not associated with religious services or themes*) became the main type of music being formally composed.

The ideas of improvisation and exaggerated use of embellishments of the Baroque period were discarded. Music became simpler and more elegant, with a melody that sang out while the other parts provided a simple accompaniment. This type of music is known as **homophony**, or *music in which there are two or more parts with similar or identical rhythms being sung or played at the same time*. The two main composers associated with this period are Franz Joseph Haydn (1732–1809) and Wolfgang Amadeus Mozart (1756–1791). Their compositions were based on balance, clarity and simplicity. At the beginning of his career, Ludwig van Beethoven (1770–1827) also wrote music in the Classical style. Later, his style evolved into the more emotional and personal style of the Romantic period.

Performance Links

When performing music of the Classical period, it is important to apply the following guidelines:

- Listen for the melody line and do not allow the accompaniment parts to overshadow it.
- Sing chords in tune.
- Make gradual, not abrupt, dynamic changes. Move smoothly through each **crescendo** (*a dynamic marking that indicates to gradually sing louder*) and **decrescendo** (*a dynamic marking that indicates to gradually sing softer*).
- Keep phrases flowing and connected.

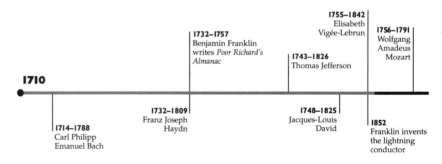

1710

1714–1788
Carl Philipp Emanuel Bach

1732–1757
Benjamin Franklin writes *Poor Richard's Almanac*

1732–1809
Franz Joseph Haydn

1743–1826
Thomas Jefferson

1748–1825
Jacques-Louis David

1755–1842
Elisabeth Vigée-Lebrun

1756–1791
Wolfgang Amadeus Mozart

1852
Franklin invents the lightning conductor

116   Beginning Unison, 2-Part/3-Part

MORE ABOUT ...

Classical Painting

The Classical period in art made use of ancient Greek and Roman sculptures as models. It stressed the importance of balanced compositions, flowing contour lines, figures modeled in light and dark, subdued colors, and noble gestures and expression. Note the artist's careful painting of details and his use of light to add drama. Point out the details in *Leopold Mozart Making Music with Wolfgang and Nannerl*. (The elaborate setting and clothing suggest that they were performing for the French king.)

Listening Links

CHORAL SELECTION

"Confutatis" from *Requiem* by Wolfgang Amadeus Mozart (1756–1791)

Wolfgang Amadeus Mozart is recognized as one of the world's greatest composers. Born in Salzburg, Austria, Mozart was a child prodigy who had mastered the keyboard at age four and had written his first composition by age five.

Although Mozart died before completing the *Requiem*, the work was completed later by his student, Franz Süssmayer, and perhaps others. Mozart's *Requiem* has been performed and loved by many for over two centuries.

The "Confutatis" begins with an energetic rhythmic drive sung by the men's section and accompanied by a moving figure in the strings. The men's voices are interrupted twice. Identify what is happening musically during these interruptions. Describe how the piece ends.

INSTRUMENTAL SELECTION

Trumpet Concerto in E♭ Major, Third Movement by Franz Joseph Haydn (1732–1809)

Franz Joseph Haydn was another child prodigy from Austria. He introduced touches of folk and gypsy music into his works. Haydn, known as the "father of the symphony," composed over one hundred symphonies.

The *Trumpet Concerto in E♭ Major* was written in 1796 for Anton Weidinger, a friend of Haydn's who invented a trumpet with valves. The concerto was designed to demonstrate the flexibility of the new instrument. The opening theme is repeated numerous times. Listen to this piece and count the number of times you hear this theme.

Check Your Understanding

1. Name two important composers who wrote during the Classical period.

2. Analyze the main characteristics of Classical music as heard in *Requiem*: "Confutatis."

3. Describe how the Greek and Roman cultures influenced the Classical period.

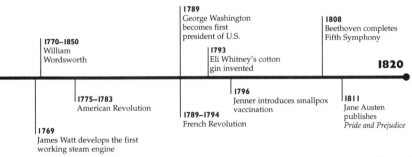

Music History *Classical*   **117**

Answers to Check Your Understanding.

1. Franz Joseph Haydn, Wolfgang Amadeus Mozart.

2. The Classical musical characteristics found in the "Confutatis" from Requiem are: strong melody line that is not overshadowed by the accompaniment, gradual dynamic changes, flowing and connected phrases.

3. People were looking for order and structure in their lives, so they turned to the early Greeks and Romans for their influences. People adapted the calm beauty and simplicity of the past and moved away from the overly decorated and embellished art from the Baroque.

ASSESSMENT

Informal Assessment

In this lesson, students showed the ability to:

- Share what they know about the Classical period.
- Describe musical characteristics, styles and forms found in Classical music.
- Describe some characteristics of Classical art.

Student Self-Assessment

Direct students to:

- Review the questions in Check Your Understanding on page 117.
- Write a paragraph answering each of the three questions about the Classical period.

ENRICHMENT

Research Project

Mozart was dying as he wrote *Requiem*. Some say he thought he was writing it for his own funeral. Indeed, after it was finished following his death, the *Requiem* was performed in a memorial service for the composer. Music is an integral part of many social and religious functions, one of which is a funeral. Ask students:

- To share any experiences of music they have heard at funerals, and the reasons they think music is played or sung at a funeral.
- Discuss what type of music would be appropriate at a funeral and give reasons for their answers. Some may feel somber music would reflect the mood, while others might suggest something lighter to lift the spirits of those in attendance, or to celebrate the life of a loved one.

117

ROMANTIC

OVERVIEW

Objectives

After completing this lesson, students will be able to:

- Describe cultural events of the Romantic period.
- Describe characteristics of Romantic music.

VOCABULARY

Have students review vocabulary in student lesson. A complete glossary of terms is found on page 246 of the student book.

Introduce the Romantic period through visual art. Analyze the painting by Pierre-Auguste Renoir on page 118. Direct students to discuss possible relationships between the two girls, and their feelings about the music and playing the piano. Is there a story in the picture? Review background information on Renoir's *Two Young Girls at the Piano* as found on page 118.

Pierre-Auguste Renoir (1841–1919) was a French impressionist who focused on people in informal gatherings. Often, their actions were important, even though there was not always an obvious suggestion of the story. His paintings captured the relationship among his subjects and their feelings. He enjoyed showing the joyful side of life.

Pierre-Auguste Renoir. *Two Young Girls at the Piano.* 1892. Oil on canvas. 111.8 x 86.4 cm (44 x 34"). The Metropolitan Museum of Art, New York, New York. Robert Lehman Collection.

118   Beginning Unison, 2-Part/3-Part

RESOURCES

Teacher Resource Binder

Music and History 10, *Romantic Music*

Music and History 11, *Franz Schubert*

Transparency 4, *Two Young Girls at the Piano*, Pierre-Auguste Renoir

Music and History 12, *Fine Art Teaching Strategy*

For additional resources, see Music and History section.

Listening Selections CD

(found in the Teacher Resource Binder)

Track 7 "Dies Irae" from *Requiem*

Track 8 "Ride of the Valkyries" from *Die Walkure*

Focus

- Describe cultural events of the Romantic period.
- Describe characteristics of Romantic music.

The Romantic Period— A Time of Drama

The **Romantic period** *(1820–1900)* was a period when composers wrote music that was filled with emotion. It was, in many ways, a reaction against the Classical period (1750–1820), when music was based on emotional restraint and formal structure.

The Romantic period was a time of tremendous change in the world. Scientific and mechanical achievements led to advances in transportation (steamboats, railways), communication (telegraph, telephone), and manufacturing (steel production, food canning). There was a move from living on farms to working in the factories. These changes helped to bring about the Industrial Revolution.

The Industrial Revolution produced a wealthy middle class. Their new wealth provided music for the masses to a far greater degree than had existed before. Musicians' incomes were now generated by the sale of concert tickets and published music rather than by the patronage of the church or the very wealthy. By not being associated with a patron, composers could show more individualism and freedom in their writing.

Visual artists of the Romantic period began to explore the world around them. They painted nature scenes, and focused on natural light in these scenes. In France, such artists were known as Impressionists; they included Edouard Manet, Edgar Degas, Pierre Renoir, and the sculptor Auguste Rodin.

Writers of the time told tales of adventure (*The Three Musketeers* by Alexandre Dumas, *Tom Sawyer* by Mark Twain), the changes in society (*Oliver Twist* by Charles Dickens), and exotic places (*Jungle Book* by Rudyard Kipling). Science fiction also became a popular theme of stories (*20,000 Leagues Under the Sea* by Jules Verne).

COMPOSERS

Ludwig van Beethoven (1770–1827)
Franz Schubert (1797–1828)
Felix Mendelssohn (1809–1847)
Frédéric Chopin (1810–1849)
Franz Liszt (1811–1886)
Richard Wagner (1813–1883)
Giuseppe Verdi (1813–1901)
Johannes Brahms (1833–1897)
Georges Bizet (1838–1875)
Peter Ilyich Tchaikovsky (1840–1893)
Antonín Dvořák (1841–1904)
Claude Debussy (1862–1918)

ARTISTS

Edouard Manet (1832–1883)
Edgar Degas (1834–1917)
Paul Cezanne (1839–1906)
Auguste Rodin (1840–1917)
Claude Monet (1840–1926)
Pierre-Auguste Renoir (1841–1919)
Mary Cassatt (1845–1926)
Paul Gauguin (1848–1903)
Vincent van Gogh (1853–1890)

AUTHORS

Alexandre Dumas (1802–1870)
Henry Wadsworth Longfellow (1807–1882)
Charles Dickens (1812–1870)
Jules Verne (1828–1905)
Louisa May Alcott (1832–1884)
Mark Twain (1835–1910)
Rudyard Kipling (1865–1905)

VOCABULARY

Romantic period

opera

mass

requiem

Music History *Romantic* **119**

LESSON PLAN

Suggested Teaching Sequence

1. Examine the Romantic period in a historical perspective.

Direct students to:

- Read and discuss the information found on student page 119.
- Turn to the time line on pages 120–121 and read the citations.
- Discuss why these are considered important dates during the Romantic period.
- Identify specific accomplishments that were made during the Romantic period and the people associated with those accomplishments.
- Compare each of these events to what occurred before and after the Romantic period.

2. Define the musical aspects of Romantic music.

Direct students to:

- Read and discuss information on Romantic music found on student page 120.
- Name several important Romantic composers.
- Define *nationalism*.

3. Discuss the performance guidelines of Romantic music.

Direct students to:

- Read the Performance Links found on student page 120.
- Discuss the performance guidelines.

National Standards

6. Listening to, analyzing, and describing music. **(a, b, c, e, f)**
8. Understanding relationships between music, the other arts, and disciplines outside the arts. **(a, b, c, d, e)**
9. Understanding music in relation to history and culture. **(a, c, d, e)**

LISTENING LESSONS

This feature is designed to expand students' appreciation of choral and instrumental music of the Romantic period.

1. Choral Selection:

"Dies Irae" from *Requiem* by Giuseppe Verdi

Direct students to:

- Read the information on student page 121 to learn more about Giuseppe Verdi and "Dies Irae" from *Requiem*.
- Define *mass* and *requiem*.
- Listen to the recorded performance to identify the middle instrumental section of the piece.
- After listening again, describe the mood of this section, and the feelings conveyed by the whole selection.

2. Instrumental Selection:

"Ride of the Valkyries" from *Die Walkure* by Richard Wagner

Direct students to:

- Read the information on student page 121 to learn more about Richard Wagner and "Ride of the Valkyries" from *Die Walkure*.
- Define *opera*.
- Listen to the recorded performance to identify the brass instruments playing the melody and the string instruments adding swirling or "flying" sounds.
- Listen again, and then discuss when and where students have heard this music before. (*cartoons, TV commercials, symphony concerts, etc.*)

Music of the Romantic Period

Composers of the Romantic period created music that was full of emotion and less structured than music of the Classical period. Melodies became longer and more expressive, and harmonies became more colorful. Larger orchestras were used to expand the available sounds in the music. Creativity was enhanced as the rules of composition were relaxed or broken.

Romantic music reflected the period's spirit of nationalism. Richard Wagner (1813–1883) highlighted German music and legends in his operas, while Giuseppe Verdi (1813–1901) wrote operas that preserved the historical and cultural traditions of his native Italy. Upon a visit to the United States, Antonin Dvorák (1841–1904), a Czech composer, wrote his famous *Symphony from the New World* to describe America.

Other composers focused on stories in works such as Modest Mussorgsky's (1839–1881) *Night on Bald Mountain* and Georges Bizet's (1838–1875) *Carmen*. Still others, like Claude Debussy (1862–1918), joined the Impressionist movement and wrote music that suggested scenes or feelings. Ludwig van Beethoven (1770–1827) crossed the bridge between the Classical and Romantic periods. His later music exhibited the emotion, rhythm, and disregard for form that was characteristic of the Romantics.

One composer most associated with the Romantic movement is Frédéric Chopin (1810–1849). His piano music explored a wide variety of strong and quiet emotions. Other composers of the period include Peter Ilyich Tchaikovsky (1840–1893) whose *Nutcracker Suite* is a staple of Christmas celebrations, and Johannes Brahms (1833–1897) whose *Lullaby* is still sung to young children across the globe.

Performance Links

When performing music of the Romantic period, it is important to apply the following guidelines:

- Perform accurately the wide range of dynamics and tempos.
- Concentrate on phrasing, making the connection between the words and the music.
- Sing with confidence in foreign languages to reflect nationalism in music.

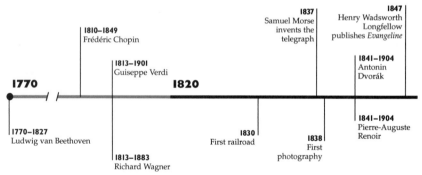

MORE ABOUT...

Romantic Painting

Emotional response is the significant feature of many Romantic paintings. Interest in exploring feelings and reaction, rather than formal structure, is typical of visual arts and music during the Romantic period. Point out the details in *Two Boys and a Girl Making Music*. Ask, "In which ways does this painter use the elements and principles of art differently than artists of other periods studied?"

Listening Links

CHORAL SELECTION
"Dies Irae" from *Requiem* by Giuseppe Verdi (1813–1901)

Giuseppe Verdi, a famous Italian composer, wrote twenty-six operas and several other works. An **opera** is *a combination of singing, instrumental music, dancing and drama that tells a story.* When Verdi died, the streets of Milan, Italy, were filled with thousands of mourners, who followed his coffin through the streets singing a chorus from one of his operas.

A **mass** is *a religious service of prayers and ceremonies.* Originating in the Roman Catholic Church it consists of spoken and sung sections. Sometimes a special mass known as a **requiem**, or *a mass for the dead,* is used. "Dies Irae" is one section of the Verdi *Requiem* that was first performed in 1874. Describe the opening section of this piece.

INSTRUMENTAL SELECTION
"Ride of the Valkyries" from *Die Walkure* by Richard Wagner (1813–1883)

Richard Wagner was a German composer whose composing style was very expressive. His music often painted a picture, and was on the grandest scale. His work greatly influenced future composers.

Wagner's *Die Walkure* is an opera based on a legend from Norse mythology. It tells the story of Wotan, the leader of the gods, who had nine daughters called Valkyries, or warrior maidens. Wotan ordered the Valkyries to bring him the world's bravest heroes, whom he would then transform into immortals to protect the gods. Act Three begins with the "Ride of the Valkyries," a scene where the warrior maidens gallop through a storm carrying the brave heroes to Valhalla, the mountaintop home of the gods. As you listen to "Ride of the Valkyries," identify when and where you have heard this music before.

Check Your Understanding

1. Name two Romantic compositions and their composers.

2. Compare musical characteristics of the Classical and Romantic periods.

3. Discuss influences on your life today that originated during the Romantic period.

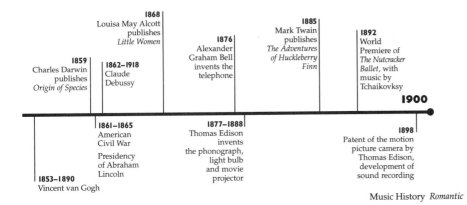

Music History *Romantic* **121**

Answers to Check Your Understanding.

1. Answers will vary. Examples: Verdi—*Requiem*, Wagner—*Die Walkure*, Dvořák—*Symphony from the New World*, Mussorgsky—*Night on Bald Mountain*, Bizet—*Carmen*, Tchaikovsky—*Nutcracker Suite*, Brahms—*Lullaby*.

2. Music of the Classical period was structured, less emotional, and emphasized clarity, repose and balance. Music of the Romantic period was full of emotion and less structured than music of the Classical period. Nationalism was an important element in Romantic music.

3. Answers will vary. For example, one might mention our current love of movies and telephones, both of which were invented during the Romantic period.

ASSESSMENT

Informal Assessment

In this lesson, students showed the ability to:

- Share what they know about the Romantic period.

- Describe musical characteristics, styles and forms found in Romantic music.

- Describe some characteristics of Romantic art.

Student Self-Assessment

Direct students to:

- Review the questions in Check Your Understanding on page 121.

- Write a paragraph answering each of the three questions about the Romantic period.

ENRICHMENT

Research Project

The Romantic period marked the beginning of the composer as a self-supporting professional. Before this time, most composers were part of a "court," or on the payroll of a wealthy family. They received commissions from the church or their patron family to create compositions for certain events, or even as study pieces for lessons. This type of patronage dwindled during the Romantic period. Since this time, composers have had to find ways to make a living either by commissions, printing and marketing their music, getting a well-known performer to present the piece, or performing it themselves. Have students research a favorite music selection to find out who the composer is and how the composer gets paid for writing the piece.

CONTEMPORARY

OVERVIEW

Objectives

After completing this lesson, students will be able to:

- Identify the major twentieth-century influences on music.
- Describe characteristics of Contemporary music.

VOCABULARY

Have students review vocabulary in student lesson. A complete glossary of terms is found on page 246 of the student book.

Introduce the Contemporary period through architecture. Analyze the picture of *Falling Water House*, designed by Frank Lloyd Wright, on page 122. Direct students to discuss the ways the house merges with its natural surroundings. Review background information on Wright's *Falling Water House* as found on page 122.

Falling Water House is one of the most inventive houses built by Frank Lloyd Wright (1867–1959). Surrounding foliage and waterfalls merge the architecture with nature. Walls are avoided almost entirely, allowing the overhangs to provide a sense of shelter.

Frank Lloyd Wright. *Falling Water House.* Bear Run, Pennsylvania. 1936. The Frank Lloyd Wright Foundation, Scottsdale, Arizona.

122 Beginning Unison, 2-Part/3-Part

RESOURCES

Teacher Resource Binder

Music and History 13, *Contemporary Music*

Music and History 14, *Carl Orff*

Transparency 5, *Falling Water House,* Frank Lloyd Wright

Music and History 15, *Fine Art Teaching Strategy*

For additional resources, see Music and History section.

Listening Selections CD

(found in the Teacher Resource Binder)

Track 9 "O Fortuna" from *Carmina Burana*

Track 10 "Fugue" from *A Young Person's Guide to the Orchestra*

Focus
- Identify the major twentieth century influences on music.
- Describe characteristics of Contemporary music.

The Contemporary Period— A Time of Change

The change from nineteenth century Romanticism to twenty-first century Modernism is as dramatic as comparing horse-drawn carriages to the rockets of the space age. The world has moved fast, and change has been constant.

New scientific discoveries and inventions began with the Industrial Revolution in the late 1800s and have continued to the present day. Technological advances were accelerated during World War I (1914–1918) and World War II (1939–1945). These advances have produced such things as the airplane, radio, television, jet propulsion, radar, atomic energy, computers and the Internet, and the exploration of outer space.

The world has become "smaller" because new technologies have made it possible to learn about world events. One can visit other parts of the world and other peoples in far less time. New ideas, sounds and trends can spread worldwide almost instantaneously.

Individualism, the principle of independent thought, combined with technology has provided artists, writers and composers with new ideas and materials for their creative endeavors. Artists such as Pablo Picasso rebelled against tradition and began to create works that were abstract. His works often did not represent objects in nature as they appeared to the eye. Some writers began to write fewer plot-driven stories and focus more on people and their thoughts and feelings.

COMPOSERS
Sergei Rachmaninoff (1873–1943)
Arnold Schoenberg (1874–1951)
Béla Bartók (1881–1945)
Igor Stravinsky (1882–1971)
Sergey Prokofiev (1891–1953)
Carl Orff (1895–1982)
Aaron Copland (1900–1990)
Benjamin Britten (1913–1976)
Leonard Bernstein (1918–1990)
John Williams (1932–)

ARTISTS
Henri Matisse (1869–1954)
Pablo Picasso (1881–1973)
Wassily Kandinsky (1866–1944)
Marc Chagall (1887–1985)
Georgia O'Keeffe (1887–1986)
Andy Warhol (1930–1987)

AUTHORS
Robert Frost (1874–1963)
Virginia Woolf (1882–1941)
Ernest Hemingway (1899–1961)
Rachel Carson (1907–1964)
James Baldwin (1924–1997)
JK Rowling (b. 1965)

VOCABULARY
synthesizer
dissonance
improvisation
fugue

National Standards
6. Listening to, analyzing, and describing music. **(a, b, c, e, f)**
8. Understanding relationships between music, the other arts, and disciplines outside the arts. **(a, b, c, d, e)**
9. Understanding music in relation to history and culture. **(a, c, d, e)**

LESSON PLAN
Suggested Teaching Sequence

1. Examine the Contemporary period in a historical perspective.

Direct students to:
- Read and discuss the information found on student page 123.
- Turn to the time line on pages 124–125 and read the citations.
- Discuss why these are considered important dates during the Contemporary period.
- Identify specific accomplishments that were made during the Contemporary period and the people associated with those accomplishments.
- Compare each of these events to what occurred before the Contemporary period.

2. Define the musical aspects of Contemporary music.

Direct students to:
- Read and discuss information on Contemporary music found on student page 124.
- Name several important Contemporary composers.
- Identify the influences of technology on music of the Contemporary period.

3. Discuss the performance guidelines of Contemporary music.

Direct students to:
- Read the Performance Links found on student page 124.
- Discuss the performance guidelines.

LISTENING LESSONS

This feature is designed to expand students' appreciation of choral and instrumental music of the Contemporary period.

1. Choral Selection:

"O Fortuna" from *Carmina Burana* by Carl Orff

Direct students to:

- Read the information on student page 125 to learn more about Carl Orff and "O Fortuna" from *Carmina Burana*.

- Listen to the recorded performance to identify repeated rhythmic patterns.

- After listening again, clap selected rhythmic patterns.

2. Instrumental Selection:

"Fugue" from *A Young Person's Guide to the Orchestra* by Benjamin Britten

Direct students to:

- Read the information on student page 125 to learn more about Benjamin Britten and "Fugue" from *A Young Person's Guide to the Orchestra*.

- Define *fugue*.

- Listen several times to the recorded performance to identify the instrument families and solo instruments as they enter playing the melody. (*woodwind family—piccolo, flute, oboe, clarinet, bassoon; string family—violin, viola, cello, bass, harp; brass family—French horn, trumpet, trombone and tuba; percussion family—snare drum, timpani, tambourine, cymbals, bass drum, xylophone*)

Music of the Contemporary Period

A great deal of change occurred in music during the late twentieth century. Technology had a large influence on these changes. Record, cassette tape and CD players made music readily available to everyone. Radios and televisions brought live music performances into people's homes. Often, acoustic instruments were replaced by the **synthesizer**, *a musical instrument that produces sounds electronically, rather than by physical vibrations.*

Like abstract art, music of this time has sought to shed itself of the musical conventions of melody, harmony, and rhythm adhered to in previous periods. Composers began to use different scales, such as Arnold Schoenberg's (1874–1951) twelve-tone system, different and complex rhythms, as in Igor Stravinsky's (1882–1971) works, and different harmonies as used by Bela Bartók (1881–1945). It was not uncommon for audiences to find this music unpleasant to the ear and filled with **dissonance** (*a combination of tones that clash*).

A new symphony form was introduced in which narrative accompanied the music. Most popular was Sergei Prokofiev's (1891–1953) *Peter and the Wolf*. Classical composers such as Aaron Copland were sought to provide music for motion pictures and ballet. Leopold Stokowski, a famous conductor, worked with Walt Disney to create the animated film *Fantasia*, based on classical music. John Williams (b. 1932), a more contemporary composer of orchestral works, has become world-famous for his themes for movies such as *Jaws* and *Star Wars*.

Performance Links

When performing music of the Contemporary period, it is important to apply the following guidelines:

- Sing on pitch, even in extreme parts of your range.
- Tune intervals carefully in the wide skips found in many melodic lines.
- Perform changing meters and unusual rhythm patterns precisely.
- Observe accurately the wide range in dynamics and tempos.

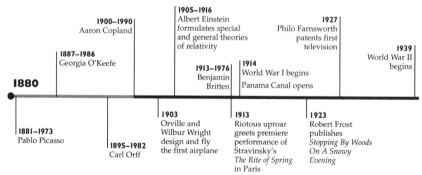

MORE ABOUT...

Contemporary Architecture

Like other applied artists, architects are faced with a double challenge. That challenge is creating works that are both useful and pleasing to the eye. Since architecture is so much a part of everyday life, the search for new solutions is never-ending. These solutions show up not only in new styles but also in new and exciting building materials. Ask students to take a close look at buildings going up in their town or city. There you are likely to see how architects combine their knowledge of engineering with an understanding of design to create buildings that are both attractive and functional.

Listening Links

CHORAL SELECTION

"O Fortuna" from *Carmina Burana* by Carl Orff (1895–1982)

Carl Orff was a German composer, perhaps best known for developing a creative approach to music education that involves speech, moving, singing, playing instruments and **improvisation** (*the art of singing or playing music, making it up as you go*).

Carmina Burana, sung in Latin and German, uses the texts from twenty-five ancient poems and love songs that were popular during the Middle Ages. It is written for solo singers, chorus and orchestra. Composed in 1937, *Carmina Burana* opens and closes with the "O Fortuna" chorus. Its text implies that life is unpredictable and fate is fickle. Orff's music often features exciting rhythms and insistent repeated note patterns. Listen for the repeated note pattern in "O Fortuna."

INSTRUMENTAL SELECTION

"Fugue" from *A Young Person's Guide to the Orchestra* by Benjamin Britten (1913–1976)

The English composer Benjamin Britten was a child genius. At the age of two, he begged his mother to teach him to play the piano. By age 16, he had composed a symphony and many other works. Benjamin Britten was highly regarded around the world, and in 1963 he was honored as England's Composer of the Year.

A Young Person's Guide to the Orchestra was written in 1945 to teach students about the instruments of the orchestra. Britten uses a fugue to highlight each section of the orchestra, and then combines them for a grand ending. A **fugue** is *a form of imitation in which a melody is performed by different instruments, entering at different times, thus adding layers of sound*. Identify each solo instrument or section as they enter.

Check Your Understanding

1. Name two important Contemporary period composers and describe their music.

2. Analyze the complex rhythms heard in "O Fortuna."

3. Summarize the changes that have made music more accessible during the twentieth century. Discuss how technology has influenced this change.

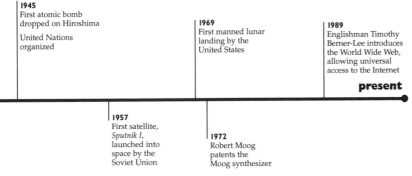

Answers to Check Your Understanding.

1. Answers will vary. Examples would include: Carl Orff—his music is often very rhythmic; Benjamin Britten—his music is often written on a grand scale; Arnold Schoenberg—12-tone music; Igor Stravinsky—his music often features complex rhythms; Bela Bartok—his music often features unusual harmonies; Sergei Prokofiev—symphony with narrative; Aaron Copland, John Williams—film music.

2. First theme—begins: quarter rest, half note, quarter note, quarter note, quarter note; Second theme—begins: half rest, half note, half note, half note, half note, half rest. Students should be able to notate the entire melody line.

3. Records, cassette tape and CD players made music accessible. Radios and televisions brought live performances into the home.

ASSESSMENT

Informal Assessment

In this lesson, students showed the ability to:

- Share what they know about the Contemporary period.

- Describe musical characteristics, styles and forms found in Contemporary music.

- Describe some characteristics of Contemporary architecture.

Student Self-Assessment

Direct students to:

- Review the questions in Check Your Understanding on page 125.

- Write a paragraph answering each of the three questions about the Contemporary period.

ENRICHMENT

Research Project

It is easy to create twelve-tone music. Have students:

- Take a chromatic set of resonator bells and arrange one octave in any order, rearranging them until the sound is interesting.

- Write down the pitches on a staff.

- Brainstorm how many ways this tone row can be played. (*For example: backward, from the middle—one way and then the other, in clusters of three or four sounds, and so on.*)

- Perform a piece made up of their choices, and evaluate what they did and did not like.

CONCERT ETIQUETTE

Objective

- Apply concert etiquette in a variety of settings.

Suggested Teaching Sequence

Direct students to:

- Read the Spotlight on Concert Etiquette on student page 126 and discuss the importance of concert etiquette in respecting the efforts of others.
- Identify the six elements that constitute proper concert etiquette.
- Compare the elements of concert etiquette to appropriate performance practices. In what ways are they related to one another?
- Apply concert etiquette during live performances in a variety of settings, such as school concerts and assemblies, professional symphony and/or opera performances, and solo recitals.
- Divide the class into small groups and assign each group one concert venue. Ask each group to make a list of five appropriate and five inappropriate behavior expectations for the assigned venue. Share findings with the class.

Progress Checkpoints

Observe students' progress in:

- ✓ Their ability to identify the elements of concert etiquette.
- ✓ Their ability to understand the importance of concert etiquette.
- ✓ Their ability to apply concert etiquette in a variety of settings.

126

 **SPOTLIGHT**

Concert Etiquette

The term **concert etiquette** describes *how we are expected to behave in formal musical performances.* Understanding appropriate concert etiquette allows you to be considerate of others, including audience members and performers. It also helps everyone attending to enjoy the performance.

Different types of musical performances dictate certain behavior guidelines. How one shows excitement at a rock concert is certainly worlds apart from the appropriate behavior at a formal concert or theater production. Understanding these differences allows audience members to behave in a manner that shows consideration and respect for everyone involved.

What are the expectations of a good audience member at a formal musical presentation?

- Arrive on time. If you arrive after the performance has begun, wait outside the auditorium until a break in the music to enter the hall.
- Remain quiet and still during the performance. Talking and moving around prevent others from hearing and enjoying the performance.
- Leave the auditorium only in case of an emergency. Try to leave during a break in the musical selections.
- Sing or clap along only when invited to do so by the performers or the conductor.
- Applaud at the end of a composition or when the conductor's arms are lowered at the conclusion of a performance. It is customary to not applaud between movements or sections of a major work.
- Save shouting, whistling and dancing for rock concerts or athletic events. These are never appropriate at formal musical performances.

Remembering these important behavior guidelines will ensure that everyone enjoys the show!

RESOURCES

Teacher Resource Binder

Evaluation Master 5, *Concert Etiquette Quiz*

National Standards

7. Evaluating music and musical performances. **(a, b)**

Choral Library

An American Folk Song Spectacular!

OVERVIEW

Composer: American Folk Songs, arranged by John Leavitt

Text: Traditional

Voicing: 2-Part

Key: G major/A♭ major/E major

Meter: 4/4, 6/8, 2/4

Form: Medley

Style: American Folk Song

Accompaniment: Piano

Programming: Festival, Concert Closer

Vocal ranges:

Objectives

After completing this lesson, students will be able to:

• Read and perform a varied repertoire of music from notation.

• Describe aurally presented music.

• Write music notation.

• Perform expressively a varied repertoire of music.

VOCABULARY

Have students review vocabulary in student lesson. Introduce terms found in the music. A complete glossary of terms is found on page 246 of the student book.

An American Folk Song Spectacular!

Composer: American Folk Songs, arranged by John Leavitt

Text: Traditional

Voicing: 2-Part

VOCABULARY

medley

folk song

$\frac{4}{4}$ meter

Focus

• Read and perform rhythmic patterns with eighth notes.

• Identify by ear and notate melodic patterns.

• Use dramatic storytelling to interpret musical content.

Getting Started

If you could pack your bags and take off tomorrow, where would you go? The call of the open road is hard to resist. Throughout the history of the American West, pioneers, cowboys, and prospectors hit the trail looking for adventure and new fortunes.

Singing and dancing have always been an important part of the American West. Not only did music lift the spirits of the pioneers, but the songs they created became records of their adventures.

🔺 SPOTLIGHT

To learn more about arranging, see page 14.

◆ History and Culture

"An American Folk Song Spectacular!" is a **medley,** or *a collection of songs musically linked together.* The four selections in this medley are examples of American folk songs. **Folk songs** are *songs that have been passed down through oral tradition and often describe a certain place or event.*

The melody to "The Red River Valley," though popular with the American cowboy, originated in New York State. After the Civil War, the Chisholm Trail provided a direct route for the longhorn cattle from Texas, through Oklahoma, to the railhead at Abilene, Kansas. Composed in the 1840s, Stephen Foster's "Oh! Susanna" was popular with the gold-seeking 49ers. "Skip to My Lou," a play-party dance, was a favorite among young people.

128 Beginning Unison, 2-Part/3-Part

RESOURCES

Beginning Sight-Singing

Sight-Singing in G Major, pages 84–89, 93

Sight-Singing the A♭ Major Scale, page 168

Sight-Singing the E Major Scale, page 168

Reading Eighth Notes, pages 23–25

Teacher Resource Binder

Teaching Master 19, *Thought Trails*

Teaching Master 20, *Creating Melodic Patterns in G Major*

Skill Builder 12, *Constructing Major Scales*

Skill Builder 14, *8-line Staff Paper*

Kodály 5, *Music Reading: Pitch*

For additional resources, see TRB Table of Contents.

Links to Learning

◆ **Vocal**

Read and perform the following examples to establish the key of G major.

do mi sol mi do   do sol do

"An American Folk Song Spectacular!" begins in the key of G major and is based on the G major scale. To locate "G" on a piano, find any set of three black keys. "G" is the white key to the left of the middle black key. This scale uses the notes G, A, B, C, D, E, F♯, G. Using the keyboard below as a guide, play the G major scale.

Sing the G major scale.

G   A   B   C   D   E   F♯ G   F♯ E   D   C   B   A   G
do re mi fa sol la ti do ti la sol fa mi re do

◆ **Theory**

Perform the following rhythmic pattern in ⁴⁄₄ **meter**, *a time signature in which there are four beats per measure and the quarter note receives the beat.*

◆ **Artistic Expression**

The cowboy sings, "I'll tell you of my troubles on the old Chisholm Trail." What troubles might he be speaking of? Imagine you are that cowboy in 1870. Write a letter to your family back home about your adventures on the Chisholm Trail.

Evaluation

Demonstrate how well you have learned the skills and concepts featured in the lesson "An American Folksong Spectacular!" by completing the following:

- Using the notes *do, mi,* and *sol,* create a four-note melodic pattern in the key of G major. Sing your pattern on "loo" and ask a classmate to identify the notes that you've sung. Have the classmate write the four notes on manuscript paper. Switch roles.
- In the character of the cowboy, present your Chisholm Trail letter to the class.

Choral Library *An American Folk Song Spectacular!* **129**

RESOURCES

Beginning Unison, 2-Part/3-Part Rehearsal/Performance CD

CD 2:1 Voices

CD 2:2 Accompaniment Only

CD 3:13 Vocal Practice Track—Part I

CD 4:14 Vocal Practice Track—Part II

National Standards

1. Singing, alone and with others, a varied repertoire of music. **(a, b, c, d)**
5. Reading and notating music. **(a, c, d)**
6. Listening to, analyzing, and describing music. **(a, c)**
9. Understanding music in relation to history and culture. **(a, b, d)**

LINKS TO LEARNING

Vocal

The Vocal section is designed to prepare students to:

- Read and sing a G major tonic triad.
- Play and sing the G major scale with accuracy.

Have students:

- Play the G major scale on the keyboard. If selected students will play the scale on the keyboard, others should follow closely on the keyboard printed on page 129.
- Sing the G major scale on note names.
- Sing the G major scale on solfège syllables.

Theory

The Theory section is designed to prepare students to:

- Understand 4/4 meter.
- Perform rhythms in 4/4 meter.

Have students:

- Tap or clap the quarter note pulse.
- Speak the rhythm pattern on a neutral syllable while tapping the quarter note pulse.
- Clap the rhythm pattern while feeling the quarter note pulse inside.

Artistic Expression

The Artistic Expression section is designed to prepare students to understand the lyrics to "The Old Chisholm Trail."

Have students:

• Read the text to "The Old Chisholm Trail."

• Imagine that they are the cowboy in the song and write a letter to family back home telling about the adventures of the Old West.

LESSON PLAN

Suggested Teaching Sequence and Performance Tips

1. Introduce

Direct students to:

• Read and discuss the information found in the Getting Started section on page 128.

• Locate the Red River of the North, the Red River of the South and the Chisholm Trail on a map.

• Identify and sing *do, mi* and *sol*, as found in the Vocal section on page 129. Create four-note patterns from these pitches.

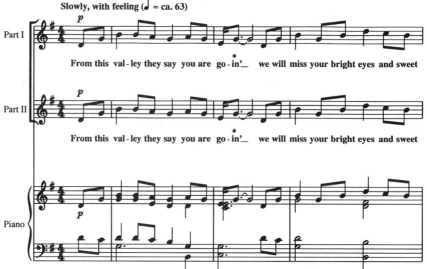

*Close to "n," sustaining.

Copyright © 1996 by HAL LEONARD CORPORATION
International Copyright Secured   All Rights Reserved

130   Beginning Unison, 2-Part/3-Part

TEACHER2TEACHER

Singing American folk songs gives students a cultural and historical connection to the rich musical heritage of our country. Folk song lyrics are a key to a treasure chest of colorful personal stories that students will enjoy exploring.

THE OLD CHISHOLM TRAIL

8 Traditional American Cowboy Song

Brightly! (♩ = ca. 138)

while.   (solo shout) He - Hah!   Well,

while.   Well,

12

come a - long boys and lis - ten to my tale,   I'll

come a - long boys and lis - ten to my tale,   I'll

tell you of my trou - bles on the old Chis - holm Trail.   My

tell you of my trou - bles on the old Chis - holm Trail.

- Practice the rhythmic patterns in 4/4 meter as found in the Theory section on page 129.
- Identify and clap, tap or sing the rhythm patterns in measures 11–23. Tap the rhythms while counting aloud. Lightly sing the rhythm patterns on solfège syllables.

Progress Checkpoints

Observe students' progress in:

✓ Their ability to read and sing in the key of G major.

✓ Their ability to locate the geographical locations mentioned in the song on a map.

✓ Their ability to read rhythmic patterns with accuracy.

Choral Library *An American Folk Song Spectacular!*   **131**

ASSESSMENT

Evaluating the Quality of a Performance

Have students:

1. Listen to a video or audio recording of this piece as performed by the choir.

2. Compare this performance to exemplary models such as other recordings or other live performances of the piece.

3. Develop constructive suggestions for improvement based on the comparison.

2. Rehearse

Direct students to:

- Find the pitches that are not *sol, do* or mi in measures 11–23. (la: *measures 15, 19; re and* la: *measure 20;* fa, *measure 21; and* la, fa, re *and* ti: *measure 22)*

- Sing "The Old Chisholm Trail" slowly on solfège syllables and correct rhythms. Repeat until comfortable. Sing with text.

- Sing measures 11–15 in a mixed-up order, as indicated by the director. Write the new arrangement as rhythm patterns with indicated solfège syllables on the chalkboard. Sing the new arrangement with correct rhythms and pitches. Sing with text. Enjoy the mixed-up sentence structures!

- Extend the activity to measures 11–12, looking for measures with similar rhythms but different solfège pitches. *(measures 12, 15, 18; measures 14 and 16; measures 20 and 22)*

MORE ABOUT...

Folk Music

Folk music is music that has been passed on from generation to generation, often in the oral tradition. Typically, folk song composers are unknown and a song may change slightly when one person learns it and then shares it with someone else. Folk songs exist in "tune families," which include all songs that originated from a specific one. Any related song in a tune family can be shorter or longer than the original, or the rhythm, melody, scale or form can be altered. For this reason, students may, at one time or another, hear the songs used in "An American Folk Song Spectacular" but with slightly different rhythm patterns, melody or text.

* Tongue clicks in alternating pitches

- Divide into two groups. Have one group sing "The Old Chisholm Trail" while the other group chants the rhythm example found in the Theory section on page 129 as an ostinato. Switch roles and repeat.

Progress Checkpoints

Observe students' progress in:

✓ Their ability to sing accurate pitches.

✓ Their ability to read and perform rhythmic patterns.

✓ Their ability to perform in two parts.

MORE ABOUT...

Careers in Music

There are many career opportunities in the field of music. Discuss the following options with the students and perhaps bring in a guest speaker from each field:

- Performer
- Composer
- Manager
- Music Technician
- Teacher
- Conductor
- Music Sales
- Music Publisher

3. Refine

Direct students to:

- Sing Part II of "The Old Chisholm Trail" (verse 2, measures 25–38), "Oh! Susanna" and "Skip to My Lou" on words.
- Identify the measures in which the voices do not sing the melody. Repeat until parts are secure.
- Work in groups of four to six to clap a rhythm pattern found in the medley. As each group performs, the rest of the class should locate the pattern in the score.
- Decide how to perform the medley with the inclusion of the cowboy letters from the activity in the Evaluation on page 129.
- Work in groups of six to ten to perform the medley in two parts, including the cowboy letters.

Progress Checkpoints

Check students' progress in:

- ✓ Their ability to sing Part II on words.
- ✓ Their ability to distinguish between melody and harmony parts.
- ✓ Their ability to perform all rhythms.

134   Beginning Unison, 2-Part/3-Part

MUSIC, SOCIETY AND CULTURE

Have students perform additional songs representing diverse cultures, including American and Texas heritage. Go to **music.glencoe.com**, the Web site for Glencoe's choral music programs, for additional music selections students can perform.

OH! SUSANNA

40 Words and Music by Stephen Collins Foster

Dance-like (♩ = ca. 120)

All voices: whistle

All voices: whistle

a few may continue to whistle

I ___

a few may continue to whistle

I ___

8va ---

46

come from A - la - ba - ma with my ban - jo on my knee, I'm ___

come from A - la - ba - ma with my ban - jo on my knee, I'm ___

ASSESSMENT

Informal Assessment

In this lesson, students showed the ability to:

- Identify and perform the melody in the keys of G major, A♭ major and E major.
- Read and perform a variety of rhythms in 4/4 meter.
- Create a unique performance of the medley.

Student Self-Assessment

Have students evaluate their individual performances based on the following:

- Diction
- Expressive Singing
- Accurate Pitches
- Accurate Rhythms
- Correct Part-Singing

Have each student rate his/her performance of this song in the areas above on a scale of 1–5, 5 being the best.

TEACHING STRATEGY

Folk Songs and Their Heritage

One of the reasons this piece is so easy to sing is because it is a medley of folk songs. Folk songs tend to feel almost second nature, and have characteristics that make them easy to sing, such as following the natural rhythm of the text and moving mostly stepwise, with easy rhythms.

Have students:

- Name the Texas folk songs used in this medley, plus list others.
- Identify the characteristics of folk songs.
- Improvise a folk tune that is four measures long in 4/4 meter, with the ensemble echoing each improvisation.

Individual Performance Assessment

To further measure growth of musical skills presented in this lesson, direct students to complete the Evaluation section on page 129.

- After each student has created a four-note melodic pattern in the key of G major, have students find a partner and perform it for each other. The listener should identify the four notes that were sung and notate them on staff paper. Switches roles and repeat.

- After writing a letter in the character of a cowboy on the Chisholm Trail, have each student read his/her letter to the class. The class should choose the best letter to be used as an introduction to this piece at your performance.

ASSESSMENT
Creating an Assessment Rubric

Have students:

1. Discuss the characteristics of a desirable performance of this piece, using all their knowledge of the performance techniques.
2. Design and identify the criteria by which they think an adjudicator might assess the performance, quality and effectiveness of this piece.
3. For each criterion, decided what characteristics will comprise an adequate, good, very good and excellent performance.
4. Create a rubric chart.
5. Use the rubric to assess quartets or small ensembles performing all or part of this song.

CULTURAL CONNECTIONS

The Root of Folk Songs

Have students:

- Identify the cultures they each have as roots.
- Collect folk songs or stories from their cultures through interviews, reading or other research.
- Arrange and notate one or several of these pieces, using their knowledge of the style to set tempo, determine texture and harmonies, and recommend vocal tone color, articulation and dynamics.
- Practice and perform their pieces as a celebration of the cultures they represent.

CONNECTING THE ARTS

Creative Dance

Have students:

- Identify the style of each of the folk songs used in this medley.
- Discuss what style of dance would be appropriate to express the same mood as the folk song (probably square dancing or clogging for the faster songs).
- Create a dance that expresses the meaning or the style of each song in the medley, without being literal.
- Perform the dances for each folk song in the medley.

Additional National Standards

The following National Standards are addressed through the Assessment, Extension, Enrichment and bottom-page activities:

2. Composing and arranging music within specific guidelines. **(b)**

3. Improvising melodies, variations and accompaniments. **(c)**

8. Understanding relationships between music, the other arts, and disciplines outside the arts. **(b)**

9. Understanding music in relation to history and culture. **(a)**

Blues, Blues, Blues

OVERVIEW

Composer: Kirby Shaw
Text: Kirby Shaw
Voicing: 2-Part
Key: C blues scale
Meter: 4/4
Form: AA'B
Style: Blues
Accompaniment: Piano
Programming: Concert, Contest, Festival

Vocal ranges:

Part I

Part II

OBJECTIVES

After completing this lesson, students will be able to:

- Perform independently with accurate rhythm.
- Create rhythmic phrases.
- Perform a varied repertoire of music representing diverse styles.

VOCABULARY

Have students review vocabulary in student lesson. Introduce terms found in the music. A complete glossary of terms is found on page 246 of the student book.

Blues, Blues, Blues

Composer: Kirby Shaw
Text: Kirby Shaw
Voicing: 2-Part

VOCABULARY

blues style
blues scale
call and response
swing rhythms
improvisation

🔺 **SPOTLIGHT**

To learn more about improvisation, see page 147.

Focus

- Compose and perform rhythmic patterns in swing style
- Perform music that represents the blues style

Getting Started

Blues style is *an original African American art form that developed in the early twentieth century in the Mississippi Delta region of the South.* The lyrics of these songs often express feelings of frustration, hardship, or longing. The best-known early blues performers include Ma Rainey, Bessie Smith and Billie Holiday. Today, the blues influence can be heard in the music of B. B. King, Susan Tedeschi and Keb'Mo'.

◆ History and Culture

Characteristics of the blues style found in "Blues, Blues, Blues" include the blues scale, call and response, and swing rhythms. The **blues scale** is *an altered major scale with lowered or flatted notes.* These flatted notes, often called the blue notes, appear in much African American music and reflect the African influence. Call and response comes from the field hollers used by slaves as they worked. In **call and response**, *a leader or group sings a phrase (call), followed by the response to that phrase by another group.* **Swing rhythms** are *rhythms made by changing two even eighth notes into two uneven eighth notes.* The first note becomes longer than the second, and a triplet feel is created. "Blues, Blues, Blues" should be performed in the swing style.

Another common characteristic of the blues style is the use of **improvisation**, or *the art of singing or playing music, making it up as you go.* It may take practice to develop this skill, but improvisation can be a lot of fun.

RESOURCES

Beginning Sight-Singing

Sight-Singing the Blues Scale, pages 172–176
Reading Swing Rhythms, pages 173–174

Teacher Resource Binder

Teaching Master 21, *Composing Rhythmic Patterns in 4/4 Meter*
Skill Builder 28, *Rhythm Challenge in 6/8 Meter*
Dalcroze 16, *Musical Style*
Reference 7, *Building a Musical Vocabulary*
For additional resources, see TRB Table of Contents.

Links to Learning

◆ **Vocal**

Perform the following examples to practice singing major and blues scales. Discuss the differences in the two.

◆ **Theory**

Read and perform the following rhythmic pattern. As you perform, move your arms and upper body in a dance-like style that reflects the triplet motion.

Read and perform this new rhythmic pattern. Continue to move your arms and upper body in the triplet style.

Now read this rhythmic pattern as even eighth notes, but perform the pattern in a swing style. Exercises 2 and 3 should sound the same. Continue to move as you perform.

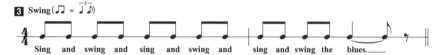

Evaluation

Demonstrate how well you have learned the skills and concepts featured in the lesson "Blues, Blues, Blues" by completing the following:

• Compose an eight-beat rhythmic pattern in $\frac{4}{4}$ meter that includes eighth notes. Perform the pattern first using even eighth notes and then again using uneven, or swing, eighth notes.

• As you sing "Blues, Blues, Blues" from memory, step or walk the beat in a dance-like manner. Demonstrate the triplet or swing feel in your movement.

Choral Library *Blues, Blues, Blues* **141**

RESOURCES

Beginning Unison, 2-Part/3-Part Rehearsal/Performance CD

CD 2:3 Voices

CD 2:4 Accompaniment Only

CD 3:14 Vocal Practice Track—Part I

CD 4:15 Vocal Practice Track—Part II

National Standards

1. Singing alone and with others a varied repertoire of music. **(b, c)**

4. Composing and arranging music within specific guidelines. **(a)**

5. Reading and notating music. **(a, c, d)**

LINKS TO LEARNING

Vocal

The Vocal section is designed to prepare students to:

• Perform a major scale and a blues scale.

• Discern the difference between the two scales.

Have students:

• Sing the C major scale on a neutral syllable or using solfège syllables.

• Sing the C blues scale on a neutral syllable.

• Discuss the differences between the two scales. *(flatted seventh, flatted fifth and flatted third in the blues scale)*

Theory

The Theory section is designed to prepare students to:

• Sing triplet and swing rhythms with movement.

• Understand the relationship between triplet patterns and swing eighth patterns.

Have students:

• Sing exercise 1 moving the arms and upper body to reflect the rhythm.

• Sing exercise 2 with the same movements.

• Sing exercise 3 noting the difference in notation and the swing marking at the beginning. Exercise 2 and 3 should sound the same.

LESSON PLAN

Suggested Teaching Sequence and Performance Tips

1. Introduce

Direct students to:

- Read and discuss the information found in the Getting Started section on page 140.

- Practice the C major scale in the Vocal section on page 141. Contrast this to the blues scale in example 2.

- Listen to the descending blues scale on the piano. Point out that in this scale the white notes alternate with the black notes. Have selected students play the scale with one finger.

- Practice the rhythmic patterns found in the Theory section on page 141.

- Practice singing the primary motive (measures 5–7) in two ways: "straight" (with even eighths) and "cool" (with swing eighths). Ask students which they prefer.

- Notice that the first motive is the blues scale. The composer uses this scale throughout the piece.

- Sing measures 5–7 either on a neutral syllable such as "doo" or with the words. Be sure to note intonation, paying particular attention to the descending minor thirds (B♭–G and E♭–C).

Blues, Blues, Blues

For 2-Part and Piano

Words and Music by
KIRBY SHAW

Copyright © 1993 Kirby Shaw Music
International Copyright Secured

142   Beginning Unison, 2-Part/3-Part

Full of opportunities for improvisation and adventure, "Blues, Blues, Blues" will be one of your students' favorite pieces. They will find the energy of the dancelike swing rhythms captivating!

scale   that   you'll nev-er lose, _   it's

scale   that   you'll nev-er lose, _   it's

fun   to   sing,   we'll   prove it to you. _

fun   to   sing,   we'll   prove it to you. _

Swing-in' rhy-thm's

Swing-in'

Choral Library *Blues, Blues, Blues*   **143**

ENRICHMENT

The blues form has so permeated the world of music that various diverse blues styles, such as "Saint Louis" and "Kansas City" have come into being. Blues has also affected classical music; the composers Maurice Ravel, Darius Mihaud, Igor Stravinsky and George Gershwin have written pieces that use blues techniques. Play a recording of Gershwin's *Rhapsody in Blue* and evaluate.

Progress Checkpoints

Observe students' progress in:

✓ Their ability to identify the blues scale and play it on the keyboard.

✓ Their ability to locate the blues scale in the score.

✓ Their ability to chant rhythms in the swing style while moving arms and upper body.

2. Rehearse

Direct students to:

• Analyze the musical score identifying sections containing the blues scale. *(measures 5–28)* Note the melodic change at measure 28. In this section, only fragments of the blues scale appear in Part II *(measures 30, 32, 34, 36)* and in both parts at measure 38.

• Listen to the recording and clap or move in a dancelike manner, beginning at measure 28. Begin to feel the swing of the rhythm as it blends with the tonality of the blues scale.

• Clap, sway or swing in a dancelike manner with a looseness in the upper body. A stiffness in the quality of movement will result in a stilted, decidedly "un-swing"-like performance.

• Chant the rhythm for measures 5–16. Compare these measures to measures 17–28. Note that the rhythms are the same, but are in a canon. *(Part II imitating Part I)* Note that this is the call-and-response style discussed in the Getting Started section on page 140.

- Chant the remainder of the song. Note that each part has the same rhythm, but not the same pitches. Which part has more of the blues scale? *(Part II)*
- Identify and discuss the three sections of the piece. *(Section A— unison, Section B—same idea in canon, and Section C—new idea with Coda)*
- Rehearse each section at half tempo, speaking the words using good diction. Be sure that the final eighth note in most motives (e.g., "fine" of "feel-in' so fine" in measure 19) has a slight accent to bring out the syncopation.

Progress Checkpoints

Observe students' progress in:

✓ Their ability to explain the form of the piece.

✓ Their ability to sing with appropriate rhythmic stress.

✓ Their energetic presentation of the text.

3. Refine

Direct students to:

- Practice parts separately at section C. Note the call-and-response style has changed and Part II seems to improvise on the idea rather than imitate it.
- Practice and secure the harmony at measures 36[beat 3]–37 and measures 40–41. Discuss and practice singing the fermatas and the slide.
- Sing the entire song one part at a time while moving to the half note in a bouncy but flowing manner.

144   Beginning Unison, 2-Part/3-Part

TEACHING STRATEGY

Swing Style

If students are not familiar with the swing-style, and are a bit stiff, have them:

- Listen to swing music.
- Move to swing music.
- Watch video footage of a swing-style performance.
- Attend a dance-band performance.

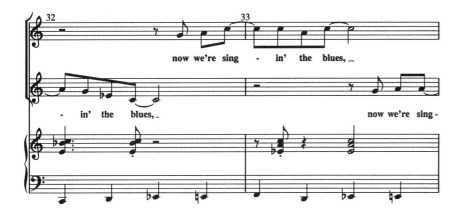

- Combine parts and partner with someone from the other section. Choose to either clap or sway on the half note. It will be fun to watch what happens when you move in unison (measures 5–15) as opposed to when you are in canon (measures 15 to the end).

- Have several groups perform for the class. Sing a second time and improvise the movement. When in canon, Part II should mirror the movements of Part I.

- Work for rhythmic and spatial precision. Remember to move to the half note.

Progress Checkpoints

Observe students' progress in:

✓ Their ability to sing and move expressively while performing two-part harmony.

✓ Their ability to identify the call-and-response style.

✓ Their ability to improvise movements in the swing style.

ASSESSMENT

Informal Assessment

In this piece, students showed the ability to:

- Maintain a steady beat while singing in the swing style.

- Perform each part while watching and listening to the other part move and sing.

- Read, perform and identify swing rhythms.

- Sing in canon.

MUSIC, SOCIETY AND CULTURE

Have students perform additional songs representing diverse cultures, including American and Texas heritage. Go to **music.glencoe.com**, the Web site for Glencoe's choral music programs, for additional music selections students can perform.

Student Self-Assessment

Have students evaluate their individual performances based on the following:

- Posture
- Breath Management
- Accurate Pitches
- Accurate Rhythms
- Correct Part-Singing

Have each student rate his/her performance of this song in the areas above on a scale of 1–5, 5 being the best.

Individual and Group Performance Evaluation

To further measure growth of musical skills presented in this lesson, direct students to complete the Evaluation section on page 141.

- After each student has composed an eight-beat rhythmic pattern in 4/4 meter that includes eighth notes, have selected students perform their pattern for the class. First, have them perform it with even eighth notes and then perform it with swing eighth notes. The class should determine which performance they prefer.
- Have all students perform "Blues, Blues, Blues" from memory, adding movement. Lead a class discussion on how movement enhances the performance.

EXTENSION

Composition

Compose a three-measure rhythmic phrase. Locate words in the phrase that contain either a triplet or a swing rhythm. Notate your phrase on the board and perform it for the class.

Additional National Standards

The following National Standards are addressed through the Assessment, Extension, Enrichment and bottom-page activities:

4. Composing and arranging music within specific guidelines. **(a)**

5. Reading and notating music. **(d)**

6. Listening to, analyzing, and describing music. **(a)**

7. Evaluating music and music performances. **(b)**

SPOTLIGHT

Improvisation

Blues style is *an original African American art form that developed in the early twentieth century in the South.* One characteristic of the blues style is call and response. In **call and response,** *a leader or group sings a phrase (call), followed by the response to that phrase by another group.* Another common characteristic of the blues style is the use of **improvisation,** or *the art of singing or playing music, making it up as you go.* Blues performers often improvise their music as they perform.

By using call and response, you can learn the first step toward improvisation.

As a class, read and perform the following call:

Call

I'm sing - in' the blues.___

Read and perform the following responses:

Response 1

Yes, you're sing - in' the blues.___

Response 2

Yes, you're sing-in',___ sing - in' the blues.___

Response 3

Yes, oh yes, you're sing - in' the blues.___

As the class sings the call, take turns individually singing one of the three responses. Now you are ready to make up your own responses. Improvise!

Spotlight *Improvisation* **147**

RESOURCES

Teacher Resource Binder

Reference 7, *Building a Musical Vocabulary*

National Standards

1. Singing, alone and with others, a varied repertoire of music. **(a, b, c)**

3. Improvising melodies, variations and accompaniments. **(a, b, c)**

IMPROVISATION

Objectives

- Create rhythmic and melodic phrases.
- Improvise rhythmic and melodic variations in a call-and-response format.

Suggested Teaching Sequence

Direct students to:

- Read the Spotlight On Improvisation on student page 147 and define *improvisation* and *call-and-response.*
- Define blues styles and list common examples of songs in the blues styles.
- Sing reponse 1 as a group after the teacher sings the call.
- Repeat this procedure for responses 2 and 3.
- Sing the call as a group and as individuals, choose a response to perform as solos.
- Sing the call as a group and as individuals, improvise their own responses.

Progress Checkpoints

Observe students' progress in:

✓ Their ability to define and describe the concept of improvisation.

✓ Their ability to demonstrate call and response.

✓ Their ability to apply improvisation techniques in call and response.

Brand New Day

OVERVIEW

Composer: Cristi Cary Miller
Text: Angela Darter Stogsdill
Voicing: 2-Part
Key: B♭ major/C major
Meter: Cut time or 2/2
Form: ABA'B'B''
Style: American Pop
Accompaniment: Piano
Programming:
 Concert/Festival

Vocal Ranges:

OBJECTIVES

After completing this lesson, students will be able to:

• Demonstrate fundamental skills while performing.

• Perform expressively a varied repertoire of music.

• Sight-read simple music in various keys.

VOCABULARY

Have students review vocabulary in student lesson. Introduce terms found in the music. A complete glossary of terms is found on page 246 of the student book.

Brand New Day

Composer: Cristi Cary Miller
Text: Angela Darter Stogsdill
Voicing: 2-Part

VOCABULARY

head voice

major tonality

🔺 **SPOTLIGHT**

To learn more about vocal production, see page 63.

Focus

• Extend the vocal range.

• Sing with expression.

• Perform music in major tonality.

Getting Started

Have you ever liked a tune so well that you could not get it out of your mind? Have you ever found yourself singing or humming the same tune all day long? "Brand New Day" is that kind of song. With its catchy melody and snappy rhythms, this song is bound to stay with you for a long time.

◆ **History and Culture**

You have often heard the phrases "dare to dream," "seize the day," and "reach for the stars." These ideas promote a positive outlook on life. They support the attitude that if we dare to dream and strive to make those dreams come true, we will find joy and purpose in our lives.

Follow your dreams and be on your way.

Start with a smile! It's a brand new day!

Scientific research has shown that music affects us physically and mentally in a positive way. Music helps develop the human mind and spirit. It allows us to express feelings and ideas in a unique way. In this song, the messages of happiness and new beginnings are conveyed from you, the performer, to the audience through the medium of music. You can share this message with your audience through your enthusiasm, the excited expression on your face, and your singing posture. These elements combine to create your overall stage presence. Let everyone see your joy in making music.

148 Beginning Unison, 2-Part/3-Part

RESOURCES

Beginning Sight-Singing

Sight-Singing in B♭ Major, pages 127–131

Sight-Singing in C Major, pages 7–12, 14–17, 27–29, 116–117

Reading Syncopation, pages 160–161

Teacher Resource Binder

Teaching Master 22, *How High Can I Sing?*

Evaluation Master 13,
 Judging Stage Presence

Skill Builder 12, *Constructing Major Scales*

Skill Builder 14, *8-line Staff Paper*

Vocal Development 11,
 Flexibility and Range

For additional resources, see TRB Table of Contents.

Links to Learning

◆ **Vocal**

Perform the following example to develop, and to practice singing in, your **head voice,** or *the higher part of your singing range.*

lah_____ lah_____ (etc.)

◆ **Theory**

"Brand New Day" begins in the key of B♭ major and is based on the B♭ major scale. *A song that is based on a major scale with "do" as its keynote, or home tone, is described as being in* **major tonality**. To locate "B♭" on a piano, find any set of three black keys. "B♭" is the top black key. This scale uses the notes B♭, C, D, E♭, F, G, A, B♭. Using the keyboard below as a guide, play the B♭ major scale.

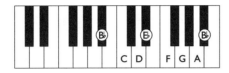

Sing the B♭ major scale.

B♭	C	D	E♭	F	G	A	B♭	A	G	F	E♭	D	C	B♭
do	re	mi	fa	sol	la	ti	do	ti	la	sol	fa	mi	re	do

Evaluation

Demonstrate how well you have learned the skills and concepts featured in the lesson "Brand New Day" by completing the following:

• Sing the vocal example above. With the help of your teacher, find the highest note in your own vocal range that can be sung relaxed, sustained, and with accurate pitch.

• Sing measures 9–17 alone or with others to show how you can express the meaning of the text through your overall stage presence.

Choral Library *Brand New Day* **149**

RESOURCES

Beginning Unison, 2-Part/3-Part Rehearsal/Performance CD

CD 2:5 Voices
CD 2:6 Accompaniment Only
CD 3:15 Vocal Practice Track—Part I
CD 4:16 Vocal Practice Track—Part II

National Standards

1. Singing, alone and with others, a varied repertoire of music. (**a, b, d**)
5. Reading and notating music. (**a, b**)

LINKS TO LEARNING

Vocal

The Vocal section is designed to prepare students to expand their vocal range by using their head voice.

Have students:

• Yawn-sigh by inhaling deeply and sighing from the top of their range to the bottom.

• Keep the feeling of the top of that sigh (head voice) and sing the exercise on "lah."

• Repeat the exercise modulating up by half steps.

Theory

The Theory section is designed to prepare students to:

• Understand the meaning of *major tonality*.

• Play and sing the B♭ major scale with accuracy.

Have students:

• Play the B♭ major scale on the keyboard. If selected students will play the scale on the keyboard, others should follow closely on the keyboard printed on page 149.

• Sing the B♭ major scale on note names.

• Sing the B♭ major scale on solfège.

LESSON PLAN

Suggested Teaching Sequence and Performance Tips

1. Introduce

Direct students to:

- Read and discuss the information found in the Getting Started section on page 148.
- Practice using their head voice while singing the Vocal section examples on page 149. Reinforce the use of breath support.
- Practice singing the B♭ major scale ascending and descending to establish the major tonality of the piece as found in the Theory section on page 149.
- Chant the rhythm of the text in measures 9–17. Locate and practice the syncopated and nonsyncopated patterns.
- Describe the overall mood of this section.

Progress Checkpoints

Observe students' progress in:

- ✓ Singing the B♭ major scale and extended pitches in tune.
- ✓ Recognizing the difference between syncopated and nonsyncopated patterns.

Dedicated to the Ralph Down Elementary School's 2001-2002 Grade Roadrunner Chorus
Oklahoma City, OK

Brand New Day

For 2-Part and Piano

Words by
ANGELA DARTER STOGSDILL

Music by
CRISTI CARY MILLER

Copyright © 2000 by HAL LEONARD CORPORATION
International Copyright Secured   All Rights Reserved

150   Beginning Unison, 2-Part/3-Part

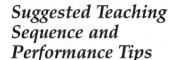

TEACHER 2 TEACHER

This optimistic, upbeat song provides an opportunity for students to sing expressively while developing the concepts of major tonality, syncopation and part-singing.

2. Rehearse

Direct students to:

- Divide into two groups. Have one group count the syncopated passages while the other group counts the steady beat.

- Draw a box around the cued notes and the words that correspond with them. *(measures 12 and 15)*

- Find the unison sections and the two-part sections in the music. Label the unison sections as Section A, and the two-part sections as Section B.

- Sing the unison sections using solfège syllables. Divide the two-part section into two-bar phrases. Read each phrase using solfège syllables.

- Locate, discuss and practice the first and second endings. *(measures 31–34)*

Progress Checkpoints

Observe students' progress in:

✓ Their ability to identify unison and two-part sections.

✓ Their ability to chant basic rhythmic notation and syncopated passages.

✓ Reading and singing passages using solfège syllables in two parts accurately.

✓ Performing the first and second endings accurately.

MORE ABOUT...

Balancing the Choir

To tune and balance the choir, consider mixing the high and low voices. Place two-thirds of the higher voices and one-third of the lower voices on Part I. Place two-thirds of the lower voices and one-third of the higher voices on Part II. This mix will cover the ranges of each individual part.

3. Refine

Direct students to:

- Sing the entire song using solfège syllables and correct rhythms.
- Stress the words that occur off the beat.
- Practice using head voice while forming and shaping pure vowel sounds to aid in the blending of voices and tuning of the vocal line.
- Keep a silent, steady beat to aid in rhythmic precision.
- Examine the text. Discuss characteristics of the music and how it reflects the text. *(syncopation adds enthusiasm)*
- Add the hand claps as indicated in the music. *(measures 35–42)* Discuss the effect hand claps have on the piece.
- Perform the entire piece with CD or piano accompaniment.

Progress Checkpoints

Observe students' progress in:

- ✓ Their ability to perform the entire song using solfège syllables with correct rhythms.
- ✓ Their balance and blend between the two parts.
- ✓ Tuning the unison and two-part sections.
- ✓ Their ability to sing expressively.

TEACHING STRATEGY

Hand Clapping

To establish balance between singing and clapping, assign half of the choir to clap while the other half imitates the action of the clap but does not make the actual sound.

ASSESSMENT

Informal Assessment

In this lesson, students showed the ability to:

- Identify the differences between syncopated and nonsyncopated rhythmic patterns in cut time.
- Count simple syncopated rhythmic patterns in cut time.
- Distinguish unison sections from two-part sections by marking their scores.
- Sing in two parts in the keys of B♭ major and C major.
- Sing in extended ranges using their head voices.

Student Self-Assessment

Have students evaluate their individual performances based on the following:

- Breath Management
- Expressive Singing
- Accurate Pitches
- Accurate Rhythms
- Correct Part-Singing

Have each student rate his/her performance of this song in the areas above on a scale of 1–5, 5 being the best.

CONNECTING THE ARTS

Creative Dance

"Brand New Day" lends itself to energetic, expressive dance. If there is a student who is a dancer, have him or her create movements to enhance the meaning of the text. Encourage attention to the musical features of the piece, such as the syncopation, as well as an interpretation of the words. The movements should fit with the energy of phrases, rhythms, pauses and melodic lines. If appropriate, teach the movement to the entire class and perform the piece with the choreography at your performance.

Individual and Group Performance Evaluation

To further measure growth of musical skills presented in this lesson, ask students to complete the Evaluation section on page 149.

- After each student has located the highest pitch in their vocal ranges, evaluate that note. Can it be sung relaxed, sustained and with accurate pitch? If not, perhaps they should re-evaluate their highest note.

- Have solos or small groups perform measures 9–17 for the rest of the class. Evaluate the performances by asking, "Did these singers express the meaning of the text through their stage presence?"

154   Beginning Unison, 2-Part/3-Part

MORE ABOUT...

Composer Cristi Miller

Graduating from Oklahoma State University with a bachelor's degree in Music education, Cristi Miller is currently a music specialist in the Putnam City School District located in Oklahoma City. She was named Putnam City's Teacher of the Year in 1992. She is an exclusive writer for Hal Leonard Corporation with over 100 pieces in print being performed worldwide.

Additional National Standards

The following National Standards are addressed through the Assessment, Extension, Enrichment and bottom-page activities:

7. Evaluating music and music performances. **(b)**

8. Understanding the relationships between music, the other arts, and disciplines outside the arts. **(a)**

Consider Yourself

OVERVIEW

Composer: Lionel Bart,
arranged by John Leavitt
Text: Lionel Bart
Voicing: 2-Part
Key: B♭ major
Meter: 6/8
Form: AABA'BA''
Style: Broadway
Accompaniment: Piano
Programming: Concert Opener

Vocal Ranges:

Objectives

After completing this lesson,
students will be able to:

• Demonstrate fundamental
skills while performing.

• Sight-read simple music in
various meters.

• Write music notation.

VOCABULARY

Have students review
vocabulary in student lesson.
Introduce terms found in the
music. A complete glossary
of terms is found on page
246 of the student book.

Consider Yourself

Composer: Lionel Bart, arranged by John Leavitt
Text: Lionel Bart
Voicing: 2-Part

VOCABULARY

half step
chromatic scale
simple meter
compound meter

Focus

• Sing chromatic pitches accurately.

• Read and write music notation in compound meter.

SPOTLIGHT

*To learn more about
concert etiquette,
see page 126.*

Getting Started

"Consider Yourself," from the musical *Oliver!*, is an energetic
song that extends an invitation to feel "at home" and to be "one
of the family." In the story, Oliver is an orphan who has been
thrown out of a poorhouse for being bold enough to ask for more
food. On his own in London, he meets a gang of pickpockets who
live on the streets. The young thieves welcome Oliver into their
group by singing "Consider Yourself." In the end, Oliver is
rescued by a kind gentleman who turns out to be his grandfather.

◆ History and Culture

Do you have a favorite television show that you enjoy
watching every week? Do you know all the characters by name?
Do you know the plot lines? Before television, ongoing stories
appeared in magazines. Like episodes of a TV show, each issue
featured a new chapter.

Oliver! is based on the novel *Oliver Twist*, by the British
author Charles Dickens (1812–1870). The story was originally
issued in 24 installments from 1837–1839. Later, it was published
as a book. Dickens wrote numerous novels and stories, the best-
known being the holiday favorite *A Christmas Carol*.

156   Beginning Unison, 2-Part/3-Part

RESOURCES

Beginning Sight-Singing

Sight-Singing in B♭ Major, pages
127–131
Reading 6/8 Meter, pages 119–121

Teacher Resource Binder

Teaching Master 23, *Creating Rhythmic
Patterns in Compound Meter*

Evaluation Master 2,
Analyzing Pitch Accuracy

Evaluation Master 13,
Judging Stage Presence

Skill Builder 15, *Emphasis on Chromatics*

For additional resources, see TRB
Table of Contents.

Links to Learning

◆ **Vocal**

A **half step** is *the smallest distance between two notes.* A **chromatic scale** is *a scale that consists of all half steps.* Perform the following example to practice singing chromatically or by half steps.

loo · · loo loo loo loo _____ loo loo
Con - sid - er your - self_____ at home.

◆ **Theory**

There are two general categories of meter: simple meter and compound meter. In **simple meter,** *the quarter note receives the beat, and the division of the beat is based on two eighth notes.* $\frac{4}{4}$ $\frac{3}{4}$, and $\frac{2}{4}$ are examples of simple meter. In **compound meter,** *the dotted quarter note receives the beat, and the division of the beat is based on three eighth notes.* $\frac{6}{8}$ meter is an example of compound meter.

Like $\frac{2}{4}$, $\frac{6}{8}$ meter is usually counted in two (except when the tempo is very slow). Read and perform the following examples to practice reading rhythmic patterns in compound meter.

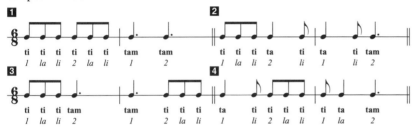

◆ **Artistic Expression**

To develop artistry through expressive singing, form a group of three to five singers. Ask one member of the group to observe facial expressions while the others sing the song. Identify expressions that communicate the invitation presented in the lyrics.

Evaluation

Demonstrate how well you have learned the skills and concepts featured in the lesson "Consider Yourself" by completing the following:

- Perform your part from measures 13–29 to demonstrate your ability to sing chromatically.
- Using the rhythmic patterns found in the Theory section above as a guide, create your own four-measure pattern in compound meter. Perform your composition for the class.

Choral Library *Consider Yourself* **157**

RESOURCES

Beginning Unison, 2-Part/3-Part Rehearsal/Performance CD

CD 2:7 Voices

CD 2:8 Accompaniment Only

CD 3:16 Vocal Practice Track - Part I

CD 4:17 Vocal Practice Track - Part II

National Standards

1. Singing, alone and with others, a varied repertoire of music. **(a, b, d)**
5. Reading and notating music. **(a, b, d)**

LINKS TO LEARNING

Vocal

The Vocal section is designed to prepare students to:

- Understand half steps and the chromatic scale.
- Sing chromatically.

Have students:

- Read the definitions of *half step* and *chromatic scale.*
- Sing the exercise on "loo," carefully tuning the half step intervals.
- Sing the exercise on the lyrics, still maintaining precise tuning of the half step intervals.
- Locate that melodic passage in their choral score.

Theory

The Theory section is designed to prepare students to:

- Understand simple versus compound meter.
- Perform rhythm patterns in compound meter.

Have students:

- Read the definitions of *simple meter* and *compound meter.*
- Perform the rhythm patterns in 6/8 meter, first on the rhythm syllables indicated and then on the counting pattern indicated.

Artistic Expression

The Artistic Expression section is designed to prepare students to sing with facial expressions appropriate for "Consider Yourself."

Have students:

- Divide into small groups, with one member of the group being the observer.
- Sing the song using appropriate facial expressions. The observer will identify the expressions that communicate the meaning of the lyrics.

LESSON PLAN

Suggested Teaching Sequence and Performance Tips

1. Introduce

Direct students to:

- Read and discuss the information found in the Getting Started section on page 156.
- Practice singing the chromatic passage used in this song as shown in the Vocal section on page 157.

From the Broadway Show OLIVER!
Consider Yourself
For 2-Part and Piano

Arranged by
JOHN LEAVITT

Words and Music by
LIONEL BART

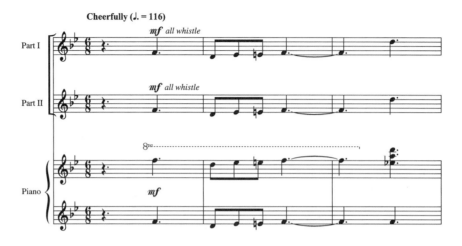

© Copyright 1960 (Renewed) Lakeview Music Co. Ltd., London, England
This arrangement © Copyright 2002 Lakeview Music Co. Ltd.
TRO – Hollis Music, Inc., New York, controls all publication rights for the U.S.A. and Canada
International Copyright Secured   All Rights Reserved Including Public Performance For Profit   Used by Permission

This arrangement is for concert use only. The use of costumes, choreography or other elements that evoke the story or characters of this musical work is prohibited.

TEACHER2TEACHER

Use "Consider Yourself" to focus on expressive stage presentation. Encourage students to use facial expressions while singing these inviting lyrics: eyes wide open, lifted eyebrows and tall smiles.

- Practice the rhythmic exercises in the Theory section on page 157 to increase their ability to read and perform rhythms in 6/8 meter.

Progress Checkpoints

Observe students' progress in:

✓ Singing chromatic passages in tune, both slowly and a tempo, accompanied and a cappella.

✓ Their ability to identify repetition of chromatic passages found in the music.

EXTENSION

Compare and Contrast

Compare the music and words of "Consider Yourself" from the top movie of 1969, *Oliver!*, with the music and words of "Be Our Guest" from the 1992 Oscar-nominated movie, *Beauty and the Beast*. In what ways are these two songs similar? Discuss how two songs written almost 30 years apart can express a similar message and still be fun to sing today.

2. Rehearse

Direct students to:

- Label measures 13–29 as Section A. Sing each phrase. Distinguish between the lyrics sung in unison and those sung in harmony. *(harmony in measures 15–16, 23–29, all else in unison)*

- Sing accurately the chromatic passage in Part II from measures 22–26.

- Label measures 29–45 as a repetition of Section A. Recognize that in comparison to Part I, Part II sings the same text and uses rhythmic imitation, but not consistent pitch imitation.

- Label measures 45–76 as Section B. Notice that the melody is constructed primarily from half steps.

- Follow the D.S. al Coda in measure 95 to return to measure 46.

- Notice that measures 87–95 repeat measures 21–29 with a new text.

- Follow the "2nd time to Coda" in measure 68 to go forward to measure 96.

ENRICHMENT

Analyze

View the 1968 movie *Oliver!* to place "Consider Yourself" within the concept of the musical. Where is Oliver when the song is sung? Who is singing it? What are the circumstances? To whom is it sung? Is the invitation accepted?

Progress Checkpoints

Observe students' progress in:
- ✓ Singing chromatic passages in tune.
- ✓ Reading rhythms correctly.
- ✓ Identifying the differences and similarities between Part I and Part II.
- ✓ Following the road map of the piece and locating the D.S. al Coda.

EXTENSION

Compare and Contrast

Compare and contrast the story line of the musical *Oliver!* with the Broadway hit *Annie.*

Answers: Both are about young people living in an orphanage. In both stories, the lead characters are adopted by wealthy, caring individuals. *Oliver!* is set in London in the mid-1800s, while *Annie* is set in New York City during the Great Depression of the 1930s.

3. Refine

Direct students to:

- Sing complete four-measure phrases in one breath, with a crescendo on tied notes.
- Sustain the vowel through tied notes and longer rhythmic values.
- Chant or count-sing the rhythms.
- Apply the dynamic markings, giving particular attention to Section B, wherein the initial phrases alternate between an energetic piano and a full forte. Also work to achieve a steady crescendo at the beginning of the last phrase. *(measures 69–72)*

VOCAL DEVELOPMENT

To encourage vocal development, have students:

- Identify where unison and part-singing occurs.
- Listen when part-singing joins into unison singing; the dynamics need to be adjusted for sudden full volume on a converging note. *(measures 29 and 45)*
- Sing with tall vowels throughout, especially on the words *us, long* and *grouse.*

Observe students' progress in:

✓ Singing phrases with energy sustained through to the end.

✓ Performing the dynamics as marked in the score.

✓ Performing rhythms and pitches with accuracy.

✓ Communicating the text effectively.

✓ Their ability to use proper word stress, precise diction and unified vowel sounds.

TEACHING STRATEGY

Reading Rhythms in 6/8 Meter

If students are unfamiliar with reading rhythms in 6/8 meter, review the Theory section on page 157. Have students:

• Construct a rhythmic pattern together, using the Theory section as a guide. Begin with one measure and then gradually add more challenging combinations for a total of four measures.

• Keep track of how well students can read and clap or chant the patterns by graphing the measure on which they made their first mistake.

• Track and graph this information for each member of the class. By the end of these trials, the students should be ready to work in 6/8 meter.

ASSESSMENT

Informal Assessment

In this lesson, students showed the ability to:

- Sing in two parts with accurate pitches and rhythms.
- Sing a chromatic passage in tune in the key of B♭ major.
- Locate in the score repetitions of chromatic passages.
- Maintain a steady beat.
- Read and perform rhythms in 6/8 meter.
- Use facial expressions to communicate the mood and message of the text.
- Follow the D.S. al Coda instruction.
- Apply dynamic markings as indicated in the score.

MORE ABOUT...

Oliver!

"Consider Yourself" is from the award-winning musical *Oliver!,* written by British composer and lyricist Lionel Bart (1930–1999). The London premiere in 1960 received 23 curtain calls. *Oliver!* opened on Broadway in 1963, receiving three Tony awards that year. The movie version was released in 1968 and earned six Academy Awards, including Best Picture.

Student Self-Assessment

Have students evaluate their individual performances based on the following:

- Diction
- Expressive Singing
- Accurate Pitches
- Accurate Rhythms
- Correct Part-Singing

Have each student rate his/her performance of this song in the areas above on a scale of 1–5, 5 being the best.

CAREERS IN MUSIC

Music as Avocation

One school activity that helps develop students' stage presence is participation in musical theatre. If your school periodically stages plays or musicals (or if there is a community theater that accepts volunteers), this might be an avocation of interest to some students. Explain that a role in the musical theatre or a play can be varied. It can range from being a member of the background chorus or "crowd scene" to playing the lead role and learning numerous lines and solo numbers. Have students compare and contrast this avocational opportunity with others they might have already pursued.

Individual and Group Performance Evaluation

To further measure growth of musical skills presented in this lesson, ask students to complete the Evaluation section on page 157.

- After individual students have performed measures 13–29 for the rest of the class, critique their performance. Were the singers able to sing chromatically?

- After each student has composed a four-measure pattern in compound meter, start at the end of the row and have each student perform his/her pattern one after another, keeping a steady beat. Evaluate their performances. Were they able to compose and perform in compound meter?

MUSIC, SOCIETY AND CULTURE

Have students perform additional songs representing diverse cultures, including American and Texas heritage. Go to **music.glencoe.com**, the Web site for Glencoe's choral music programs, for additional music selections students can perform.

EXTENSION

Chromatic Pitches

The term *chromatic* derives from the Greek word *khroma,* meaning "color." Chromatic tones add color by using pitches not already in the scale or key signature.

Relate the sound of the recurring chromatic passage (D-E♭-E-F) to its physical placement on a keyboard. Distribute a picture of a blank keyboard and ask students to write in the letter names of the keys. Locate D-E♭-E-F on the keyboard. Stress that chromatic pitches are adjacent keys one half step apart. Locate other chromatic passages in the score *(measures 45–46, 53–54, 58–60)* and their placement on the keyboard. To assess student comprehension, ask them to name four consecutive half-step pitches that are chromatic and to play them at the keyboard.

Choral Library *Consider Yourself* **167**

Additional National Standards

The following National Standards are addressed through the Assessment, Extension, Enrichment and bottom-page activities:

4. Composing and arranging music within specific guidelines. **(a)**

6. Listening to, analyzing, and describing music. **(b)**

7. Evaluating music and music performances. **(b)**

8. Understanding the relationships between music, the other arts, and disciplines outside the arts. **(a)**

Hine ma tov

OVERVIEW

Composer: Hebrew Folk Song, arranged by Henry Leck

Text: Traditional

Voicing: 2-Part

Key: E minor/F# minor

Meter: 2/4

Form: Canonic/ABA'

Style: Hebrew Folk Song

Accompaniment: Piano

Programming: Concert, Contest, Festival, Multicultural

Vocal ranges:

Objectives

After completing this lesson, students will be able to:

• Sight-read simple music in various keys.

• Create rhythmic phrases.

• Perform a varied repertoire of music representing styles from diverse cultures.

VOCABULARY

Have students review vocabulary in student lesson. Introduce terms found in the music. A complete glossary of terms is found on page 246 of the student book.

Hine ma tov

Composer: Hebrew Folk Song, arranged by Henry Leck

Text: Traditional

Voicing: 2-Part

VOCABULARY

minor tonality

²⁄₄ meter

Focus

• Perform music in minor tonality.

• Compose rhythmic phrases.

• Perform music that represents the Hebrew culture.

Getting Started

Imagine that you are at a festive occasion. Perhaps it is a celebration such as a wedding, a birthday party, or a bar mitzvah. You hear the host ask the guests to come join in a dance. The people begin to sing and dance in a circle while holding hands or interlocking arms. "Hine ma tov" is the type of song that might be performed for this occasion.

◆ History and Culture

People have always danced as a means of expression. This is particularly true in Israel. Despite the fact that its people have a heritage that spans thousands of years, Israel did not achieve statehood until 1948.

Over the years, Jewish people have developed a rich tradition of folk art, music, and dance. "Hine ma tov" is an example of this rich heritage. The English translation is: "Behold, how good and pleasant it is for brethren to dwell together in unity."

On page 232 in this book you will find the lesson "Unity." Although "Unity" is written in the African American gospel tradition, it uses the same text as "Hine ma tov." Listen to both songs and discuss the ways in which two different cultures have chosen to express a similar theme of unity and peace.

🎲 **SKILL BUILDERS**

To learn more about the key of E minor, see Beginning Sight-Singing, page 94.

168 Beginning Unison, 2-Part/3-Part

RESOURCES

Beginning Sight-Singing

Sight-Singing in E minor, pages 94–101

Sight-Singing the F# Minor Scale, page 168

Reading 2/4 Meter, page 59

Reading Dotted Notes, pages 43–45, 92, 110

Teacher Resource Binder

Teaching Master 24, *Pronunciation Guide for "Hine ma tov"*

Teaching Master 25, *Composing a Rhythmic Composition in 2/4 Meter*

Skill Builder 30, *Solfège Hand Signs*

Evaluation Master 2, *Analyzing Pitch Accuracy*

For additional resources, see TRB Table of Contents

Links to Learning

◆ **Vocal**

"Hine ma tov" begins in the key of E minor and is based on the E minor scale. *A song that is based on a minor scale with* la *as its keynote, or home tone, is described as being in* **minor tonality**. Sing the E minor scale.

Read and perform the following examples to practice singing some of the melodic patterns found in "Hine ma tov."

◆ **Theory**

Read and speak the following rhythmic patterns. Silently mouth the syllables in parentheses to help feel the space needed for the longer note values. To develop a strong sense of two beats per measure, put extra emphasis on the word "boom" each time it occurs. **²/₄ meter** is *a time signature in which there are two beats per measure and the quarter note receives the beat.*

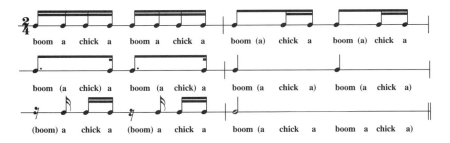

Evaluation

Demonstrate how well you have learned the skills and concepts featured in the lesson "Hine ma tov" by completing the following:

- Sing measures 5–20 to show that you can sing in minor tonality.
- Compose a four-measure rhythmic composition in ²/₄ meter using the rhythms presented in this lesson. Perform your composition for the class.

RESOURCES

Beginning Unison, 2-Part/3-Part Rehearsal/Performance CD

CD 2:9 Voices

CD 2:10 Accompaniment Only

CD 3:17 Vocal Practice Track—Part I

CD 4:18 Vocal Practice Track—Part II

National Standards

1. Singing, alone and with others, a varied repertoire of music. **(a, b, c, d)**

4. Composing and arranging music within specific guidelines. **(a)**

5. Reading and notating music. **(a, b, c, d)**

Vocal

The Vocal section is designed to prepare students to:

- Understand minor tonality.
- Sing the E minor scale.

Have students:

- Read the definition of minor tonality.
- Sing the E minor scale on note names.
- Sing the E minor scale on solfège syllables.
- Sing the two melodic examples and locate those patterns in their choral score.

Theory

The Theory section is designed to prepare students to:

- Understand 2/4 meter.
- Read and perform rhythmic patterns in 2/4 meter.

Have students:

- Read the definition of 2/4 meter.
- Tap or clap the quarter-note pulse.
- Speak the rhythm exercise slowly while tapping the quarter note pulse.
- Speak the rhythm exercise while feeling the quarter note pulse inside. Repeat increasing tempo when comfortable.

LESSON PLAN

Suggested Teaching Sequence and Performance Tips

1. Introduce

Direct students to:

- Read and discuss the information found in the Getting Started section on page 168.
- Practice the rhythm patterns in the Theory section on page 169.
- Chant and clap measures 5–12, noting the repetition. Read measures 13–20, noting the continued repetition of this idea in Part I through measure 28, where it shifts to Part II and continues through measure 36.
- Chant Part II, measures 37–49, noting the repetition.
- Chant Part I, measures 50 to the end. Note the key change and the return of the motive first found in measure 13.
- Mark the form as: Introduction (measures 1–12), A (measures 13–36), B (measures 37–49), A' (measures 50–62).

Progress Checkpoints

Observe students' progress in:

- ✓ Their ability to read rhythmic patterns with accuracy, giving space to the longer notes.
- ✓ Their ability to locate repeated patterns in the song.
- ✓ Their ability to recognize the form of the song.

Hine ma tov

For 2-Part and Piano

Arranged by
HENRY LECK

Hebrew Folk Song

Copyright © 1996 Colla Voce Music, Inc.
International Copyright Secured   All Rights Reserved

TEACHER 2 TEACHER

This vital piece of music will give your students an insight into the undying hope for peace and solidarity that is held by the people of Israel.

ne ma tov u - mah na - yim she - vet a - chim gam ya - chad! Hi -

ne ma tov u - mah na - yim she - vet a - chim gam ya - chad! Hi -

ne ma tov u - mah na - yim she - vet a - chim gam ya - chad! Hi -

Hi - ne she - vet a - chim gam ya - chad!

2. Rehearse

Direct students to:

- Practice the Vocal section on page 169 to get familiar with the E minor scale and melodic patterns in E minor used in this piece.

- Sing from your hand signs the *la-do-mi* and *re-fa-la* triads. Once this is secure, sing measures 5–6 to establish the tonality of the piece. Continue sight-singing using solfège syllables.

- Sight-sing Part I, measures 13–28 and then sight-sing Part II, measures 29–36. Be sure to tune the D (*sol*) to secure the feeling of minor tonality.

- Sight-sing Part II, measures 37–49. Secure the pitches and rhythms. Be sure to tune the C# (*fi*).

- Study measures 50 to the end. Locate the imitation between parts. Isolate and practice measures 56–end in both parts.

- Sight-sing Part I, measures 29–36. When accurate, add Part II.

- Sight-sing Part I, measures 41–49. Note the E minor triad (*la-do-mi*) in measure 41 of Part I. When accurate, add Part II.

Progress Checkpoints

Observe students' progress in:

✓ Their rhythmic precision, especially in the B section.

✓ Singing pitches accurately.

✓ Singing their parts securely.

EXTENSION

Moving to the Music

Create a dance! The driving rhythm of "Hine ma tov" inspires the singer to move while singing. Divide into groups and create movement to fit the style of the song. Consider the following ideas while creating your dance:

- Stepping or clapping on pulses.
- Moving arm in arm.
- Changing direction or movement from a line to a circle.
- Changing the movement to match changes in the music. (*measures 29— Descant enters, measures 37—B section, measure 50—imitation, and measures 60 to end—Coda*)

3. Refine

Direct students to:

- Chant the text in small sections with special attention to word stress. The Hebrew pronunciation guide for "Hine ma tov" is found in the Teacher Resource Binder, Teaching Master 24.
- Sing small sections with parts separate until secure. Put all parts together once vocal independence is established.
- Sustain with energy and forward motion on longer rhythmic values to create a feeling of singing over the bar line.
- Sing lightly to articulate the shorter rhythmic values.
- Sing with a strong stress on beat 1.

Progress Checkpoints

Observe students' progress in:

✓ Singing their parts securely with the text.

✓ Singing with clear, understandable diction.

✓ Presenting the text energetically.

✓ Their ability to move forward on longer rhythmic values.

✓ Lightly articulating shorter rhythmic values.

172 Beginning Unison, 2-Part/3-Part

ENRICHMENT

Hebrew Language

Although the Hebrew written in this song looks much like English, Hebrew is actually written in a very different way than English. Research the Hebrew alphabet and try writing the title of this song in Hebrew script.

Informal Assessment

In this lesson, students showed the ability to:

- Sing accurately in a minor key.
- Read and perform a variety of rhythms in 2/4 meter.
- Sing in the Hebrew language.

Student Self-Assessment

Have students evaluate their individual performances based on the following:

- Hebrew Diction
- Expressive Singing
- Accurate Pitches
- Accurate Rhythms
- Correct Part-Singing

Have each student rate his/her performance of this song in the areas above on a scale of 1–5, 5 being the best.

TEACHING STRATEGY

Identifying a Key as Minor

Have students discuss and identify strategies for determining whether a piece is in a major or minor key. Some possible strategies include:

- Look at the key signature, and determine the possible major key.
- Look at the notation, especially the beginning chord, and the chords at the ends of phrases, identifying the tonal center.
- Determine if the tonal center matches the major key, or is a third below, indicating the relative minor.
- If minor, look for altered tones. If there are none, it is natural minor. If there are altered tones, it is possibly harmonic minor.

Individual and Group Performance Evaluation

To further measure growth of musical skills presented in this lesson, direct students to complete the Evaluation section on page 169.

- Have solos or small groups or sections sing measures 5–20 while the rest of the class listens. Evaluate their performances by asking, "Were these singers able to sing in minor tonality?"

- After each student has composed a four-measure rhythmic pattern in 2/4 meter, start at the end of the row and have each student perform his/her pattern one after another, keeping a steady beat. Evaluate their performances. Were they able to compose and perform in 2/4 using the rhythms presented in this lesson?

Music, Society and Culture

Have students perform additional songs representing diverse cultures, including American and Texas heritage. Go to **music.glencoe.com**, the Web site for Glencoe's choral music programs, for additional music selections students can perform.

174   Beginning Unison, 2-Part/3-Part

Additional National Standards

The following National Standards are addressed through the Assessment, Extension, Enrichment and bottom-page activities:

4. Composing and arranging music within specific guidelines. **(a)**

5. Reading and notating music. **(d)**

7. Evaluating music and music performances. **(a)**

8. Understanding the relationships between music, the other arts, and disciplines outside the arts. **(a)**

SPOTLIGHT

Careers In Music

Composer/Arranger

Composers turn their ideas into music just as authors write original stories and artists paint original pieces of art. A **composer** is *a person who takes a musical thought and writes it out in musical notation to share with others.* There are no special degree requirements to be a composer, but a thorough knowledge of music and music technology is helpful. Some composers write their music with the use of a MIDI and music software on the computer. Others write their music compositions out by hand on manuscript paper.

Composing is a very competitive field. Some composers are able to make a good living from writing, but not all. It depends on whether there is a demand for the type of music they write and whether they have connections with those who can get it published.

As a young aspiring composer, it is necessary for you to listen to as much variety of music as possible, including classical, jazz, world music, and popular. Broaden your musical knowledge. Study the music of the composers you really like. Begin by emulating their style, then branch out to create your own style. Look for ways to make your compositions unique.

Also, composers may use their talents to write arrangements of existing tunes. An **arranger** is *a composer who takes an original or existing melody and adds extra features or changes the melody in some way.* Look through the songs in this book and find one example of an original composition and one example of an arrangement.

Spotlight *Careers In Music* **175**

RESOURCES

Teacher Resource Binder

Reference 7, *Building a Musical Vocabulary*
Reference 15, *Exploring Careers in Music*

National Standards

7. Evaluating music and musical performances. **(a, b)**

CAREERS IN MUSIC

Objective

• Describe music-related vocations and avocations.

Suggested Teaching Sequence

Direct students to:

• Read the Spotlight on Careers in Music on page 175 and identify the career opportunities as a composer/arranger.

• Divide into small groups and make lists of composers they are familiar with. Share the lists with the class. Do they overlap?

• Discuss the difficulties of breaking into the composition field as a career. Compare those to the rewards.

• Share their personal favorites of composers. If possible, share a recording of their work with the class.

• Discuss the differences between an arranger and a composer.

• Find examples of arrangements and compositions in the music they are singing.

Progress Checkpoints

Observe students' progress in:

✓ Their ability to identify the difference between an arranger and a composer.

✓ Their ability to describe the difficulties and rewards of being a career composer.

✓ Their ability to locate examples of compositions and arrangements.

Little David, Play On Your Harp

OVERVIEW

Composer: African American Spiritual, arranged by Emily Crocker

Text: Traditional

Voicing: 2-Part

Key: E♭ major/F major

Meter: 4/4

Form: AA'BA'BA''A''Coda

Style: Spiritual

Accompaniment: Piano

Programming: Americana Program, Festival, Multicultural

Vocal Ranges:

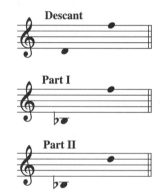

Objectives

After completing this lesson, students will be able to:

• Use standard terminology to explain musical performances and notation.

• Perform independently with accurate rhythm.

• Perform a varied repertoire of music representing styles from diverse cultures.

VOCABULARY

Have students review vocabulary in student lesson. Introduce terms found in the music. A complete glossary of terms is found on page 246 of the student book.

Little David, Play On Your Harp

Composer: African American Spiritual, arranged by Emily Crocker

Text: Traditional

Voicing: 2-Part

VOCABULARY

syncopation

spiritual

imitation

descant

Focus

• Define *imitation.*

• Identify and perform syncopated and non-syncopated rhythms.

• Perform music that represents the African American spiritual.

🎲 **SKILL BUILDERS**

To learn more about sixteenth and eighth note combinations, see Beginning Sight-Singing, page 74.

Getting Started

Imagine yourself at a football game. The cheerleaders are cheering the team to victory, and the band is playing the fight song. The unique rhythms that you hear grab your attention and encourage you to move to the beat. This excitement in the music is caused by syncopation. **Syncopation** occurs when *the accent is moved from a strong beat to a weak beat or the weak portion of a beat.* Enjoy singing the many syncopated rhythms in "Little David, Play On Your Harp."

◆ History and Culture

"Little David, Play On Your Harp" is an example of a spiritual. A part of the African American tradition, **spirituals** are *songs that are often based on biblical themes or stories and were first sung by the slaves.* What spirituals do you know?

In this arrangement, two musical devices—imitation and descant—are used to create interest and variety. **Imitation** occurs when *one part copies what the other part has just sung.* A **descant** is *a special part that is added to the other parts in a song and is usually sung higher than the other parts.* Find examples of imitation, and locate the descant in this song.

RESOURCES

Beginning Sight-Singing

Sight-Singing in E♭ Major, pages 147–151

Sight-Singing in F Major, pages 38–40, 60, 76–77, 118, 121–122

Reading Syncopation, pages 160–161

Teacher Resource Binder

Skill Builder 20, *Naming Intervals*

Skill Builder 23, *Rhythm and Kodály*

Skill Builder 24, *Rhythm Challenge Using Syncopation*

Kodály 6, *Music Reading: Rhythm*

Reference 7, *Building a Musical Vocabulary*

For additional resources, see TRB Table of Contents.

Links to Learning

◆ **Vocal**

Perform the following example below to practice singing intervals found in "Little David, Play On Your Harp."

la la la la la la la la la la la la la la la la la la la la

◆ **Theory**

Read and perform the following syncopated and non-syncopated rhythmic patterns used in "Little David, Play On Your Harp."

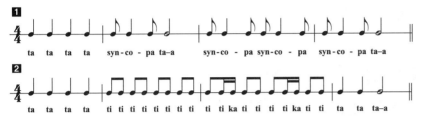

1

ta ta ta ta syn-co - pa ta–a syn-co - pa syn-co - pa syn-co - pa ta–a

2

ta ta ta ta ti ti ti ti ti ti ti ti ti ti ka ti ti ti ti ka ti ti ta ta ta–a

Evaluation

Demonstrate how well you have learned the skills and concepts featured in the lesson "Little David, Play On Your Harp" by completing the following:

• As a duet or in a small group, perform measures 1–19 to show your understanding of imitation while singing.

• Look in your music at measures 4 and 12. Which measure is an example of syncopation and which is an example of non-syncopation? Support your answer. Find other examples of each in your music.

LINKS TO LEARNING

Vocal

The Vocal section is designed to prepare students to sing the intervals found in "Little David, Play On Your Harp."

Have students:

• Sing the example using solfège syllables.

• Sing the example on "la" as indicated, concentrating on accurate pitches and tuning the intervals.

• Locate these intervals in the choral score.

Theory

The Theory section is designed to prepare students to sing the syncopated and nonsyncopated rhythms used in "Little David, Play On Your Harp."

Have students:

• Tap or clap the quarter-note pulse.

• Speak exercise 1 while tapping the quarter-note pulse.

• Speak exercise 1 while feeling the quarter-note pulse inside.

• Repeat this procedure for exercise 2.

• Locate these rhythms in the choral score.

RESOURCES

Beginning Unison, 2-Part/3-Part Rehearsal/Performance CD

CD 2:11 Voices

CD 2:12 Accompaniment Only

CD 3:18 Vocal Practice Track—Part I

CD 4:19 Vocal Practice Track—Part II

National Standards

1. Singing, alone and with others, a varied repertoire of music. **(a, b, c)**

6. Listening to, analyzing, and describing music. **(a, b, c)**

9. Understanding music in relation to history and culture. **(a)**

LESSON PLAN

Suggested Teaching Sequence and Performance Tips

1. Introduce

Direct students to:

- Read and discuss the information found in the Getting Started section on page 176.

- Practice singing the intervals used in this song as shown in the Vocal section on page 177.

- Practice chanting and clapping the syncopated and nonsyncopated rhythms used in this song as shown in the Theory section on page 177.

- Echo clap several nonsyncopated rhythms and contrast them to syncopated rhythms. Present a series of rhythms, both syncopated and nonsyncopated, and have the students identify. (NOTE: Include this exercise in your daily warm-up to reinforce the concept.)

This arrangement for
Priscilla Gaston and the Crockett Sixth Grade Choir

Little David, Play On Your Harp

For 2-Part and Piano

Arranged by
EMILY CROCKER

African American Spiritual

Copyright © 1989 HAL LEONARD CORPORATION
International Copyright Secured All Rights Reserved

TEACHER 2 TEACHER

The arrangement of this spiritual perfectly embodies the enthusiasm and joy for singing we strive to develop in our young singers! The clever rhythms and charming melody serve as a format for teaching challenging part-singing.

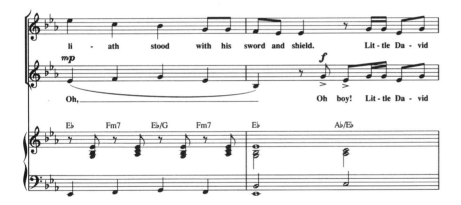

- Chant measures 3–7. This is the A theme (also known as the chorus). Locate, discuss and chant the variations in the two-sixteenth-note, two-eighth-note motive when this theme returns. *(measures 7, 15, 25, 29 of Part II)* Mark these sections with an A.

Progress Checkpoints

Observe students' progress in:

✓ Their ability to perform a syncopated pattern with rhythmic accuracy.

✓ Their ability to aurally discriminate a nonsyncopated rhythm from a syncopated one.

✓ Their ability to sing intervals in tune.

✓ Their ability to study the score and find the recurring A section.

EXTENSION

Composition

Research the story of David and Goliath and create two additional verses for measures 11–15 and measures 21–25. Decide how to place these verses in the song and perform it with the class.

2. Rehearse

Direct students to:

- Sing Part II, measures 3–11. Pay particular attention to rhythmic accuracy. Note that Part II has the melody.

- Sing Part I, beginning with the pick-up to measures 12–15. Mark this as the B section (also known as the verse).

- Locate and sing the repeat of the B section. *(measures 22–25)*

- Discuss the key change from E♭ major to F major at measure 30. This raises the pitch of the song a half step and creates a feeling of energy and excitement.

- Isolate and chant the three parts at measures 30–43. Note the repeated rhythms in all parts. When accurate, chant all parts together.

- Tap the beat while sight-singing Part II in measures 30–43. Make sure to hold the half note its full value. When accurate, combine with Part III.

- Tap the pulse while sight-singing Part I at measures 8–11 and measures 16–19. Note that these are repetitions of Part I at measure 30 in the key of E♭.

180   Beginning Unison, 2-Part/3-Part

Progress Checkpoints

Observe students' progress in:

✓ Their rhythmic precision, particularly with syncopation and longer notes.

✓ Their independence of vocal lines.

✓ Their ability to identify form.

CULTURAL CONNECTIONS

Spirituals

Spirituals are slave songs created in the United States by African Americans. Considered to be one of the first American musical forms, these songs of sorrow and songs of hope were important tools for motivating and sustaining African Americans during the slavery experience. Many of these songs were composed in the fields during labor, which means that movement often coincided with the rhythms and expressions of these pieces. The texts of spirituals often carry multiple meanings, depicting religious desires for heavenly peace, as well as physical desires for freedom and equality.

3. Refine

Direct students to:

- Sing the entire song using crisp, clear diction. Omit the descant part. Encourage the students to sing with energy by articulating lightly with shorter rhythmic values.

- Sight-sing the descant down an octave. Note the repetition of measures 30–33 and measures 34–37. Practice several yawn-sighs before singing measures 30–37 as written. Encourage students to sing lightly with forward placement in this upper register. Listen to the students sing the descant in small groups and choose four to six singers to perform the part.

- Chant the coda (measures 38–43). When accurate, add pitches and text. For balance purposes, you may wish to re-voice the choir on the coda.

Progress Checkpoints

Observe students' progress in:

✓ Singing pitches and rhythms accurately.

✓ Singing with crisp, clear diction.

✓ Their energetic presentation of the text.

✓ Using their light head voice on the descant.

TEACHING STRATEGY

Sight-Singing: Making Mistakes

The goal of sight-singing is to perform a piece of music at first sight, without studying it beforehand. At the beginning, students are likely to make a lot of mistakes. Help them understand that mistakes are how people learn, and that with practice they will get much better. Discuss how laughing at the mistakes of others can be hurtful, but that if everyone laughs together during these first few attempts, it will reduce the pressure until everyone's sight-singing improves.

ASSESSMENT

Informal Assessment

In this lesson, students showed the ability to:

- Locate and perform syncopated and nonsyncopated rhythms in 4/4 meter.
- Locate differences and similarities between parts to facilitate learning a song.
- Sing with energy by using crisp, clear diction and creating space between notes.

Student Self-Assessment

Have students evaluate their individual performances based on the following:

- Posture
- Diction
- Accurate Pitch
- Accurate Rhythms
- Correct Part-Singing

Have each student rate his/her performance of this song in the areas above on a scale of 1–5, 5 being the best.

MORE ABOUT...

Arranger Emily Crocker

Emily Holt Crocker, Director of the Milwaukee Children's Choir, is recognized nationally as one of the leading experts in children's choirs. After a successful 15-year career as a music teacher and choral director in her native Texas, she joined the music publishing industry, and now holds the position of Vice President of Choral Publications for Hal Leonard Corporation in Milwaukee and is Senior Author and Editor of the *Essential Elements for Choir* textbook series.

She holds degrees from the University of North Texas and Texas Woman's University, and has done additional study at UNT (choral conducting), Westminster Choir College (conducting and voice-building), TWU (vocal pedagogy) and Sam Houston State University (Kodály methods).

Individual and Group Performance Evaluation

To further measure growth of musical skills presented in this lesson, direct students to complete the Evaluation section on page 177.

- Have duets or small groups perform measures 1–19 for the rest of the class. The class should evaluate. Did these singers understand and perform imitation correctly?

- Have all students locate measures 4 and 12 and determine which measure is an example of syncopation and which is an example of nonsyncopation. Call on selected students to share their answers and support their choice. Have student find other examples of each in these pieces of music.

TEACHING STRATEGY

Assessment Jitters

Some students might find the pressure of the evaluation process very difficult, if not impossible. Students should be encouraged to take the risk, but also be allowed to pass and wait until they are ready to perform in such a pressure situation.

Music, Society and Culture

Have students perform additional songs representing diverse cultures, including American and Texas heritage. Go to **music.glencoe.com**, the Web site for Glencoe's choral music programs, for additional music selections students can perform.

Additional National Standards

The following National Standards are addressed through the Assessment, Extension, Enrichment and bottom-page activities:

4. Composing and arranging music within specific guidelines. **(a)**

6. Listening to, analyzing, and describing music. **(a, c)**

7. Evaluating music and music performances. **(b)**

9. Understanding music in relation to history and culture. **(c)**

Pokare Kare Ana

Composer: Paware Tomoana, arranged by Mark O'Leary
Text: Paware Tomoana
Voicing: 2-Part

Pokare Kare Ana

OVERVIEW

Composer: Paware Tomoana, arranged by Mark O'Leary
Text: Paware Tomoana
Voicing: 2-Part
Key: G major / A major
Meter: 4/4
Form: AA'A"A'''
Style: New Zealand Love Song
Accompaniment: Piano or guitar with optional flutes
Programming: Concert, Festival

Vocal Ranges:

VOCABULARY

diction
syllabic stress
skip-wise motion

Focus

- Perform music with correct diction and syllabic stress.
- Understand music in relation to history and culture.

Getting Started

In any language, vocal music can be used to express emotions or to tell a story. Therefore, when singing, it is important to convey the meaning of the text through your body language and facial expression. It is also important to use proper **diction** *(the pronunciation of words while singing)* and correct syllabic stress so that you can be clearly understood.

Syllabic stress is *the stressing of one syllable over another.* For example, in the word *music,* you would stress the first syllable more than the second. You would sing, "MU-sic," rather than "mu-SIC." Discuss where you would place the syllabic stress on the words *father, telephone,* and *America.*

◆ **History and Culture**

"Pokare Kare Ana" is a love song from New Zealand. Sung in the Maori language, it tells the story of Princess Hinemoa and Tutaneki, a warrior who lived on an island nine miles from shore. Hinemoa's father would not allow the couple to see each other. Every night Tutaneki would serenade Hinemoa by playing his flute, and the sound would travel across the water to her. One night, Hinemoa decided to swim to her warrior's island. Soon after, Hinemoa and Tutaneki were married, and many tribes developed from the descendants of this couple.

SPOTLIGHT

To learn more about diction, see page 33.

Objectives

After completing this lesson, students will be able to:

- Demonstrate fundamental skills while performing.
- Relate music to history and culture.

VOCABULARY

Have students review vocabulary in student lesson. Introduce terms found in the music. A complete glossary of terms is found on page 246 of the student book.

Choral Library *Pokare Kare Ana* **185**

RESOURCES

Beginning Sight-Singing

0Sight-Singing in G Major, pages 84–89, 93
Sight-Singing in A Major, pages 162–165

Teacher Resource Binder

Teaching Master 26, *Pronunciation Guide for "Pokare Kare Ana"*
Teaching Master 27, *The Language of Music*
Skill Builder 21, *Pitch and Kodály*
Skill Builder 30, *Solfège Hand Signs*
Reference 23, *Text Emphasis in Singing*
For additional resources, see TRB Table of Contents.

LINKS TO LEARNING

Vocal

The Vocal section is designed to prepare students to develop accurate intonation while singing intervals in skip-wise motion.

Have students:

- Clap, tap or chant the rhythm of the example.
- Speak the pitch names using solfège syllables.
- Sing the example as written once the rhythm and pitch are secure.

Theory

The Theory section is designed to prepare students to practice singing the opening phrase of "Pokare Kare Ana."

Have students:

- Clap, tap or chant the rhythm of the example.
- Sing the example on "loo," paying attention to the skip-wise motion and to intonation.

Artistic Expression

The Artistic Expression section is designed to prepare students to sing with proper diction and syllabic stress.

Have students:

- Chant the example, placing a slight stress on the syllables in capital letters.
- Sing the example, placing a slight stress on the syllables in capital letters.

Links to Learning

◆ Vocal

Skip-wise motion means *to skip two or more notes away from a given note on the staff.* Read and perform the following example to develop accurate intonation while singing in skip-wise motion.

do   sol   do   sol   do   mi   do   sol   mi   do

◆ Theory

Perform the following example to practice singing the opening phrase of "Pokare Kare Ana." Notice the skip-wise motion.

loo   loo loo loo loo   loo   loo,_____   loo   loo loo loo loo   loo   loo,___

_____   loo loo loo loo loo   loo   loo,_____   loo   loo loo loo loo   loo

◆ Artistic Expression

To develop artistry in singing through proper diction and syllabic stress, chant and sing the following example. Place a slight stress on the syllables that are printed in capital letters.

Po - KA-re KA-re   A - na,_____   nga   WAI o Ro-to-RU - a,___

___ WHI-ti A-tu KO-e HI - ne,_____   MA - RI-no A-na   E.

Evaluation

Demonstrate how well you have learned the skills and concepts featured in the lesson "Pokare Kare Ana" by completing the following:

- Apply your knowledge of syllabic stress by singing the second verse of "Pokare Kare Ana" (measures 9–16) with correct diction and syllabic stress.
- Describe the cultural background of this piece in your own words.

186   Beginning Unison, 2-Part/3-Part

RESOURCES

Beginning Treble Rehearsal/Performance CD

CD 2:13 Voices

CD 2:14 Accompaniment Only

CD 3:19 Vocal Practice Track—Part I

CD 4:20 Vocal Practice Track—Part II

National Standards

1. Singing, alone and with others, a varied repertoire of music. **(a, b, c, d)**

5. Reading and notating music. **(a, b, c)**

9. Understanding music in relation to history and culture. **(a)**

Pokare Kare Ana

For 2-Part and Piano or Guitar* with Optional Flutes**

Arranged by
MARK O'LEARY

Words and Music by
PAWARE TOMOANA

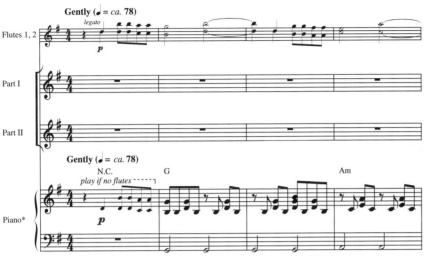

* Although originally scored for guitar, piano may be used. Pianist should imitate smooth, guitar-like playing.
  Guitar should use chord symbols above piano and rhythms indicated in piano.

**Flute part found on page 196.

© 1991 MARK O'LEARY MUSIC PUBLISHING
International Copyright Secured   All Rights Reserved

Choral Library *Pokare Kare Ana*   **187**

LESSON PLAN

Suggested Teaching Sequence and Performance Tips

1. Introduce

Direct students to:

- Read and discuss the information found in the Getting Started section on student page 185. (*FA-ther, TEL-e-phone, a-MER-i-ca*)

- Review the Links to Learning section before singing measures 9–16 with text.

- Sight-sing measures 17–24 using solfège syllables. (*NOTE: In solfège, the altered pitch F-natural [measure 17] is te. C♯ [measure 23, Part II] is fi.*)

- Chant the text in rhythm, then add pitches.

TEACHER 2 TEACHER

Each verse of the song expresses the warrior Tutaneki's love for Hinemoa, the Maori Princess. Encourage the students to convey the emotions of the text through dynamic changes and expressive singing.

187

Observe students' progress in:

✓ Their ability to perform with tonal and rhythmic accuracy in both vocal parts.

✓ Using correct pronunciation and syllabic stress in the Maori language.

188   Beginning Unison, 2-Part/3-Part

TEACHING STRATEGY

Sight-Singing: Making Mistakes

The goal of sight-singing is to perform a piece of music at first sight, without studying it beforehand. At the beginning, students are likely to make a lot of mistakes. Help them understand that mistakes are how people learn, and that with practice, their sight-singing skills will improve. Discuss how laughing at others' mistakes can be hurtful, but if everyone laughs during the early attempts, it will reduce the pressure until everyone's skills improve.

E hi - ne e, _____ Ho - ki mai ra, _____

E hi - ne e, _____ Ho - ki mai ra, _____

_____ Ka ma - te a - hau i - te a - ro - ha e.

_____ Ka ma - te a - hau i - te a - ro - ha e.

(to m. 9)

2. Rehearse

Direct students to:

- Analyze the music of verse 3 *(measures 25–40)* and compare this section to the music found in measures 9–24. Describe the similarities and differences. *(The melody is the same, but the different words require different rhythmic treatment. The harmony is different in measures 25–33, where the second part imitates the first. The dynamics in measures 9–24 begin* piano *and* crescendo *to mezzo piano, in contrast to the dynamics at measures 25–40, which begin at mezzo piano to mezzo forte.)*

- Sight-sing this new section using solfège syllables, and then add the text.

MUSIC, SOCIETY AND CULTURE

Have students perform additional songs representing diverse cultures, including American and Texas heritage. Go to **music.glencoe.com**, the Web site for Glencoe's choral music programs, for additional music selections students can perform.

- Ask students to sight-sing measures 41–65 using solfège syllables. Compare this passage to the previous one. *(Key change up a step from G Major to A Major. The dynamic level is increasing, moving from mezzo forte to forte to fortissimo.)*

- Chant the text of this passage in rhythm, then perform.

190   Beginning Unison, 2-Part/3-Part

ASSESSMENT

Evaluating the Quality of a Performance

Have students:

1. Listen to a video or audio recording of this piece as performed by the choir.

2. Compare this performance to exemplary models such as other recordings or other live performances of the piece.

3. Develop constructive suggestions for improvement based on the comparison.

Progress Checkpoints

Observe students' progress in:

✓ Their ability to locate the imitative writing style employed in the passage.

✓ Their ability to locate the key change.

✓ Their ability to locate dynamic changes in the score.

✓ Accurate pronunciation of all words.

CULTURAL CONNECTIONS

Research

Have students use the Internet as a source for learning more about Maori culture. Have students share their findings with the class and discuss the relationship of what they have learned to the music of "Pokare Kare Ana."

3. Refine

Direct students to sing the entire song in the Maori language.

Progress Checkpoints

Observe students' progress in:

✓ Their ability to sing with energy and listen for a good balance of parts.

✓ Their ability to sing the longer rhythmic values with expression and forward motion.

✓ Their ability to articulate with crisp, clear diction and syllabic stress.

EXTENSION

Improvisation

Using Orff keyboard instruments, have students improvise an accompaniment for this piece. Use the chord symbols provided in the score as a guide.

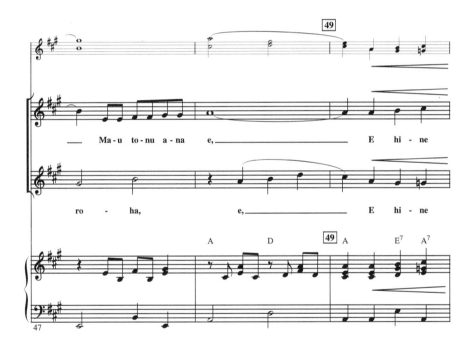

Informal Assessment

In this lesson, students showed the ability to:

- Perform "Pokare Kare Ana" with attention to variations in dynamics and imitative passages.
- Articulate the Maori language with accurate pronunciation and syllabic stress.

TEACHING STRATEGY

Concert Etiquette

Have students:

1. Identify and exhibit appropriate concert etiquette in a variety of settings (formal concerts, information concerts, large concert halls, small concert halls, and so forth).
2. Attend a variety of live performances
3. Discuss the appropriate and inappropriate concert behaviors observed.
4. Write a short analysis of appropriate concert etiquette for each setting.

Student Self-Assessment

Have students evaluate their individual performances based on the following:

- Breath Management
- Phrasing
- Diction
- Accurate Rhythms
- Accurate Pitches

Have each student rate his/her performance of this song in the areas above on a scale of 1–5, 5 being the best.

TEACHING STRATEGY

Diction

Clear pronunciation requires attention to both vowels and consonants. Have students:

- Discuss which choral techniques will produce clear diction. *(uniform vowels, crisp beginning and ending consonants, quick mouth movement to shape sounds)*
- Sing through the piece slowly with only vowels, keeping the jaw lowered, and blending the vowels.
- Add the consonants, keeping the vowels blended.
- Sing through the piece, paying attention to clear diction.

Individual and Group Performance Evaluation

To further measure growth of musical skills presented in this lesson, direct students to complete the Evaluation section on page 186.

- Have students sing verse 2 of this. *(measures 9–16)* Prepare a checklist including specific measures where diction and syllabic stress are a challenge. Videotape the class singing the piece and use the checklist to critique their performance.

- Describe the Maori culture and the story of "Pokare Kare Ana."

Additional National Standards

The following National Standards are addressed through the Assessment, Extension, Enrichment and bottom-page activities:

3. Improvising melodies, variations and accompaniments. **(a)**

5. Reading and notating music. **(a, b)**

7. Evaluating music and music performances. **(b)**

Pokare Kare Ana

For 2-Part and Piano or Guitar with Optional Flutes

FLUTE 1, 2

Words and Music by PAWARE TOMOANA
Arranged by MARK O'LEARY

© 1991 MARK O'LEARY MUSIC PUBLISHING
International Copyright Secured   All Rights Reserved

196   Beginning Unison, 2-Part/3-Part

Río, Río

Composer: Chilean Folk Song, arranged by Audrey Snyder
Text: Traditional Spanish
Voicing: 2-Part

Río, Río

OVERVIEW

Composer: Chilean Folk Song, arranged by Audrey Snyder
Text: Traditional Spanish
Voicing: 2-Part
Keys: F major/G major
Meter: 6/8
Form: ABA'C'A'B'
Style: Chilean Folk Song
Accompaniment: Piano
Programming: Contest/Festival

Vocal Ranges:

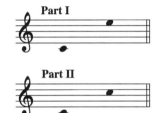

Objectives

After completing this lesson, students will be able to:

- Use standard terminology to explain music.
- Relate music to culture and to other concepts outside the arts.
- Evaluate the quality and effectiveness of their own performances.

VOCABULARY
$\frac{6}{8}$ meter
tied notes
unison

Focus

- Recognize the difference between unison and part-singing.
- Relate other subjects to music.
- Develop criteria for evaluating music.

Getting Started

Why are people so fascinated by rivers? Through the course of time, artists have been inspired to write songs, poems, and books about rivers. Often, human feelings and emotions are used to describe them. Country singer Garth Brooks sings, "You know a dream is like a river, ever changing as it flows." The famous poet Solaz wrote, "I am a fathomless river; untold riches and treasures are hidden in my deeps." As you learn "Río, Río," you will notice the human characteristics given to the river.

◆ History and Culture

The people of Chile have a tradition of living life with enthusiasm. This lifestyle is reflected in vibrant music, flavorful food, and festive celebrations. Rivers play an important part in the lives of the Chilean people. These rivers are tourist attractions as well as sources of enjoyment and productivity.

Written in Spanish, "Río, Río" (translated "River, River") is a folk song of unknown origin. However, a historic tale of a Chilean military leader and his wife parallels its text. The military leader went off to war and his wife longed for his return. Read the words found in "Río, Río." Do you think this story fits the text?

SPOTLIGHT

To learn more about pitch matching, see page 83.

Choral Library *Río, Río* **197**

VOCABULARY

Have students review vocabulary in student lesson. Introduce terms found in the music. A complete glossary of terms is found on page 246 of the student book.

RESOURCES

Beginning Sight-Singing

Sight-Singing in F Major, pages 38–40, 60, 76–77, 118, 121–122

Sight-Singing in G Major, pages 84–89, 93

Reading 6/8 Meter, pages 119–121

Teacher Resource Binder

Teaching Master 28, *Pronunciation Guide for "Río Río"*

Evaluation Master 17, *Self Observation/Self-Assessment*

Skill Builder 28, *Rhythm Challenge in 6/8 Meter*

Interdisciplinary 21-22, *Language Arts*

Reference 20, *Rhythm Challenge Chart*

For additional resources, see TRB Table of Contents.

LINKS TO LEARNING

Vocal

The Vocal section is designed to prepare students to sing some of the melodic patterns found in the song.

Have students:

- Speak the pitches on note names or solfège syllables.
- Clap, tap or chant the rhythm in the example.
- Sing the example once notes and rhythms are secure.

Theory

The Theory section is designed to prepare students to:

- Read simple rhythms in 6/8 meter.
- Distinguish between unison and 2-part music.

Have students:

- Tap or clap a steady pulse.
- Speak the exercise while tapping the pulse.
- Speak the exercise while feeling the pulse inside.
- Locate the unison sections in their music.

Links to Learning

◆ **Vocal**

Perform the following example to practice singing some of the melodic patterns found in "Río, Río."

◆ **Theory**

Read and perform the following example to practice rhythmic patterns in $\frac{6}{8}$ **meter,** *a time signature in which there are six beats to a measure and the dotted quarter note receives the beat.* Observe the **tied notes** *(two notes of the same pitch that are joined together to form one longer note)* in the example.

Although this arrangement of "Río, Río" is written in two parts, there are sections throughout where both parts sing in **unison** *(all parts sing the same notes at the same time).* Look at the music and locate the parts that are sung in unison.

◆ **Artistic Expression**

Poets have often written about rivers. Find a poem about a river to read to the class. As a class, discuss the various characteristics given to rivers in each poem.

Evaluation

Demonstrate how well you have learned the skills and concepts featured in the lesson "Río, Río" by completing the following:

- Sing measures 14–29 with another student, one on each part. Write a short self-evaluation of your performance by answering the following questions:
  - When singing in unison, did your voices match pitch?
  - When singing in harmony, could both parts be heard?
  - Could the melody line be heard over the harmony line?
  - Was the rhythm performed correctly?

  Collect feedback from several students by asking them the same questions. Compare your answers. Share what you have learned.

- As a class, decide which poems should be read at a performance of "Río, Río."

RESOURCES

Beginning Treble Rehearsal/Performance CD

- **CD 2:15** Voices
- **CD 2:16** Accompaniment Only
- **CD 3:20** Vocal Practice Track - Part I
- **CD 4:21** Vocal Practice Track - Part II

National Standards

1. Singing, alone and with others, a varied repertoire of music. **(a, b, c, d)**
5. Reading and notating music. **(a, b, c)**
7. Evaluate music and music performances. **(b)**
8. Understanding relationships between music, the other arts and disciplines outside the arts. **(b)**

Río, Río
(River, River)

For 2-Part and Piano

Arranged by
AUDREY SNYDER

Chilean Folk Song

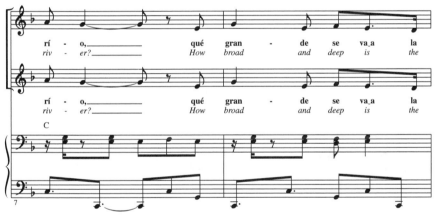

Copyright © 2001 by HAL LEONARD CORPORATION
International Copyright Secured All Rights Reserved

Choral Library *Río, Río* **199**

TEACHER2TEACHER

Students will enjoy singing this delightful Spanish song in 6/8 meter. The repetitive vocal line serves as an ideal tool for teaching the art of part-singing. Add a guitar to embellish the piano accompaniment.

Artistic Expression

The Artistic Expression section is designed to prepare students to relate literature to music.

Have students:

- Locate a poem about a river.
- Share their poem with the class.
- Compare and contrast the various characteristics given to rivers by each poet.

LESSON PLAN

Suggested Teaching Sequence and Performance Tips

1. Introduce

Direct students to:

- Read and discuss the information found in the Getting Started section on student page 197.
- Practice the vocal example, paying special attention to intonation.
- Practice the rhythmic example found in the Theory section. (*Note: Counting this example in two, as opposed to six, helps the meter to flow and also simplifies the tied note passages.*)
- Locate the unison passages in the music. (*measures 6–13, 19–21, 27–29, 60–62, 68–72*)
- Sing measures 6–13. Locate in the score every instance where this melodic idea occurs. (*measures 31–38 and measures 47–54 in Part II*)

- Sing measures 14–29. Locate in the score every instance where this melodic idea occurs. (*measures 55–70 in Part I*)
- Sing measures 39–46. This is a transitional section that occurs only once.
- Locate and practice the key change at measure 47.

Progress Checkpoints

Observe students' progress in:

✓ Their ability to sing in F major and G major.

✓ Their ability to read simple rhythms in 6/8 meter.

✓ Their ability to distinguish unison from 2-part music.

MORE ABOUT...

Arranger Audrey Snyder

Audrey Snyder completed her bachelor's and master's degrees in music education from the University of Oregon and did additional postgraduate work in England. During her many successful years as a public school music teacher, she began to write choral music for her own students, publishing her first choral piece in 1978. Since that time Audrey has published numerous original choral compositions and arrangements. Widely recognized as one of the top educational choral writers today, Audrey composes music with rare beauty, simplicity and charm. She is a highly regarded educator, clinician, editor and producer.

2. Rehearse

Direct students to:

- Chant in rhythm the note names or solfège syllables from the beginning to the end of each section while maintaining a steady beat. Pay special attention to the tied notes.
- Sing each section using solfège syllables. Pause at unison sections, checking for accurate intonation and student recognition of unison and harmony.

Progress Checkpoints

Observe students' progress in:

- ✓ Their ability to distinguish between melody and harmony in each part.
- ✓ Their ability to recognize and sing the key change.
- ✓ Their ability to chant text with rhythmic accuracy.

Choral Library *Río, Río* **201**

3. Refine

Direct students to:

- Sing each part separately using solfège syllables. Pay particular attention to pitch and rhythmic accuracy.

- Combine both parts, singing one section at a time. Check for accuracy and independence of parts.

- Speak the Spanish diction in echo-style with the teacher, using appropriate word stress. Modify any words spoken incorrectly.

- Sing the song in Spanish one section at a time. Pay attention to diction, musical phrasing and word stress.

- Apply the arranger's dynamic markings. Create a true contrast between the *mezzo forte* in measures 6–21 and the *piano* at measures 22–25. The *subito piano* at measure 70 should contrast to the *fortissimo* ending, beginning in measure 72.

Progress Checkpoints

Observe students' progress in:

✓ Their ability to sing with accurate pitches and rhythms.

✓ Singing with clear Spanish diction.

✓ Using contrasting dynamics.

ASSESSMENT
Creating an Assessment Rubric

Have students:

1. Discuss the characteristics of a desirable performance of this piece, using all their knowledge of the performance techniques.

2. Design and identify the criteria by which they think an adjudicator might assess the performance, quality and effectiveness of this piece.

3. For each criterion, decided what characteristics will comprise an adequate, good, very good and excellent performance.

4. Create a rubric chart.

5. Use the rubric to assess quartets or small ensembles performing all or part of this song.

ASSESSMENT

Informal Assessment

In this lesson, students showed the ability to:

- Read melodic passages in F and G major.
- Read and perform rhythms in 6/8 meter.
- Recognize unison and 2-part passages in music.
- Create audible contrasts between dynamic levels.
- Relate literature to music.

Student Self-Assessment

Have students evaluate their individual performances based on the following:

- Diction
- Foreign Language
- Expressive Singing
- Accurate Pitch
- Accurate Rhythms

Have each student rate his/her performance of this song in the areas above on a scale of 1–5, 5 being the best.

COMMUNITY CONNECTIONS

Spanish Music in Your Community

Have students:

- Attend a concert of Spanish music in your community.
- Explore recordings of various styles of Spanish music and assess the quality of each.
- Invite a Spanish-speaking music performer, composer or other artist from your community to come to the class and discuss Spanish music with them.

Individual and Group Performance Evaluation

To further measure growth of musical skills presented in this lesson, direct students to complete the Evaluation section on page 198.

- Work with the students as they sing their parts and evaluate themselves based on the criteria given.

- Listen to the poems the class collected about rivers and help decide which one(s) could be read at a performance.

Beginning Unison, 2-Part/3-Part

CULTURAL CONNECTIONS

Characteristics of Spanish Music

Spanish music, like the music of any major cultural group, has many styles and, therefore, many different characteristics based on its function, region of origin, and musical form. Encourage students to research types of Spanish music that are different than "Río, Río" to see just how diverse the musical characteristics within one culture can be.

EXTENSION

Add Spanish-sounding instruments such as a guitar, guiro, claves and/or maracas to capture the flavor of the piece. Have students improvise on the rhythm instruments. Encourage them to use a variety of dynamics and rhythms.

TEACHING STRATEGY

Concert Etiquette

Have students:

1. Identify and exhibit appropriate concert etiquette in a variety of settings (formal concerts, information concerts, large concert halls, small concert halls, and so forth).

2. Attend a variety of live performances

3. Discuss the appropriate and inappropriate concert behaviors observed.

4. Write a short analysis of appropriate concert etiquette for each setting.

ENRICHMENT

Geography

Draw a map of Chile. Be sure to bring out the details of the rivers. Label the names and feature them with special color highlights. Decorate your map with bright colors.

CURRICULUM CONNECTIONS

Creative Writing

Have each student write a poem about a river. Poems could center around an imaginary or specific river or focus on the feelings students have when they see a river. Encourage each student to be creative and enjoy the process.

Music, Society and Culture

Have students perform additional songs representing diverse cultures, including American and Texas heritage. Go to **music.glencoe.com**, the Web site for Glencoe's choral music programs, for additional music selections students can perform.

Additional National Standards

The following National Standards are addressed through the Assessment, Extension, Enrichment and bottom-page activities:

3. Improvising melodies, variations and accompaniments. **(b)**

6. Listening to, analyzing and describing music. **(b)**

Sourwood Mountain

OVERVIEW

Composer: American Folk Song, arranged by Shirley W. McRae

Text: Traditional

Voicing: 3-Part Treble

Key: F major/G major

Meter: 2/4

Form: Strophic

Style: Southern Folk Song

Accompaniment: Piano and Flute

Programming: Americana, Folk Songs

Vocal Ranges:

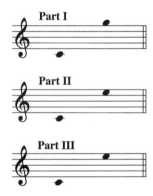

Objectives

After completing this lesson, students will be able to:

• Identify music form presented through music notation.

• Perform expressively and accurately music from diverse cultures, including American folk music.

• Read music notation, including sixteenth notes.

VOCABULARY

Have students review vocabulary in student lesson. Introduce terms found in the music. A complete glossary of terms is found on page 246 of the student book.

Sourwood Mountain

Composer: American Folk Song, arranged by Shirley W. McRae
Text: Traditional
Voicing: 3-Part Treble

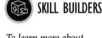

VOCABULARY
strophic
strophe
refrain
$\frac{2}{4}$ meter

Focus

• Identify musical form.

• Sing with expression and technical accuracy.

• Read rhythmic patterns with sixteenth notes.

Getting Started

Like many folk songs, "Sourwood Mountain" is **strophic,** in that *the melody repeats while the words change from verse to verse.* For example, the melody of the first **strophe,** or *verse,* is the same as both the second and third strophes. Although the melody repeats, the rhythms vary slightly to accommodate the words in each strophe. What other strophic folk songs do you know?

Another feature common to folk music is the **refrain,** *a repeated section at the end of each phrase.* In "Sourwood Mountain," the refrain is made up of the nonsense syllables, "hi-o, hi-o, diddle-i-day."

SKILL BUILDERS

To learn more about $\frac{2}{4}$ meter, see Beginning Sight-Singing, *page 59.*

◆ History and Culture

Though it is likely that the song "Sourwood Mountain" arrived with the eighteenth-century pioneers from the British Isles, its history in the United States lies in the southern Appalachian Mountains. The Appalachians form the second-largest mountain range in North America. They extend from Quebec, Canada, to Alabama. Southern Appalachia includes parts of West Virginia, Virginia, Kentucky, Tennessee, North and South Carolina, Georgia, and Alabama. This area was originally inhabited by Native Americans, including the Cherokee.

RESOURCES

Beginning Sight-Singing

Sight-Singing in F Major, pages 38–40, 60, 76–77, 118, 121–122

Sight-Singing in G Major, pages 84–89, 93

Reading 2/4 Meter, page 59

Reading Sixteenth Notes, pages 58–59, 74–75, 82–83

Teacher Resource Binder

Teaching Master 29, *Evaluating Accuracy of Intonation, Rhythm, and Diction*

Evaluation Master 8, *Evaluating Rhythmic Accuracy*

Skill Builder 29, *Singing in Three Parts*

Vocal Development 17, *Warmup: Intonation and Choral Blend*

For additional resources, see TRB Table of Contents.

Links to Learning

◆ **Vocal**

Read and perform the following example to practice three-part singing.

◆ **Theory**

$\frac{2}{4}$ **meter** is *a time signature in which there are two beats per measure and the quarter note receives the beat.* Read and perform the following examples to practice reading rhythmic patterns with sixteenth notes in $\frac{2}{4}$ meter.

Evaluation

Demonstrate how well you have learned the skills and concepts featured in the lesson "Sourwood Mountain" by completing the following:

• Find the fourth and fifth strophe in the music to show that you understand strophic form.

• Sing one strophe alone to demonstrate accurate intonation, precise rhythm, and clear diction.

• Alone or with others, read and clap the rhythmic patterns found in the Theory section above. Evaluate how well you did.

Choral Library *Sourwood Mountain* **209**

RESOURCES

Beginning Unison, 2-Part/3-Part Rehearsal/Performance CD

CD 2:17 Voices
CD 2:18 Accompaniment Only
CD 3:21 Vocal Practice Track—Part I
CD 4:22 Vocal Practice Track—Part II
CD 4:23 Vocal Practice Track—Part III

National Standards

1. Singing, alone and with others, a varied repertoire of music. **(a, b, c, d)**
5. Reading and notating music. **(a, b, c)**
6. Listening to, analyzing and describing music. **(c)**

LINKS TO LEARNING

Vocal

The Vocal section is designed to prepare students to practice three-part singing.

Have students:

• Sing each part separately.

• Combine all three parts and sing together once each part is secure.

• Listen to each other to make sure that each chord is in tune.

Theory

The Theory section is designed to prepare students to:

• Read rhythmic patterns in 2/4 meter.

• Read rhythmic patterns with sixteenth notes.

Have students:

• Tap or clap a steady pulse.

• Speak each exercise while tapping the pulse.

• Speak each exercise while feeling the pulse inside.

LESSON PLAN

Suggested Teaching Sequence and Performance Tips

1. Introduce

Direct students to:

- Read and discuss the information found in the Getting Started section on student page 208.
- Practice the vocal example, paying special attention to intonation. Allow each student to sing each of the three parts. After mastering the pitches, divide into two, then three, parts.
- Practice the rhythmic examples found in the Theory section. Encourage students to begin at a slower tempo until the rhythms are secure, and then gradually increase the speed to tempo as students are able.
- Locate each strophe in the music. (*measures 5–12, 19–26, 29–36, 43–50, 53–60*)

Progress Checkpoints

Observe students' progress in:

- ✓ Their ability to sing the chords in tune.
- ✓ Their ability to sing in three parts.
- ✓ Their ability to read the sixteenth note rhythms accurately while maintaining a steady pulse.
- ✓ Their ability to recognize each strophe in the music.

This arrangement dedicated to the
1996 North Carolina Summer Institute in Choral Art
Elementary Choir, Henry Leck, Director

Sourwood Mountain

For 3-Part Treble and Piano with Optional Flute**

Arranged by
SHIRLEY W. McRAE

American Folk Song

1. Chick-ens crow-in' on Sour-wood Moun-tain, Hi - o, hi - o, did-dle-i - day,

Get your dog and we'll go hunt-in', Hi - o, hi - o, did-dle-i - day.

* Pronounced dih-duhl-eye-day.
** Flute part found on page 217.

Copyright © 1996 Plymouth Music Co., Inc.
International Copyright Secured   All Rights Reserved

TEACHER 2 TEACHER

The simple melody and strophic arrangement of "Sourwood Mountain" provides an opportunity to focus on clear diction when singing in English.

2. Rehearse

Direct students to:

- Count the melodic rhythm for each strophe. Chant the lyrics with accurate rhythms before adding pitches, making students aware of accented and unaccented syllables. Note that the two phrases of each strophe end identically.

- Count the rhythms for non-melodic Parts II and III in strophe 3. *(measure 29)* Chant the lyrics in rhythm before adding pitches.

- Sing strophe 3 with all parts. Direct all parts to listen for the off-beat entrances in Part II found in measures 31 and 35.

- Count the rhythms for nonmelodic Part I in strophe 5. *(measure 53)* Chant the lyrics in rhythm before adding pitches.

CURRICULUM CONNECTIONS

Technology in Music

Have students:

1. Identify technology used in music (computer, midi, mp3, CD, audio/video recordings, synthesizer, sound equipment, electronic sounds, and so forth.

2. Discuss what effect technology has on music.

3. Create a musical composition using a form of technology.

4. Perform a solo or small ensemble for the class incorporating technology.

- Sing strophe 5 with all parts. Direct Part I to listen for the melody while singing their harmony part.
- Count the rhythms in the coda. *(measure 61)* Chant the lyrics and add pitches. Secure the initial pitch for Parts II and III at measure 65 by remembering their final pitch in measure 64. Drill this entrance.

Progress Checkpoints

Observe students' progress in:

✓ Their ability to sing with accurate melodic pitches and rhythms.

✓ Use of proper word stress.

✓ Exact rhythmic placement of off-beat entrances in Part II at measure 31.

✓ In-tune unisons on the downbeats of measures 53, 54, 56 in strophe 5, as well as a balanced G major triad on the final syllable in the strophe.

CURRICULUM CONNECTIONS

Geography

Have students research the geography of the Appalachian Mountains. Locate them on a map and discuss various aspects of the mountains, such as which states the range runs through, elevations, landmarks, famous Americans from the Appalachian region, etc.

'Bout as cute and twice as la - zy, Hi - o, hi - o, did-dle-i - day.

Hi, hi, did-dle-i - day.

Hi, hi, did-dle-i - day.

37 Flute

mf

3. Refine

Direct students to:

- Sing the entire song using solfège syllables and correct rhythms.
- Sing the lyrics. Form tall, rounded vowel sounds and articulate, crisp consonants.
- Create four-measure phrases.
- Sing with appropriate word stress, with unstressed syllables softer than stressed syllables.
- Use the head voice throughout, creating a lovely sound.

Progress Checkpoints

Observe students' progress in:

✓ Their ability to sing with accurate pitches and rhythms.

✓ Singing with proper diction.

✓ Their ability to shape each four-measure phrase.

✓ The use of proper syllabic stress.

✓ The use of proper tone quality.

Choral Library *Sourwood Mountain* **213**

 **Online**

MUSIC, SOCIETY AND CULTURE

Have students perform additional songs representing diverse cultures, including American and Texas heritage. Go to **music.glencoe.com**, the Web site for Glencoe's choral music programs, for additional music selections students can perform.

ASSESSMENT

Informal Assessment

In this lesson, the students showed the ability to:

- Define and locate strophic form in music.
- Sing in parts to create three-voice chords.
- Read and perform sixteenth notes in rhythmic patterns.
- Perform English text with tall, rounded vowels, correct word stress and good diction.

Student Self-Assessment

Have students evaluate their individual performances based on the following:

- Diction
- Tall Vowels
- Accurate Pitch
- Accurate Rhythms
- Correct Part-Singing

Have each student rate his/her performance of this song in the areas above on a scale of 1–5, 5 being the best.

214   Beginning Unison, 2-Part/3-Part

MORE ABOUT...

Arranger Shirley McRae

Shirley McRae is an active clinician in Orff Schulwerk and children's choirs. Her work draws upon many years of experience as an elementary school music specialist and children's choir director. Her compositions have won national awards, and she has published music for choir and a recorder method book, among other works.

214

Individual and Group Performance Evaluation

To further measure growth of musical skills presented in this lesson, direct students to complete the Evaluation section on page 209.

- Direct students to find the fourth and fifth strophe in this song.
- Direct students to choose a strophe to sing alone, making sure they sing with accurate intonation, rhythm and diction.
- Students are to choose an example from the Theory section and perform it either alone or in a small group. Guide them as they evaluate their performance, having them check for correct rhythms and how well they maintained a steady pulse.

TEACHING STRATEGY

Extra Help—Tuning Chords

To help students listen to one another, form three groups and have one student in each section choose a pitch and hold it out until everyone in the section is singing the same pitch, using a neutral syllable such as "ooh" or "ah." Point to one student from one of the sections. That student changes the group pitch, and everyone must listen and move to that pitch. Continue to point to individual students in each of the groups, waiting each time until that group has tuned to the new pitch. The chords will be very interesting, and sometimes dissonant, which requires even more careful listening. Encourage soft singing, and listening to one another within and between each section.

EXTENSION

The melody of "Sourwood Mountain" is pentatonic, in that it contains only the notes F, G, A, C, D. Notate this pentatonic scale on the board, placing C and D both above and below F so it reads: C, D, F, G, A, C, D. Point and sing a three- to four-note motive and have the students echo it. When the students are secure with echo singing, only point, allowing them to create the musical sounds independently. Begin with a three-note motive and progressively expand the length to seven to ten notes. Ask a student to come point a motive while the class sings.

Additional National Standards

The following National Standards are addressed through the Assessment, Extension, Enrichment and bottom-page activities:

7. Evaluating music and music performances. **(a, b)**

8. Understanding relationships between music, the other arts and disciplines outside the arts. **(b)**

9. Understanding music in relation to history and culture. **(a)**

Sourwood Mountain

FLUTE

Southern Folk Song
Arranged by SHIRLEY W. McRAE

Copyright © 1996 Plymouth Music Co., Inc.
International Copyright Secured   All Rights Reserved

Choral Library *Sourwood Mountain*   **217**

Music, Society and Culture

Have students perform additional songs representing diverse cultures, including American and Texas heritage. Go to **music.glencoe.com**, the Web site for Glencoe's choral music programs, for additional music selections students can perform.

Tinga Layo

OVERVIEW

Composer: West Indies Folk Song, arranged by Cristi Cary Miller

Text: Traditional

Voicing: 3-Part Mixed

Key: C/D Major

Meter: 4/4

Form: ABA' ABA' C A"B'A'''

Style: West Indies Folk Song

Accompaniment: Piano, Percussion

Programming: Multicultural

Vocal Ranges:

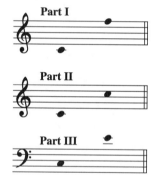

Objectives

After completing this lesson, students will be able to:

- Demonstrate ensemble performance techniques by singing in three-part harmony.
- Identify and perform music symbols referring to dynamics.
- Perform music representative of diverse cultures, including music of the West Indies.

VOCABULARY

Have students review vocabulary in student lesson. Introduce terms found in the music. A complete glossary of terms is found on page 246 of the student book.

218

Tinga Layo

Composer: West Indies Folk Song, arranged by Cristi Cary Miller

Text: Traditional

Voicing: 3-Part Mixed

VOCABULARY

calypso

chord

harmony

dynamics

Focus

- Sing in three-part harmony.
- Identify and perform standard notation for dynamics.
- Perform music that represents calypso of the West Indies.

Getting Started

Perhaps you know the song "Tinga Layo." It is a popular children's folk song from the Caribbean and a perfect example of calypso music. **Calypso** is *a style of music that comes from the West Indies and features syncopated rhythms and comical lyrics.* In this calypso song, you will sing about a donkey that walks, talks, and eats with a fork and spoon!

◆ History and Culture

The Caribbean region (West Indies) encompasses a chain of islands stretching over 2,000 miles from the southern coast of Florida to the northern coast of Venezuela, South America. Historically, the West Indies are known for producing sugar cane, coconuts, and bananas. Today some of these islands, which include Barbados, Puerto Rico, and the Virgin Islands, are popular tourist destinations. They provide tropical paradises and feature exciting music, lush vegetation, beautiful beaches, and crystal-clear seas.

 SPOTLIGHT

To learn more about the changing voice, see page 231.

RESOURCES

Beginning Sight-Singing

Sight-Singing in C Major, pages 7–12, 14–17, 27–29, 116–117

Sight-Singing in D Major, pages 102–109

Reading Syncopation, pages 160–161

Teacher Resource Binder

Evaluation Master 14, *Performance Evaluation: Part Singing*

Skill Builder 1, *Building Harmony*

Skill Builder 24, *Rhythm Challenge Using Syncopation*

Skill Builder 29, *Singing in Three Parts*

Kodály 5, *Music Reading: Pitch*

For additional resources, see TRB Table of Contents.

Links to Learning

◆ **Vocal**

When *three or more notes are sung together*, a **chord** is formed and harmony is created. **Harmony** occurs *when two or more different notes or melodies are sung at the same time*. Practice the following chords to develop the skill of singing in harmony.

◆ **Theory**

Read and perform the following examples to practice reading rhythmic patterns with syncopation.

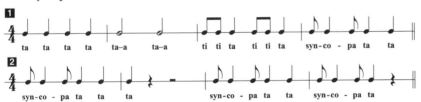

◆ **Artistic Expression**

One way to add expression to a musical performance is through the use of **dynamics**, or *symbols that indicate to a musician how loud or soft to sing or play*. In the Vocal examples above, sing example 1 *mf*, or *mezzo forte* (medium loud); sing example 2 *mp*, or *mezzo piano* (medium soft); and sing example 3 *f*, or *forte* (loud).

Evaluation

Demonstrate how well you have learned the skills featured in the lesson "Tinga Layo" by completing the following:

• In a trio with one singer on each part, perform measures 4–12 of "Tinga Layo." How well were you able to sing in three-part harmony?

• Sing measures 5–24. As you perform, adjust your dynamic levels as marked at measures 5–6 (*mp*), measures 12–13 (*f*), measures 16–17 (*mf*), and measures 20–21 (*mp*).

Choral Library *Tinga Layo* **219**

RESOURCES

Beginning Unison, 2-Part/3-Part Rehearsal/Performance CD

CD 2:19 Voices

CD 2:20 Accompaniment Only

CD 3:22 Vocal Practice Track—Part I

CD 4:24 Vocal Practice Track—Part II

CD 4:25 Vocal Practice Track—Part III

National Standards

1. Singing, alone and with others, a varied repertoire of music. **(a, b, c, d)**

5. Reading and notating music. **(a, b, c)**

9. Understanding music in relation to history and culture. **(a, b)**

LINKS TO LEARNING

Vocal

The Vocal section is designed to prepare students to form chords and sing in three-part harmony.

Have students:

• Sing each part separately.

• Combine all three parts and sing together once each part is secure.

• Listen to each other to make sure that each chord is in tune.

Theory

The Theory section is designed to prepare students to read and perform syncopated rhythms in 4/4 meter.

Have students:

• Tap or clap a steady pulse.

• Speak each exercise while tapping the pulse.

• Speak each exercise while feeling the pulse inside.

Artistic Expression

The Artistic Expression section is designed to prepare students to use dynamics to enhance their musical performance of "Tinga Layo."

Have students:

• Sing the Vocal section three times, each time observing each dynamic marking as directed.

LESSON PLAN

Suggested Teaching Sequence and Performance Tips

1. Introduce

Direct students to:

- Read and discuss the information found in the Getting Started section on student page 218.
- Practice singing the chords in three-part harmony as shown in the Vocal section. Direct students to listen to one another so each chord is in tune.
- Locate every instance of these three chord progressions in the score. *(Progression #1: measures 7–8, 15–16, 19–20; Progression #2: measures 11–12, 23–24; Progression #3: measures 13–14, 17–18)*
- Practice reading syncopated rhythms as shown in the Theory section.

Tinga Layo

For 3-Part Mixed and Piano with Optional Percussion**

Arranged by
CRISTI CARY MILLER

West Indies Folk Song

*Pronounced "ting-gah lay-oh."

**Percussion part found on pages 229 and 230.

Copyright © 2000 by HAL LEONARD CORPORATION
International Copyright Secured   All Rights Reserved

220   Beginning Unison, 2-Part/3-Part

TEACHER 2 TEACHER

With its Calypso beat, "Tinga Layo" is an energetic and fun piece to perform. Include the optional percussion instruments to give this folk song a true island flavor.

- Locate in the score every instance of the syncopated texts "Run, little donkey, run" *(measures 7–8, 11–12, 23–24, 31–32, 35–36, 38–39, 41–42, 45–46, 53–54, 56–57)* and "Tinga layo." *(measures 13, 15, 17, 19, 47, 48, 49)*
- Find in the score the other texts that are syncopated. *(e.g., measures 5–6 in Part I, measures 29–30 in Part III)*

Progress Checkpoints

Observe students' progress in:

✓ Singing three-part harmonic progressions.

✓ Their ability to locate the progressions in the music.

✓ Reading and performing syncopated rhythms.

✓ Their ability to locate syncopated rhythmic patterns in the music.

EXTENSION

Improvise!

Have students memorize the chord progression in the passage from measures 47–50. Sing the pitches that occur on the downbeat of each measure. (If desired, in measure 49, Part II may sing E followed by C# so as to include the leading tone.) Sustain each chord for four beats. Repeat so as to create a continuous loop. Provide guidelines for the improvising singer: (1) Begin each chord with the pitch your part is singing; (2) Add two to three more pitches per measure in a 4/4 pattern; (3) Relax and remember that this is spontaneous music-making. Repeat often with other songs so students can become more comfortable with the improvisational process.

2. Rehearse

Direct students to:

- Count the rhythms for Part II in measures 5–24.
- Sight-sing the melody first presented in Part II, measures 5–24. Notice the similarities between measures 5–8 and 9–12, as well as the repetition of measures 9–12 in measures 21–24. Label the ABA′ form whose sections begin at measure 5, measure 13, and measure 21.
- Count the rhythms for Part III in measures 29–38. Keep counting through the measures of rest. When accurate, add pitches and text.
- Count rhythms for Parts I and II in measures 31–38. When accurate, add pitches and text.
- Chant the text with all parts on their own line in measures 29–38. Ensure that entrances are exact, particularly Part III in measures 38. When accurate, add pitches.

TEACHING STRATEGY

Reading Rhythms

The Conga Drums part provides a wonderful opportunity to teach reading rhythms and placing accents. Notated in 4/4 meter, it may be easier to begin by thinking in 8/8 meter. In eight, the accents in measures 1–3 fall on beats 1, 4 and 7, creating three groups. The first and second group each contain three counts, leaving the third group with only two. Try counting 1-2-3, 1-2-3, 1-2, so that all the 1's receive the same accented weight.

- When secure, add Part I entering with the melody at measure 38 and continue.
- At measure 40, chant the rhythms for Parts II and III, noting that when both parts sing, they share a text and rhythms. Chant texts in rhythm, adding pitches when secure.
- Begin at measure 38 with all parts together.
- Return to measure 5 to learn Parts I and III. When rhythms and pitches are secure, put all three parts together.

Progress Checkpoints

Observe student's progress in:
- ✓ Their ability to identify ABA form.
- ✓ Their use of proper vocal tone to sing the melody.
- ✓ Their ability to sing in three-part harmony.
- ✓ Their rhythmic precision, particularly in the syncopated patterns.

3. Refine

Direct students to:

- Sing the entire song using solfège syllables and correct rhythms.

- Apply the arranger's dynamic markings. Create a true contrast between the *mezzo piano* in measures 5–12 and the *forte* at measure 13. Similarly, create a true contrast between Part III in measure 29 and Parts I & II at measure 31.

- Sustain with energy and forward momentum the longer rhythmic values; e.g., whole notes and half notes.

- Articulate syncopated rhythms and shorter rhythmic values with a lightness, as if a long staccato.

- Sing gently the final syllable of a phrase when it is a downbeat quarter note, as in measures 8, 16 and 50. Sustain the full rhythmic value and avoid "punching" the syllable.

Progress Checkpoints

Observe students' progress in:

- ✓ The use of accurate pitches and rhythms.
- ✓ Their ability to sing with proper diction.
- ✓ Giving an energetic presentation of the text.
- ✓ Making an audible contrast in dynamics.
- ✓ Placing articulations that lighten shorter rhythmic values and sustain longer ones.

224   Beginning Unison, 2-Part/3-Part

ASSESSMENT

Informal Assessment

In this lesson, the students showed the ability to:

- Read and perform syncopated rhythms, as well as locate them in a score.
- Sing chord progressions in three-part harmony, as well as locate them in a score.
- Create audible contrasts between dynamic levels.
- Perform music that represents the calypso style of the West Indies.

Student Self-Assessment

Have students evaluate their individual performances based on the following:

- Posture
- Breath Management
- Diction
- Expressive Singing
- Correct Part-Singing

Have each student rate his/her performance of this song in the areas above on a scale of 1–5, 5 being the best.

CURRICULUM CONNECTIONS

Geography

Although many of the West Indies islands are now independent countries, all were former territories of Spain, the United Kingdom, France, the Netherlands, or the United States. Direct students to locate the West Indies on a map.

Individual Performance Assessment

To further measure growth of musical skills presented in this lesson, direct students to complete the Evaluation section on page 219.

- Direct students to form trios and sing measures 4–12 of the song. Assist them as they evaluate how well they were able to stay in tune and on their part.
- Have the students sing each section of the song from measures 5–24, applying the dynamic contrasts as marked in the music. Make sure there is a distinct and audible contrast between each dynamic.

MORE ABOUT...

The History of Calypso Music

Calypso music is probably derived from the carnival folk music of Trinidad, West Indies. Song themes are usually stories of local interest. Originally, the only music accompaniment to calypso songs might have been a guitar, maracas or a combination of instruments. Around 1945, singers in calypso bands began to include steel drums, which is now a characteristic sound in calypso music. A common vocal technique in this style of music is the shifting of emphasis onto unexpected syllables of words. Singer Harry Belafonte is a well-known musician who sings in the calypso style.

VOCAL DEVELOPMENT

The Cambiata Voice

As a boy's voice changes, it reaches a stage called the cambiata voice, which begins to stretch lower but is still able to sing into the higher pitches of the boy's voice. It is important not to stretch this voice too low, as it can become strained. It is fascinating for young men to track their development through the year as they are able to sing lower and lower.

Music, Society and Culture

Have students perform additional songs representing diverse cultures, including American and Texas heritage. Go to **music.glencoe.com**, the Web site for Glencoe's choral music programs, for additional music selections students can perform.

228 Beginning Unison, 2-Part/3-Part

Additional National Standards

The following National Standards are addressed through the Assessment, Extension, Enrichment and bottom-page activities:

3. Improvising melodies, variations and accompaniments. **(b)**

7. Evaluating music and music performances. **(b)**

8. Understanding relationships between music, the other arts and disciplines outside the arts. **(b)**

9. Understanding music in relation to history and culture. **(a, b)**

Tinga Layo

PERCUSSION
(Cowbell, Maracas, Conga Drums)

West Indies Folk Song
Arranged by
CRISTI CARY MILLER

Copyright © 2000 by HAL LEONARD CORPORATION
International Copyright Secured   All Rights Reserved

Music, Society and Culture

Have students perform additional songs representing diverse cultures, including American and Texas heritage. Go to **music.glencoe.com**, the Web site for Glencoe's choral music programs, for additional music selections students can perform.

SPOTLIGHT

Changing Voice

As we grow in size and maturity, we don't always grow at the same rate. Just look around your school or neighborhood. Some thirteen-year-olds tower over others, while some are quite small.

As the voice matures, it changes in both pitch and **timbre** *(tone quality)*. Just like growing in stature, this process is not the same for every person. One person's voice might drop an octave almost overnight, while another person's might not seem to have changed at all.

The Male Voice

As a young male singer, you will face several challenges as your voice matures. Certain pitches that were once easy to sing suddenly may be out of your vocal range. While every voice change is unique, many male singers progress through several identifiable stages:

1. The voice is a treble voice with no obvious signs of changing.

2. The upper range sounds slightly breathy or hoarse.

3. The singer is able to sing lower pitches than before. Higher pitches continue to sound breathy. The speaking and singing voices are noticeably lower. There is an obvious "break" around middle C.

4. The voice "settles" into **Bass** *(the lowest-sounding male voice)* or "rises" to **Tenor** *(the highest-sounding male voice)*. Higher pitches can now be sung in **falsetto,** *a register in the male voice that extends far above the natural high voice.*

With practice and attention to the principles of good singing, you can get through this transition without too much difficulty.

The Female Voice

As a young female singer, you will not face the same challenges that young male singers face. However, your voice will go through changes, too.

Between the ages of eleven and sixteen, you might notice breathiness in your vocal tone, difficulty in moving between your chest voice and head voice, and a general lack of vocal resonance.

By using the good vocal techniques of posture, breath and vowel formation, you can establish all the qualities necessary for success. You should use your full vocal range and gain experience in singing both **Alto** *(the lowest-sounding female voice)* and **Soprano** *(the highest-sounding female voice)*, since your actual voice category may not be evident until you reach your middle-to-late teens.

Spotlight *Changing Voice* **231**

RESOURCES

Teacher Resource Binder

Teaching Master 30, *Checking on My Changing Voice*
Reference 7, *Building a Musical Vocabulary*
Reference 25, *What's My Vocal Range?*

National Standards

7. Evaluating music and musical performances. **(a, b)**

CHANGING VOICE

Objectives

- Demonstrate characteristic vocal timbre individually and in groups.

Suggested Teaching Sequence

Direct students to:

- Read Spotlight on Changing Voice on student page 231 and identify the four stages of the male changing voice and the characteristics of the voice in each stage.

- Test their vocal ranges to determine their highest and lowest comfortable singing note. Check their ranges throughout the year.

- Discuss changes that occur in a female changing voice.

- Describe the four main voice categories for singers: Soprano, Alto, Tenor and Bass.

- Record themselves singing "America" at the beginning of the year, the middle of the year and the end of the year. Compare the three recordings and document changes in the voice that have occurred during the course of the year.

Progress Checkpoints

Observe students' progress in:

✓ Their ability to identify the four stages of change in the male voice.

✓ Their ability to discuss the changes that occur in the female changing voice.

✓ Their ability to discover the progress of change in their individual voice.

Unity

OVERVIEW

Composer: Glorraine B. Moone and Rev. Freddie Washington, arranged by Daniel M. Cason II

Text: Psalm 133:1 with additional text by Glorraine B. Moone

Voicing: SSA

Key: F major

Meter: 4/4

Form: AABB′

Style: Gospel

Accompaniment: Piano

Programming: Multicultural

Vocal Ranges:

Soprano I

Soprano II

Alto

OBJECTIVES

After completing this lesson, students will be able to:

• Perform music while demonstrating fundamental skills.

• Read music notation, including sixteenth notes.

• Perform music representative of different genres, including the gospel style.

VOCABULARY

Have students review vocabulary in student lesson. Introduce terms found in the music. A complete glossary of terms is found on page 246 of the student book.

Unity

Composer: Glorraine B. Moone and Rev. Freddie Washington, arranged by Daniel M. Cason II

Text: Psalm 133:1, with additional text by Glorraine B. Moone

Voicing: SSA

VOCABULARY

gospel music

rote

chest voice

Focus

• Extend your vocal range.

• Read and perform rhythmic patterns with sixteenth notes.

• Perform music in the gospel style.

SKILL BUILDERS

To learn more about dotted eighth and sixteenth note combinations, see Beginning Sight-Singing, page 92.

Getting Started

Unity can be defined as "many standing together as one." Throughout history, people have demonstrated unity through both good and bad times. On a more personal basis, friends often stand together united as one. By singing "Unity," you can express the importance of unity, peace, and friendship in your life.

◆ History and Culture

Gospel music is *religious music that originated in the African American churches of the South.* During the early 1900s, the gospel sound spread to other parts of the United States. As many African Americans migrated to the North and the West, they took with them their songs of praise—their gospel music.

Originally, gospel music was taught by **rote,** or *taught by singing a song over and over again.* Today, many printed arrangements exist, making gospel music accessible to more people. In this arrangement, the composer draws from the biblical text, "Behold how good and how pleasant it is for brethren to dwell together in unity," and combines it with her own text. The result is an expressive song that calls for unity among all people.

On page 168 in this book, you will find the lesson to "Hine ma tov," a Hebrew folk song. It is based on the same text as "Unity." Listen to both songs and discuss the ways in which two different cultures have chosen to express a similar theme of unity and peace.

RESOURCES

Beginning Sight-Singing

Sight-Singing in F Major, pages 38–40, 60, 76–77, 118, 121–122

Reading Eighth and Sixteenth Note Combinations, page 92.

Teacher Resource Binder

Teaching Master 31, *What's My Vocal Range?*

Teaching Master 32, *African American Influences on Music*

Skill Builder 27, *Rhythm Challenge in 4/4 Meter*

Reference 7, *Building a Musical Vocabulary*

Reference 20, *Rhythm Challenge Chart*

For additional resources, see TRB Table of Contents.

Links to Learning

◆ **Vocal**

The melody in "Unity" begins in the **chest voice,** or *the lower part of your vocal range.* Perform the following example to gently develop and expand your chest voice. Keep the "ah" vowel relaxed and not forced.

mee____ ah_____   mee____ ah_____ (etc.)

◆ **Theory**

Perform the following sixteenth-note patterns used in "Unity." Form two groups. At the same time, one group pats the steady quarter notes while the other group taps the rhythm. Keep the tempo slow and relaxed to reflect the gospel style. Switch roles.

Evaluation

Demonstrate how well you have learned the skills and concepts featured in lesson "Unity" by completing the following:

- Sing the Vocal example above. With the help of your teacher, find the lowest note in your own vocal range that can be sung relaxed, sustained, and with accurate pitch.

- Perform measures 12–19 of "Unity" in small groups to show the correct usage of the sixteenth-note rhythmic patterns.

- African American history and culture are the foundation for many important musical styles, including spirituals, jazz, gospel, rap, and rhythmn and blues. Make a chart of the songs that you know for each style of music listed above. Sing one of the songs and demonstrate the style for your friends.

Choral Library *Unity* **233**

RESOURCES

Beginning Unison, 2-Part/3-Part Rehearsal/Performance CD

CD 2:21 Voices

CD 2:22 Accompaniment Only

CD 3:23 Vocal Practice Track—Sop. I

CD 3:24 Vocal Practice Track—Sop. II

CD 4:26 Vocal Practice Track—Alto

National Standards

1. Singing, alone and with others, a varied repertoire of music. **(a, b, c, d)**

5. Reading and notating music. **(a, b, c)**

7. Evaluating music and music performances. **(b)**

9. Understanding music in relation to history and culture. **(a, b)**

LINKS TO LEARNING

Vocal

The Vocal section is designed to prepare students to extend their vocal ranges by developing their chest voices.

Have students:

- Begin at the middle of their range and gradually work their way down to the bottom of their range.

- Take special care not to force the lower notes, but to keep the "ah" vowel relaxed.

Theory

The Theory section is designed to prepare students to read rhythms that use eighth and sixteenth note combinations.

Have students:

- Form two groups as directed in the lesson.

- Make sure the pulse is relaxed, but steady, to reflect the gospel style.

- Clap or tap the patterns accurately.

- Reverse roles when secure.

LESSON PLAN

Suggested Teaching Sequence and Performance Tips

1. Introduce

Direct the students to:

- Read and discuss the information found in the Getting Started section on student page 232.
- Follow along and actively listen to measures 2–10 of the vocal line to determine if this song begins in the upper (head voice) or lower (chest voice).
- Find and identify the lowest pitch in the phrase. *(measures 3–6 ledger line A is the lowest pitch)*
- Practice singing the vocal warm-up in a gentle, relaxed and peaceful tone quality. Start in D major, descending to A major.
- Hum measures 3–10 with a relaxed and open throat while feeling a forward facial buzz. Strive for a smooth transition to head voice at first space F.
- Sing the first and second endings on text.
- Read and practice the rhythmic examples found in the Theory section.
- Locate and define the various repeat signs and endings of measures 19–22.

Unity

For SSA and Piano

Arranged and Scored by
DANIEL M. CASON II

Words from Psalm 133:1
Additional text by GLORRAINE B. MOONE
Music by GLORRAINE B. MOONE
and REV. FREDDIE WASHINGTON

Copyright © 1989 by Professionals for Christ Publications, Post Office Box 3800-F, Birmingham, AL 35208
The Exclusive Distributor Of This Arrangement: Plymouth Music Co., Inc.
170 N.E. 33rd Street, Ft. Lauderdale, FL 33334
International Copyright Secured   Made in U.S.A.   All Rights Reserved

234   Beginning Unison, 2-Part/3-Part

"Unity" is a smooth, relaxed gospel piece. Consider adding drums and bass to your performance. Encourage the pianist to feel free to embellish and improvise.

Progress Checkpoints

Observe students' progress in:

✓ Their ability to use a relaxed and accurate vocal tone in their chest voice.

✓ Their ability to locate and sing the first and second endings.

✓ Their ability to read and perform rhythmic patterns with eighth and sixteenth note combinations.

2. Rehearse

Direct students to:

- Chant, then sing, measures 12–19. Bring out moving tones in Soprano II and Alto lines.

- Have students identify the AABB' form. (*Note: Section A measures 1–10 and repeated with second ending. Section B measures 12–19 and repeated with special endings.*)

- Create forward-moving phrases in the B sections by applying a slight crescendo to all half and dotted half notes.

- Sing measures 20–22 in three parts.

Progress Checkpoints

Observe students' progress in:

✓ The correct use of a variety of repeat signs and endings.

✓ The correct identification of AABB' form.

✓ Their ability to sing in three-part harmony.

HISTORICAL CONNECTIONS

Compare and Contrast

Compare the song "Unity" with "We Shall Overcome" from the 1960s civil rights movement. Discuss how the two songs written 30 years apart express a similar message. What is the same or different about these songs? (Both compositions are based on a single repeated motive. Both begin slowly and develop with intensity. "Unity" has a more driving rhythm, encouraging people to pull together. "We Shall Overcome" has a smoother, more reflective style.)

3. Refine

Direct students to:

- Sing the entire song applying the indicated breath marks, dynamics and gospel style.

- Have students suggest ways to create variation in the repeated section. *(measures 12–19)* Apply these suggestions to the song. *(Variations could include solo improvisations on sustained beat, hand claps and dynamic contrasts.)*

- Articulate the text in the lower register of the voice in a light tone with accurate pitch. Avoid a heavy chest voice sound.

Progress Checkpoints

Observe students' progress in:

✓ The use of audible contrasting dynamics.

✓ The effective communication of the text.

✓ The ability to perform contrasting repeated sections.

✓ The correct use of chest voice.

ASSESSMENT

Informal Assessment

In this lesson, students showed the ability to:

- Sing appropriately in chest voice to allow shifts into head voice.

- Read and perform eighth and sixteenth note combinations.

- Sing in three-part harmony in an appropriate gospel style.

236   Beginning Unison, 2-Part/3-Part

CULTURAL CONNECTIONS

Gospel Style

Gospel music is a genre of the twentieth century, originating with the sacred songs of the African-American churches of South. Gospel singers have been known to take simple melodies and vocally embellish them, such as using full falsetto voices, shouting, humming, growling, moaning, whispering, crying or screaming. Fancy melismas, syncopated rhythms, blue notes and repeated fragments of the text are musical ways of improvising a gospel song. Much of the blues and soul styles found in today's pop music can be traced to the gospel style.

u - ni - ty,—— Lord, we pray for

u - ni - ty,—— Lord, we pray for

1, 2, 3, etc.

u - ni - ty.

Final ending

u - ni - ty.

u - ni - ty.

u - ni - ty.

8va

(Repeat as desired)
last time poco rit.

Lord, we pray for u - ni - ty.

last time poco rit.

Lord, we pray for u - ni - ty.

last time poco rit.

Additional National Standards

The following National Standards are addressed through the Assessment, Extension, Enrichment and bottom-page activities:

3. Improvising melodies, variations and accompaniments. **(b, c)**

Student Self-Assessment

Have students evaluate their individual performances based on the following:

- Diction
- Phrasing
- Expressive Singing
- Posture
- Accurate Rhythms

Have each student rate his/her performance of this song in the areas above on a scale of 1–5, 5 being the best.

Individual and Group Performance Evaluation

To further measure growth of musical skills presented in this lesson, direct students to complete the Evaluation section on page 233.

- Aid each student in charting the lowest pitch in his/her vocal range by singing the exercise in the Vocal section.
- Direct students to form small groups and perform the eighth and sixteenth note combinations found in the song.
- Aid the class in brainstorming and listing songs they know that can trace their origins to African American history and culture.

EXTENSION

Improvisation

To "improvise" means to "make something up on the spot." It is a key element in many styles of music from the African American culture, including gospel, jazz and rap music. A performer can improvise both melodic and harmonic variations, as well as changes in text.

Encourage students to create a solo vocal improvisational line over the B section of the song.

Yonder Come Day

OVERVIEW

Composer: Georgia Sea Islands Spiritual, arranged by Judith Cook Tucker

Text: Traditional, with additional words by Judith Cook Tucker

Voicing: 3-Part, Any Combination

Key: D major

Meter: 4/4

Form: AA'A"A'''A"

Style: African American Folk Song

Accompaniment: Optional Piano

Programming: Americana program, Concert Opener, Thematic programming

Vocal Ranges:

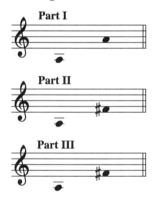

OBJECTIVES

After completing this lesson, students will be able to:

- Sing while demonstrating good breath support.
- Evaluate the effectiveness of musical performances.
- Perform music from the Georgia Sea Islands.

VOCABULARY

Have students review vocabulary in student lesson. Introduce terms found in the music. A complete glossary of terms is found on page 246 of the student book.

238

Yonder Come Day

Composer: Georgia Sea Islands Spiritual, arranged by Judith Cook Tucker
Text: Traditional, with additional words by Judith Cook Tucker
Voicing: 3-Part, Any Combination

VOCABULARY

body percussion

a cappella

breath support

patsch

SPOTLIGHT

To learn more about breath management, see page 21.

Focus

- Sing with good breath support.
- Evaluate the quality and effectiveness of performances.
- Perform music from the Georgia Sea Islands.

Getting Started

What kind of games do you enjoy playing? What kind of games do you think children played many years ago before there was electricity? Possibly, the children played "Kick the Can" or "Hide and Seek." At other times, they might have played singing games. Often, while singing, they would add **body percussion** by *clapping, stepping, or slapping their thighs.* Make a game of "Yonder Come Day" by adding the suggested body percussion movements, or make up your own!

◆ History and Culture

"Yonder Come Day" comes from the Georgia Sea Islands, which are located along the outer banks of Georgia. From the late 1700s until the Civil War, slaves worked on the plantations found on these islands. Geographically, the slaves were cut off from the mainland, as connecting bridges were not built until many years later. As a result, the rich African culture, songs, and games were preserved. The native people developed their own language, a mixture of English and African dialect known as *Gullah.* Their songs were traditionally sung **a cappella,** or *without instruments.* In place of instruments, a common practice was the use of body percussion to accompany these songs.

238   Beginning Unison, 2-Part/3-Part

RESOURCES

Beginning Sight-Singing

Sight-Singing in D Major, pages 102–109

Teacher Resource Binder

Evaluation Master 1, *Accuracy in Performance*

Evaluation Master 4, *Checking Out Phrasing*

Vocal Development 13, *Posture and Breathing*

Reference 7, *Building a Musical Vocabulary*

For additional resources, see TRB Table of Contents.

Links to Learning

◆ Vocal

Breath support, or *a constant airflow,* is necessary to produce sound for singing. Perform the following exercise to help develop this skill.

> Breathe in air through an imaginary straw. Exhale on a "hiss." First inhale and exhale over 6 counts, then 10 counts, then 12.

For more practice, place the palm of one hand three or four inches from your mouth. As you sing the following example, you should feel a steady stream of warm air on your palm. Then take your hand away, but continue to sing in the manner above.

◆ Artistic Expression

To develop artistry through movement, perform the opening phrase of "Yonder Come Day" (measures 3–10) while doing the body percussion movements indicated below. The word **patsch** means *to slap your hands on your thighs.*

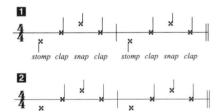

Evaluation

Demonstrate how well you have learned the skills and concepts featured in the lesson "Yonder Come Day" by completing the following:

- To show that you can sing with appropriate breath support, sing measures 3–10, taking a breath only at the end of measure 6.

- With the assistance of your teacher, videotape your class performing "Yonder Come Day." View the video and evaluate how well you were able to use the body percussion movements during your performance.

Vocal

The Vocal section is designed to prepare students to sing with proper breath support.

Have students:

- Breathe in air through an imaginary straw as directed.

- Sing the example at a moderate tempo, on one breath, once they are able to exhale over the full 12 counts.

Artistic Expression

The Artistic Expression section is designed to prepare students to add movement and body percussion to their performance of "Yonder Come Day."

Have students:

- Use body percussion expressively to support the musical performance of the composition.

- Create their own movements as they sing the song.

RESOURCES

Beginning Unison, 2-Part/3-Part Rehearsal/Performance CD

CD 2:23 Voices

CD 2:24 Accompaniment Only

CD 3:25 Vocal Practice Track—Part I

CD 4:27 Vocal Practice Track—Part II

CD 4:28 Vocal Practice Track—Part III

National Standards

1. Singing, alone and with others, a varied repertoire of music. **(a, b, c, d)**

5. Reading and notating music. **(a, b, c)**

7. Evaluating music and music performances. **(b)**

9. Understanding music in relation to history and culture. **(a, c)**

LESSON PLAN

Suggested Teaching Sequence and Performance Tips

1. Introduce

Direct students to:

- Read and discuss the information found in the Getting Started section on student page 238.
- Read and practice performing the body percussion used in this song as found in the Artistic Expression section.
- Perform the body percussion as a full ensemble and also in small groups.
- Apply information from Getting Started to the performance of the body percussion. ("How would the motions and sounds change if the day were stormy? Cold? Blazing hot?")

Progress Checkpoints

Observe students' progress in:

- ✓ Their ability to establish and maintain a steady beat.
- ✓ Performing body percussion with musical and stylistic sensitivity.
- ✓ Their ability to change the expressiveness of the body percussion in response to changing performance contexts.

Yonder Come Day

For 3-Part, Any Combination, a cappella

Arranged by
JUDITH COOK TUCKER

Based on the traditional
Georgia Sea Islands Spiritual
Additional words and music by
JUDITH COOK TUCKER

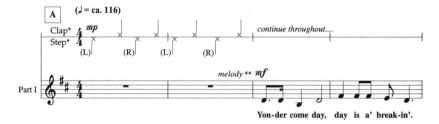

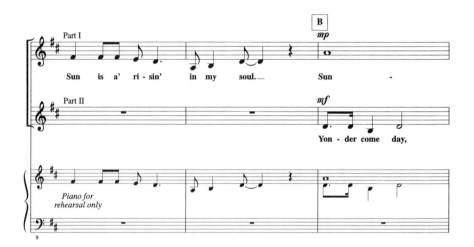

*Begin with step/clap for two measures.
**Sing melody once or twice through in unison before layering in parts.

© 1985 Judith Cook Tucker
All Rights Reserved

240 Beginning Unison, 2-Part/3-Part

TEACHER2TEACHER

Use "Yonder Come Day" to focus on developing and building part-singing skills and vocal independence. Have the students learn and sing each of the three independent vocal lines before designating specific lines for individuals and/or sections.

*At D.S., repeat Section C as many times as desired. On the last repeat, observe ritard and hold last note.

2. Rehearse

Direct students to:

- Analyze the score and identify body percussion (pages 240, 243).
- Individually read, practice and perform the body percussion in different-sized groups.
- Perform the body percussion beginning in measure 1 with the CD. Repeat and only perform the body percussion in measures 27–34.
- Read and perform the melody in the Vocal section.
- Use the exercises in the Vocal section to develop and apply breath support.
- Use the score and find and perform Part III. *(measures 19–26 with variation at the end)*
- Divide into two groups and perform Part III and body percussion with the CD.
- Divide into two groups and sing Parts I and II with the CD, both with and without the music.
- Divide into three groups and sing Parts I, II, and III with and without the score and CD.
- Add body percussion and perform again.

Progress Checkpoints

Observe students' progress in:

- ✓ Aural and music reading skills are evident when performing.
- ✓ Their ability to perform with enhanced breath support.

EXTENSION

Create Additional Melodies or Rhythms

Partner songs lend themselves to adding additional "partners." As students become more familiar with "Yonder Come Day," some may do what students have done for years: create new parts, words, etc. If you observe this taking place, provide a structured opportunity for students to add melodic or rhythmic parts to the song. Have students notate their "partners" and then teach them to the class. Assess their efforts in terms of being musically accurate in terms of notation and style.

3. Refine

Direct the students to:

- Perform each rhythmic value accurately so as to help avoid "pushing" or "rushing" the tempo.
- Accurately perform and sustain the rhythms in the spoken section, page 243, top line, measures 27–34, especially the syn-CO-pa passages as appropriate.
- Emphasize performing with a strong-beat/weak-beat feeling as they experience the steady pulse when performing.
- Articulate clear diction when performing spoken and sung passages.
- Listen to and adjust their dynamics to help maintain balance between individual parts when performing. ("Which part should be the most prominent? Which in the background?")
- Establish and maintain breath support when singing, especially when there are long tones.

Progress Checkpoints

Observe students' progress in:

- ✓ Their ability to maintain a steady tempo throughout a performance.
- ✓ Keeping good breath support to help maintain vocal energy when singing and speaking.
- ✓ Their ability to sing in tune throughout the song.

242 Beginning Unison, 2-Part/3-Part

ENRICHMENT

Expanding Musical Expression

View a DVD of the group Stomp to see examples of how repetitive rhythms and percussive sounds are becoming more and more a part of the musical landscape. What are the instruments they are playing? How important is body movement to the musical ideas being presented? (Brooms, hubcaps, trash cans, basketballs, dumpsters, cards, buckets, are some of the sources of sounds heard in this DVD. Body movement with clapping and stomping are important to the musical as well as visual aspect of the performance.)

Additional National Standards

The following National Standards are addressed through the Assessment, Extension, Enrichment and bottom-page activities:

3. Improvising melodies, variations and accompaniments. **(b, c)**

6. Listening to, analyzing and describing music. **(c)**

8. Understanding relationships between music, the other arts and disciplines outside the arts. **(a)**

ASSESSMENT

Informal Assessment

In this lesson, students showed the ability to:

- Sing with good breath support.
- Perform body percussion expressively.
- Self-evaluate their performances.
- Learn a song through a kinesthetic, aural and visual approach.

Student Self-Assessment

Have students evaluate their individual performances based on the following:

- Diction
- Breath Support
- Posture
- Accurate Pitch
- Accurate Rhythms

Have each student rate his/her performance of this song in the areas above on a scale of 1–5, 5 being the best.

Individual and Group Performance Evaluation

To further measure growth of musical skills presented in this lesson, direct students to complete the Evaluation section on page 239.

- Direct students to use good breath support and sing measures 3–10, only taking a breath at the end of measure 6.
- Create performance criteria for "Yonder Come Day" by videotaping the class singing this song. Discuss areas that are performed well and also those areas that need improvements.

Glossary

2/2 meter   A time signature in which there are two beats per measure and the half note receives the beat.

2/4 meter   A time signature in which there are two beats per measure and the quarter note receives the beat.

3/2 meter   A time signature in which there are three beats per measure and the half note receives the beat.

3/4 meter   A time signature in which there are three beats per measure and the quarter note receives the beat.

3/8 meter   A time signature in which there is one group of three eighth notes per measure and the dotted quarter note receives the beat. When the tempo is very slow, this meter can be counted as having three beats per measure, with the eighth note receiving the beat.

4/4 meter   A time signature in which there are four beats per measure and the quarter note receives the beat.

5/8 meter   A time signature in which there are five beats per measure and the eighth note receives the beat.

6/4 meter   A time signature in which there are two groups of three quarter notes per measure and the dotted half note receives the beat. When the tempo is very slow, this meter can be counted as having six beats per measure, with the quarter note receiving the beat.

6/8 meter   A time signature in which there are two groups of three eighth notes per measure and the dotted quarter note receives the beat. When the tempo is very slow, this meter can be counted as having six beats per measure, with the eighth note receiving the beat.

9/8 meter   A time signature in which there are three groups of three eighth notes per measure and the dotted quarter note receives the beat. When the tempo is very slow, this meter can be counted as having nine beats per measure, with the eighth note receiving the beat.

12/8 meter   A time signature in which there are four groups of three eighth notes per measure and the dotted quarter note receives the beat.

A

a cappella *(ah-kah-PEH-lah)*   [It.] A style of singing without instrumental accompaniment.

a tempo *(ah TEM-poh)*   [It.] A tempo marking which indicates to return to the original tempo of a piece or section of music.

ABA form   A form in which an opening section (A) is followed by a contrasting section (B), which leads to the repetition of the opening section (A).

accelerando *(accel.)* *(ah-chel-leh-RAHN-doh)* [It.] A tempo marking that indicates to gradually get faster.

accent   A symbol placed above or below a given note to indicate that the note should receive extra emphasis or stress. ( )

accidental   Any sharp, flat or natural that is not included in the key signature of a piece of music.

adagio *(ah-DAH-jee-oh)*   [It.] Slow tempo, but not as slow as *largo*.

ad libitum *(ad. lib.)*   [Lt.] An indication that the performer may vary the tempo or add or delete a vocal or instrumental part.

Aeolian scale *(ay-OH-lee-an)*   [Gk.] A modal scale that starts and ends on *la*. It is made up of the same arrangement of whole and half steps as a natural minor scale.

al fine *(ahl FEE-neh)*   [It.] To the end.

aleatory music *(AY-lee-uh-toh-ree)*   A type of music in which certain aspects are performed randomly. Also known as chance music.

alla breve   Indicates cut time; a duple meter in which there are two beats per measure, and half note receives the beat. *See* cut time.

allargando (*allarg.*) (*ahl-ahr-GAHN-doh*) [It.] To broaden, become slower.

allegro (*ah-LEH-groh*) [It.] Brisk tempo; faster than *moderato*, slower than *vivace*.

allegro non troppo (*ah-LEH-groh nohn TROH-poh*) [It.] A tempo marking that indicates not too fast. Not as fast as *allegro*.

altered pitch Another name for an accidental.

alto (*AL-toh*) The lowest-sounding female voice.

andante (*ahn-DAHN-teh*) [It.] Moderately slow; a walking tempo.

andante con moto (*ahn-DAHN-teh kohn MOH-toh*) [It.] A slightly faster tempo, "with motion."

animato Quickly, lively; "animated."

anthem A choral composition in English using a sacred text.

arpeggio (*ahr-PEH-jee-oh*) [It.] A chord in which the pitches are sounded successively, usually from lowest to highest; in broken style.

arrangement A piece of music in which a composer takes an existing melody and adds extra features or changes the melody in some way.

arranger A composer who takes an original or existing melody and adds extra features or changes the melody in some way.

art song A musical setting of a poem.

articulation The amount of separation or connection between notes.

articulators The lips, teeth, tongue and other parts of the mouth and throat that are used to produce vocal sound.

avocational Not related to a job or career.

barbershop A style of *a cappella* singing in which three parts harmonize with the melody. The lead sings the melody while the tenor harmonizes above and the baritone and bass harmonize below.

barcarole A Venetian boat song.

baritone The male voice between tenor and bass.

barline A vertical line placed on the musical staff that groups notes and rests together.

Baroque period (*bah-ROHK*) [Fr.] The historical period in Western civilization from 1600 to 1750.

bass The lowest-sounding male voice.

bass clef A clef that generally indicates notes that sound lower than middle C.

basso continuo (*BAH-soh cun-TIN-you-oh*) [It.] A continually moving bass line, common in music from the Baroque period.

beat The steady pulse of music.

bebop style Popular in jazz, music that features notes that are light, lively and played quickly. Often the melodic lines are complex and follow unpredictable patterns.

blues scale An altered major scale that uses flatted or lowered third, fifth and seventh notes: *ma* (lowered from *mi*), *se* (lowered from *sol*) and *te* (lowered from *ti*).

blues style An original African American art form that developed in the early twentieth century in the Mississippi Delta region of the South. The lyrics often express feelings of frustration, hardship or longing. It often contains elements such as call and response, the blues scale and swing.

body percussion The use of one's body to make a percussive sound, such as clapping, snapping or stepping.

breath mark A symbol in vocal music used to indicate where a singer should take a breath. (◊)

breath support A constant airflow necessary to produce sound for singing.

cadence A melodic or harmonic structure that marks the end of a phrase or the completion of a song.

call and response A derivative of the field hollers used by slaves as they worked. A leader or group sings a phrase (call) followed by a response of the same phrase by another group.

calypso A style of music that originated in the West Indies and which features syncopated rhythms and comical lyrics.

canon A musical form in which one part sings a melody, and the other parts sing the same melody, but enter at different times. Canons are sometimes called rounds.

cantabile *(con-TAH-bee-leh)* [It.] In a lyrical, singing style.

cantata *(con-TAH-tah)* [It.] A large-scale musical piece made up of several movements for singers and instrumentalists. Johann Sebastian Bach was a prominent composer of cantatas.

cantor *(CAN-tor)* A person who sings and/or teaches music in a temple or synagogue.

canzona [It.] A rhythmic instrumental composition that is light and fast-moving.

chamber music Music performed by a small instrumental ensemble, generally with one instrument per part. The string quartet is a popular form of chamber music, consisting of two violins, a viola and a cello. Chamber music was popular during the Classical period.

chantey *See* sea chantey.

chanteyman A soloist who improvised and led the singing of sea chanteys.

chest voice The lower part of the singer's vocal range.

chorale *(kuh-RAL)* [Gr.] Congregational song or hymn of the German Protestant Church.

chord The combination of three or more notes played or sung together at the same time.

chromatic scale *(kroh-MAT-tick)* [Gk.] A scale that consists of all half steps and uses all twelve pitches in an octave.

Classical period The historical period in Western civilization from 1750 to 1820.

clef The symbol at the beginning of a staff that indicates which lines and spaces represent which notes.

coda A special ending to a song. A concluding section of a composition. (♦)

common time Another name for 4/4 meter. Also known as common meter. (**C**)

composer A person who takes a musical thought and writes it out in musical notation to share it with others.

compound meter Any meter in which the dotted quarter note receives the beat, and the division of the beat is based on three eighth notes. 6/8, 9/8 and 12/8 are examples of compound meter.

con moto *(kohn MOH-toh)* [It.] With motion.

concert etiquette A term used to describe what is appropriate behavior in formal or informal musical performances.

concerto *(cun-CHAIR-toh)* [Fr., It.] A composition for a solo instrument and orchestra.

concerto grosso *(cun-CHAIR-toh GROH-soh)* [Fr., It.] A multimovement Baroque piece for a group of soloists and an orchestra.

conductor A person who uses hand and arm gestures to interpret the expressive elements of music for singers and instrumentalists.

conductus A thirteenth-century song for two, three or four voices.

consonance Harmonies in chords or music that are pleasing to the ear.

Contemporary period The historical period from 1900 to the present.

countermelody A separate melodic line that supports and/or contrasts the melody of a piece of music.

counterpoint The combination of two or more melodic lines. The parts move independently while harmony is created. Johann Sebastian Bach is considered by many to be one of the greatest composers of contrapuntal music.

contrary motion A technique in which two melodic lines move in opposite directions.

crescendo (*creh-SHEN-doh*) [It.] A dynamic marking that indicates to gradually sing or play louder.

cut time Another name for 2/2 meter. (¢)

D

da capo (D.C.) (*dah KAH-poh*) [It.] Go back to the beginning and repeat; *see also* dal segno *and* al fine.

dal segno (D.S.) (*dahl SAYN-yah*) [It.] Go back to the sign and repeat.

D. C. al Fine (*FEE-nay*) [It.] A term that indicates to go back to the beginning and repeat. The term *al fine* indicates to sing to the end, or *fine*.

decrescendo (*DAY-creh-shen-doh*) [It.] A dynamic marking that indicates to gradually sing or play softer.

descant A special part in a piece of music that is usually sung higher than the melody or other parts of the song.

diatonic scale (*die-uh-TAH-nick*) A scale that uses no altered pitches or accidentals. Both the major scale and the natural minor scale are examples of a diatonic scale.

diction The pronunciation of words while singing.

diminished chord A minor chord in which the top note is lowered one half step from *mi* to *me*.

diminuendo (*dim.*) (*duh-min-yoo-WEN-doh*) [It.] Gradually getting softer; *see also* decrescendo.

diphthong A combination of two vowel sounds.

dissonance A combination of pitches or tones that clash.

dolce (*DOHL-chay*) [It.] Sweetly.

dominant chord A chord built on the fifth note of a scale. In a major scale, this chord uses the notes *sol, ti* and *re*, and it may be called the **V** ("five") chord, since it is based on the fifth note of the major scale, or *sol*. In a minor scale, this chord uses the notes *mi, sol* and *ti* (or *mi, si* and *ti*), and it may be called the **v** or **V** ("five") chord, since it is based on the fifth note of the minor scale, or *mi*.

Dorian scale (*DOOR-ee-an*) [Gk.] A modal scale that starts and ends on *re*.

dot A symbol that increases the length of a given note by half its value. It is placed to the right of the note.

dotted half note A note that represents three beats of sound when the quarter note receives the beat.

double barline A set of two barlines that indicate the end of a piece or section of music.

D. S. al coda (*dahl SAYN-yoh ahl KOH-dah*) [It.] Repeat from the symbol (𝄋) and skip to the coda when you see the sign. (⊕)

duet A group of two singers or instrumentalists.

dynamics Symbols in music that indicate how loud or soft to sing or play.

E

eighth note A note that represents one half beat of sound when the quarter note receives the beat. Two eighth notes equal one beat of sound when the quarter note receives the beat.

eighth rest A rest that represents one half beat of silence when the quarter note receives the beat. Two eighth rests equal one beat of silence when the quarter note receives the beat.

expressive singing To sing with feeling.

F

falsetto [It.] The register in the male voice that extends far above the natural voice. The light upper range.

fermata (*fur-MAH-tah*) [It.] A symbol that indicates to hold a note or rest for longer than its given value. (⌢)

fine (*fee-NAY*) [It.] A term used to indicate the end of a piece of music.

flat A symbol that lowers the pitch of a given note by one half step.(♭)

folk music Music that passed down from generation to generation through oral tradition. Traditional music that reflects a place, event or a national feeling.

folk song A song passed down from generation to generation through oral tradition. A song that reflects a place, event or a national feeling.

form The structure or design of a musical composition.

forte (*FOR-tay*) [It.] A dynamic that indicates to sing or play loud. (*f*)

fortissimo (*for-TEE-see-moh*) [It.] A dynamic that indicates to sing or play very loud. (*ff*)

fugue (*FYOOG*) A musical form in which the same melody is performed by different instruments or voices entering at different times, thus adding layers of sound.

fusion Music that is developed by the act of combining various types and cultural influences of music into a new style.

G

gospel music Religious music that originated in the African American churches of the South. This music can be characterized by improvisation, syncopation and repetition.

grand staff A staff that is created when two staves are joined together.

H

grandioso [It.] Stately, majestic.

grave (*GRAH-veh*) [It.] Slow, solemn.

grazioso (*grah-tsee-OH-soh*) [It.] Graceful.

Gregorian chant A single, unaccompanied melodic line sung by male voices. Featuring a sacred text and used in the church, this style of music was developed in the medieval period.

H

half note A note that represents two beats of sound when the quarter note receives the beat. ♩

half rest A rest that represents two beats of silence when the quarter note receives the beat. ▬

half step The smallest distance (interval) between two notes on a keyboard; the chromatic scale is composed entirely of half steps.

harmonic minor scale A minor scale that uses a raised seventh note, *si* (raised from *sol*).

harmonics Small whistle-like tones, or overtones, that are sometimes produced over a sustained pitch.

harmony A musical sound that is formed when two or more different pitches are played or sung at the same time.

head voice The higher part of the singer's vocal range.

homophonic (*hah-muh-FAH-nik*) [Gk.] A texture where all parts sing similar rhythm in unison or harmony.

homophony (*haw-MAW-faw-nee*) [Gk.] A type of music in which there are two or more parts with similar or identical rhythms being sung or played at the same time. Also, music in which melodic interest is concentrated in one voice part and may have subordinate accompaniment.

hushed A style marking indicating a soft, whispered tone.

I

imitation The act of one part copying what another part has already played or sung.

improvisation The art of singing or playing music, making it up as you go, or composing and performing a melody at the same time.

International Phonetic Alphabet (IPA) A phonetic alphabet that provides a notational standard for all languages. Developed in Paris, France, in 1886.

interval The distance between two notes.

intonation The accuracy of pitch, in-tune singing.

Ionian scale *(eye-OWN-ee-an)* [Gk.] A modal scale that starts and ends on *do*. It is made up of the same arrangement of whole and half steps as a major scale.

J

jazz An original American style of music that features swing rhythms, syncopation and improvisation.

jongleur [Fr.] An entertainer who traveled from town to town during medieval times, often telling stories and singing songs.

K

key Determined by a song's or scale's home tone, or keynote.

key signature A symbol or set of symbols that determines the key of a piece of music.

L

ledger lines Short lines that appear above, between treble and bass clefs, or below the bass clef, used to expand the notation.

legato *(leh-GAH-toh)* [It.] A connected and sustained style of singing and playing.

lento *(LEN-toh)* [It.] Slow; a little faster than *largo*, a little slower than *adagio*.

lied *(leet)* [Ger.] A song in the German language, generally with a secular text.

liturgical text A text that has been written for the purpose of worship in a church setting.

lute An early form of the guitar.

Lydian scale *(LIH-dee-an)* [Gk.] A modal scale that starts and ends on *fa*.

lyrics The words of a song.

M

madrigal A poem that has been set to music in the language of the composer. Featuring several imitative parts, it usually has a secular text and is generally sung *a cappella*.

maestoso *(mah-eh-STOH-soh)* [It.] Perform majestically.

major chord A chord that can be based on the *do, mi,* and *sol* of a major scale.

major scale A scale that has *do* as its home tone, or keynote. It is made up of a specific arrangement of whole steps and half steps in the following order: W + W + H + W + W + W + H.

major tonality A song that is based on a major scale with *do* as its keynote, or home tone.

mangulina A traditional dance from the Dominican Republic.

marcato *(mar-CAH-toh)* [It.] A stressed and accented style of singing and playing.

Mass A religious service of prayers and ceremonies originating in the Roman Catholic Church consisting of spoken and sung sections. It consists of several sections divided into two groups: proper (text changes for every day) and ordinary (text stays the same in every mass). Between the years 1400 and 1600, the Mass assumed its present form consisting of the Kyrie, Gloria, Credo, Sanctus and Agnus Dei. It may include chants, hymns and psalms as well. The Mass also developed into large musical works for chorus, soloists and even orchestra.

measure The space between two barlines.

medieval period The historical period in Western civilization also known as the Middle Ages (400–1430).

medley A collection of songs musically linked together.

melisma (*muh-LIZ-mah*) [Gk.] A group of notes sung to a single syllable or word.

melismatic singing (*muh-liz-MAT-ik*) [Gk.] A style of text setting in which one syllable is sung over many notes.

melodic contour The overall shape of the melody.

melodic minor scale A minor scale that uses raised sixth and seventh notes: *fi* (raised from *fa*) and *si* (raised from *sol*). Often, these notes are raised in ascending patterns, but not in descending patterns.

melody A logical succession of musical tones.

meter A way of organizing rhythm.

meter signature *See* time signature.

metronome marking A sign that appears over the top line of the staff at the beginning of a piece or section of music that indicates the tempo. It shows the kind of note that will receive the beat and the number of beats per minute as measured by a metronome.

mezzo forte (*MEH-tsoh FOR tay*) [It.] A dynamic that indicates to sing or play medium loud. (*mf*)

mezzo piano (*MEH-tsoh pee-AH-noh*) [It.] A dynamic that indicates to sing or play medium soft. (*mp*)

mezzo voce (*MEH-tsoh VOH-cheh*) [It.] With half voice; reduced volume and tone.

minor chord A chord that can be based on the *la, do,* and *mi* of a minor scale.

minor scale A scale that has *la* as its home tone, or keynote. It is made up of a specific arrangement of whole steps and half steps in the following order: W + H +W + W + H + W + W.

minor tonality A song that is based on a minor scale with *la* as its keynote, or home tone.

mixed meter A technique in which the time signature or meter changes frequently within a piece of music.

Mixolydian scale (*mix-oh-LIH-dee-an*) [Gr.] A modal scale that starts and ends on *sol*.

modal scale A scale based on a mode. Like major and minor scales, each modal scale is made up of a specific arrangement of whole steps and half steps, with the half steps occurring between *mi* and *fa*, and *ti* and *do*.

mode An early system of pitch organization that was used before major and minor scales and keys were developed.

modulation A change in the key or tonal center of a piece of music within the same song.

molto [It.] Very or much; for example, *molto rit.* means "much slower."

motet (*moh-teht*) Originating as a medieval and Renaissance polyphonic song, this choral form of composition became an unaccompanied work, often in contrapuntal style. Also, a short, sacred choral piece with a Latin text that is used in religious services but is not a part of the regular Mass.

motive A shortened expression, sometimes contained within a phrase.

music critic A writer who gives an evaluation of a musical performance.

music notation Any means of writing down music, including the use of notes, rests and symbols.

musical A play or film whose action and dialogue are combined with singing and dancing.

musical theater An art form that combines acting, singing, and dancing to tell a story. It often includes staging, costumes, lighting and scenery.

mysterioso [It.] Perform in a mysterious or haunting way; to create a haunting mood.

N

narrative song A song that tells a story.

national anthem A patriotic song adopted by nations through tradition or decree.

nationalism Patriotism; pride of country. This feeling influenced many Romantic composers such as Wagner, Tchaikovsky, Dvorák, Chopin and Brahms.

natural A symbol that cancels a previous sharp or flat, or a sharp or flat in a key signature. (♮)

natural minor scale A minor scale that uses no altered pitches or accidentals.

no breath mark A direction not to take a breath at a specific place in the composition. (N.B.)

non troppo (*nahn TROH-poh*) [It.] Not too much; for example, *allegro non troppo*, "not too fast."

notation Written notes, symbols and directions used to represent music within a composition.

O

octave An interval of two pitches that are eight notes apart on a staff.

ode A poem written in honor of a special person or occasion. These poems were generally dedicated to a member of a royal family. In music, an ode usually includes several sections for choir, soloists and orchestra.

opera A combination of singing, instrumental music, dancing and drama that tells a story.

optional divisi (*opt.div.*) Indicating a split in the music into optional harmony, shown by a smaller cued note.

oral tradition Music that is learned through rote or by ear and is interpreted by its performer(s).

oratorio (*or-uh-TOR-ee-oh*) [It.] A dramatic work for solo voices, chorus and orchestra presented without theatrical action. Usually, oratorios are based on a literary or religious theme.

ostinato (*ahs-tuh-NAH-toh*) [It.] A rhythmic or melodic passage that is repeated continuosly.

overture A piece for orchestra that serves as an introduction to an opera or other dramatic work.

P

palate The roof of the mouth; the hard palate is at the front, the soft palate is at the back.

parallel motion A technique in which two or more melodic lines move in the same direction.

parallel sixths A group of intervals that are a sixth apart and which move at the same time and in the same direction.

parallel thirds A group of intervals that are a third apart and which move at the same time and in the same direction.

part-singing Two or more parts singing an independent melodic line at the same time.

patsch The act of slapping one's hands on one's thighs.

pentatonic scale A five-tone scale using the pitches *do, re, mi, sol* and *la*.

perfect fifth An interval of two pitches that are five notes apart on a staff.

perfect fourth An interval of two pitches that are four notes apart on a staff.

phrase A musical idea with a beginning and an end.

Phrygian scale (*FRIH-gee-an*) [Gk.] A modal scale that starts and ends on *mi*.

pianissimo (*pee-ah-NEE-see-moh*) [It.] A dynamic that indicates to sing or play very soft. (*pp*)

piano (*pee-AH-noh*) [It.] A dynamic that indicates to sing or play soft. (*p*)

pitch Sound, the result of vibration; the highness or lowness of a tone, determined by the number of vibrations per second.

pitch matching In a choral ensemble, the ability to sing the same notes as those around you.

piu (*pew*) [It.] More; for example, *piu forte* means "more loudly."

poco (*POH-koh*) [It.] Little; for example *poco dim.* means "a little softer."

poco a poco (*POH-koh ah POH-koh*) [It.] Little by little; for example, *poco a poco cresc.* means "little by little increase in volume."

polyphony (*pah-LIH-fun-nee*) [Gk.] Literally, "many sounding." A type of music in which there are two or more different melodic lines being sung or played at the same time. Polyphony was refined during the Renaissance, and this period is sometimes called "golden age of polyphony."

polyrhythms A technique in which several different rhythms are performed at the same time.

presto (*PREH-stoh*) [It.] Very fast.

program music A descriptive style of music composed to relate or illustrate a specific incident, situation or drama; the form of the piece is often dictated or influenced by the nonmusical program. This style commonly occurs in music composed during the Romantic period.

Q

quarter note A note that represents one beat of sound when the quarter note receives the beat.

quarter rest A rest that represents one beat of silence when the quarter note receives the beat.

quartet A group of four singers or instrumentalists.

R

rallentando (*rall.*) (*rahl-en-TAHN-doh*) [It.] Meaning to "perform more and more slowly." *See also* ritard.

refrain A repeated section at the end of each phrase or verse in a song. Also known as a chorus.

register, vocal A term used for different parts of the singer's range, such as head register, or head voice (high notes); and chest register, or chest voice (low notes).

relative minor scale A minor scale that shares the same key signature as its corresponding major scale. Both scales share the same half steps, between *mi* and *fa*, and *ti* and *do*.

Renaissance period The historical period in Western civilization from 1430 to 1600.

repeat sign A symbol that indicates that a section of music should be repeated.

repetition The restatement of a musical idea; repeated pitches; repeated "A" section in ABA form.

requiem (*REK-wee-ehm*) [Lt.] Literally, "rest." A mass written and performed to honor the dead and comfort the living.

resonance Reinforcement and intensification of sound by vibration.

rest A symbol used in music notation to indicate silence.

rhythm The combination of long and short notes and rests in music. These may move with the beat, faster than the beat or slower than the beat.

ritard *(rit.) (ree-TAHRD)* [It.] A tempo marking that indicates to gradually get slower.

Romantic period The historical period in Western civilization from 1820 to 1900.

rondo form A form in which a repeated section is separated by several contrasting sections.

rote The act of learning a song by hearing it over and over again.

round *See* canon.

rubato *(roo-BAH-toh)* [It.] The freedom to slow down and/or speed up the tempo without changing the overall pulse of a piece of music.

S

sacred music Music associated with religious services or themes.

scale A group of pitches that are sung or played in succession and are based on a particular home tone, or keynote.

scat singing An improvisational style of singing that uses nonsense syllables instead of words. It was made popular by jazz trumpeter Louis Armstrong.

sea chantey A song sung by sailors, usually in rhythm with their work.

secular music Music not associated with religious services or themes.

sempre *(SEHM-preh)* [It.] Always, continually.

sempre accelerando *(sempre accel.)* *(SEHM-preh ahk-chel)* [It.] A term that indicates to gradually increase the tempo of a piece or section of music.

sequence A successive musical pattern that begins on a higher or lower pitch each time it is repeated.

serenata [It.] A large-scale musical work written in honor of a special occasion. Generally performed in the evening or outside, it is often based on a mythological theme.

sforzando *(sfohr-TSAHN-doh)* [It.] A sudden strong accent on a note or chord. (*sfz*)

sharp A symbol that raises the pitch of a given note one half step. ()

shekere An African shaker consisting of a hollow gourd surrounded by beads.

sight-sing Reading and singing music at first sight.

simile *(sim.) (SIM-ee-leh)* [It.] To continue the same way.

simple meter Any meter in which the quarter note receives the beat, and the division of the beat is based on two eighth notes. 2/4, 3/4 and 4/4 are examples of simple meter.

singing posture The way one sits or stands while singing.

sixteenth note A note that represents one quarter beat of sound when the quarter note receives the beat. Four sixteenth notes equal one beat of sound when the quarter note receives the beat.

sixteenth rest A rest that represents one quarter beat of silence when the quarter note receives the beat. Four sixteenth rests equal one beat of silence when the quarter note receives the beat.

skip-wise motion The movement from a given note to another note that is two or more notes above or below it on the staff.

slur A curved line placed over or under a group of notes to indicate that they are to be performed without a break.

solfège syllables Pitch names using *do, re, mi, fa, sol, la, ti, do,* etc.

solo One person singing or playing an instrument alone.

sonata-allegro form A large ABA form consisting of three sections: exposition, development and recapitulation. This form was made popular during the Classical period.

soprano The highest-sounding female voice.

sostenuto (*SAHS-tuh-noot-oh*) [It.] The sustaining of a tone or the slackening of tempo.

sotto voce In a quiet, subdued manner; "under" the voice.

spirito (*SPEE-ree-toh*) [It.] Spirited; for example, *con spirito* ("with spirit").

spiritual Songs that were first sung by African American slaves, usually based on biblical themes or stories.

staccato (*stah-KAH-toh*) [It.] A short and detached style of singing or playing.

staff A series of five horizontal lines and four spaces on which notes are written. A staff is like a ladder. Notes placed higher on the staff sound higher than notes placed lower on the staff.

stage presence A performer's overall appearance on stage, including enthusiasm, facial expression and posture.

staggered breathing In ensemble singing, the practice of planning breaths so that no two singers take a breath at the same time, thus creating the overall effect of continuous singing.

staggered entrances A technique in which different parts and voices enter at different times.

stanza A section in a song in which the words change on each repeat. Also known as a verse.

step-wise motion The movement from a given note to another note that is directly above or below it on the staff.

strophe A verse or stanza in a song.

strophic A form in which the melody repeats while the words change from verse to verse.

style The particular character of a musical work; often indicated by words at the beginning of a composition, telling the performer the general manner in which the piece is to be performed.

subdominant chord A chord built on the fourth note of a scale. In a major scale, this chord uses the notes *fa*, *la* and *do*, and it may be called the **IV** ("four") chord, since it is based on the fourth note of the major scale, or *fa*. In a minor scale, this chord uses the notes *re*, *fa* and *la*, and it may be called the **iv** ("four") chord, since it is based on the fourth note of the minor scale, or *re*.

subito (sub.) (*SOO-bee-toh*) [It.] Suddenly.

suspension The holding over of one or more musical tones in a chord into the following chord, producing a momentary discord.

swing rhythms Rhythms in which the second eighth note of each beat is played or sung like the last third of triplet, creating an uneven, "swing" feel. A style often found in jazz and blues. Swing rhythms are usually indicated at the beginning of a song or section.

syllabic *See* syllabic singing.

syllabic singing A style of text setting in which one syllable is sung on each note.

syllabic stress The stressing of one syllable over another.

symphonic poem A single-movement work for orchestra, inspired by a painting, play or other literary or visual work. Franz Liszt was a prominent composer of symphonic poems. Also known as a tone poem.

symphony A large-scale work for orchestra.

syncopation The placement of accents on a weak beat or a weak portion of the beat, or on a note or notes that normally do not receive extra emphasis.

synthesizer A musical instrument that produces sounds electronically, rather than by the physical vibrations of an acoustic instrument.

tempo   Terms in music that indicate how fast or slow to sing or play.

tempo I or tempo primo   *See* a tempo.

tenor   The highest-sounding male voice.

tenuto *(teh-NOO-toh)*   [It.] A symbol placed above or below a given note indicating that the note should receive stress and/or that its value should be slightly extended.

text   Words, usually set in a poetic style, that express a central thought, idea or narrative.

texture   The thickness of the different layers of horizontal and vertical sounds.

theme   A musical idea, usually a melody.

theme and variation form   A musical form in which variations of the basic theme make up the composition.

third   An interval of two pitches that are three notes apart on a staff.

tie   A curved line used to connect two or more notes of the same pitch together in order to make one longer note.

tied notes   Two or more notes of the same pitch connected together with a tie in order to make one longer note.

timbre   The tone quality of a person's voice or musical instrument.

time signature   The set of numbers at the beginning of a piece of music. The top number indicates the number of beats per measure. The bottom number indicates the kind of note that receives the beat. Time signature is sometimes called meter signature.

to coda   Skip to (⊕) or CODA.

tone color   That which distinguishes the voice or tone of one singer or instrument from another; for example, a soprano from an alto, or a flute from a clarinet. *See also* timbre.

tonic chord   A chord built on the home tone, or keynote of a scale. In a major scale, this chord uses the notes *do, mi* and *sol*, and it may be called the **I** ("one") chord, since it is based on the first note of the major scale, or *do*. In a minor scale, this chord uses the notes *la, do* and *mi*, and it may be called the **i** ("one") chord, since it is based on the first note of the minor scale, or *la*.

treble clef   A clef that generally indicates notes that sound higher than middle C.

trio   A group of three singers or instrumentalists with usually one on a part.

triplet   A group of notes in which three notes of equal duration are sung in the time normally given to two notes of equal duration.

troppo *(TROHP-oh)*   [It.] Too much; for example, *allegro non troppo* ("not too fast").

tutti *(TOO-tee)*   [It.] Meaning "all" or "together."

twelve-tone music   A type of music that uses all twelve tones of the scale equally. Developed in the early twentieth century, Arnold Schoenberg is considered to be the pioneer of this style of music.

two-part music   A type of music in which two different parts are sung or played.

unison   All parts singing or playing the same notes at the same time.

variation   A modification of a musical idea, usually after its initial appearance in a piece.

vivace *(vee-VAH-chay)*   [It.] Very fast; lively.

vocal jazz   A popular style of music characterized by strong prominent meter, improvisation and dotted or syncopated patterns. Sometimes sung *a cappella*.

W

whole note   A note that represents four beats of sound when the quarter note receives the beat.   o

whole rest   A rest that represents four beats of silence when the quarter note receives the beat.   ▬

whole step   The combination of two successive half steps.

word painting   A technique in which the music reflects the meaning of the words.

word stress   The act of singing important parts of the text in a more accented style than the other parts.

Y

yoik   A vocal tradition of the Sámi people of the Arctic region of Sampi that features short melodic phrases that are repeated with slight variations.

Classified Index

Index of Songs and Spotlights

Spotlights

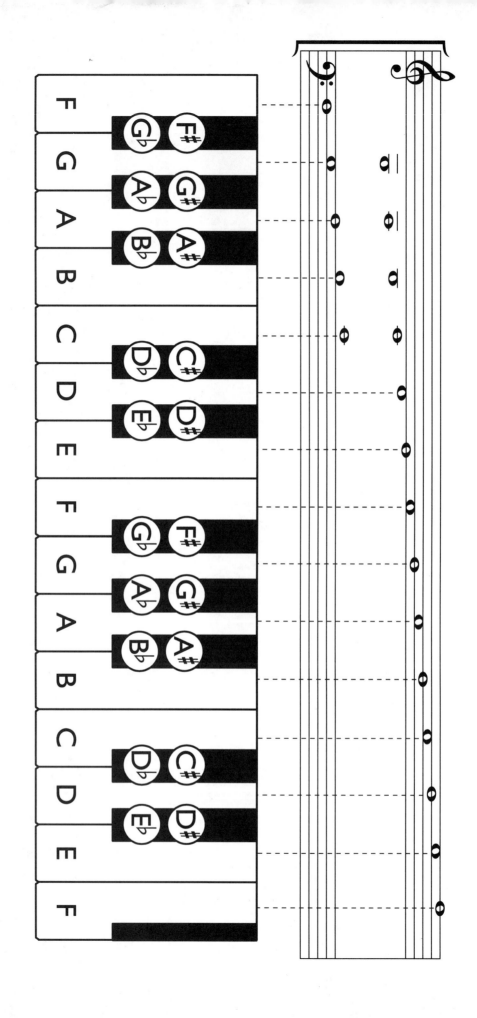